Gotcha Good!

Nonfiction Books to Get Kids Excited About Reading

**Kathleen A. Baxter and
Marcia Agness Kochel**

**LIBRARIES
UNLIMITED**

A Member of the Greenwood Publishing Group

Westport, Connecticut • London

Library of Congress Cataloging-in-Publication Data

Baxter, Kathleen A.
  Gotcha good! : nonfiction books to get kids excited about reading / Kathleen A. Baxter and Marcia Agness Kochel.
    p. cm.
  Includes bibliographical references and indexes.
  ISBN 978-1-59158-654-8 (alk. paper)
    1. Children—Books and reading—United States. 2. Preteens—Books and reading—United States. 3.
  Children's literature, American—Bibliography. 4. Book talks—United States. I. Kochel, Marcia Agness. II. Title.
  Z1037.B39 2008
  028.5'5—dc22   2008010350

British Library Cataloguing in Publication Data is available.

Library of Congress Control Number: 2008010350
ISBN: 978-1-59158-654-8

First published in 2008

Libraries Unlimited, 88 Post Road West, Westport, CT 06881
A Member of the Greenwood Publishing Group, Inc.
www.lu.com

Printed in the United States of America

The paper used in this book complies with the
Permanent Paper Standard issued by the National
Information Standards Organization (Z39.48–1984).

10 9 8 7 6 5 4 3 2 1

Contents

Chapter 1

American Journeys

American history is not all about politics and wars. It is full of intriguing, complicated people, strange events, and citizens fighting against injustice. In this chapter you will find some topics you might expect (such as stories of Jamestown and women's suffrage and the Civil Rights movement), but you will also read about cheeseburgers, cotton, Alcatraz, and the Miracle on Ice hockey game. Booktalking a wide variety of history books will let your listeners know that American history is much more than what can be found in a textbook.

Adler, David A., and Michael S. Adler. *A Picture Book of John Hancock*. Illustrated by Ronald Himler. Holiday House, 2007. ISBN 0823420051. Unpaged. Grades 2–4.

John Hancock had a terrible thing happen to him when he was seven years old. His father, a minister, died, and John's mother split up his family. He went to live with his aunt and uncle, who were wealthy, and they raised John and treated him like their own son. When John was twenty-four years old, his uncle died, and John became one of the wealthiest men in the colonies.

He cared a lot about principles, more than he cared about money. He felt that England was treating her colonies in America badly, and he became involved in the cause of freedom. By the time the Second Continental Congress formed in 1775, John was chosen president. Then, a year later, on July 4, 1776, John signed his name really big on the Declaration of Independence.

He was one of our greatest patriots, one of the founders of our country, and this is an excellent introduction to his life story.

Armstrong, Jennifer. *The American Story: 100 True Tales from American History.* Illustrated by Roger Roth. Knopf Books for Young Readers, 2006. ISBN 0375812563. 358 p. Grades 4–up.

Is there anybody anywhere who doesn't like a good story? American history is full of good stories, and Jennifer Armstrong tells us one hundred of them in this colorful book.

She starts in 1565 with the building of the first city still in existence—Saint Augustine, Florida. She goes on to tell us about the first American democracy—the Confederacy of the Five Nations, begun in about 1570 by five native tribes. Along the way, she describes the Salem Witch Trials, one of Ben Franklin's rather unfortunate experiments with electricity (man, did he get a shock!), two great events that happened on the same day in different parts of the United States: Alexander Graham Bell's first public introduction of the telephone (it was a hit!) and the Battle of Little Bighorn. She describes maybe the most famous painting in American history. Here's a clue: almost everyone owns a copy of it. Do you know what it is? (Answer: Gilbert Stuart's painting of George Washington, which is on the dollar bill.)

She tells us the first time bananas were brought into New York City. No one knew what they were and no one bought any, so they rotted. Now they are the most popular fruit in the country. She describes the whale that paid back the whalers who were trying to kill him by ramming and sinking their ship. She tells us about the furry men with bat wings who live on the moon. You didn't know about those? Well, it was a hoax made up to sell newspapers, and it worked.

She tells us about the gunfight at the O.K. Corral, the Valentine's Day Massacre in Chicago, the elephants that walked across the Brooklyn Bridge, and the first dinosaur fossils found in the United States. You'll love learning these great stories, and you'll want to know more about almost every one.

Up Close: Robert F. Kennedy by Marc Aronson.

Aronson, Marc. *Up Close: Robert F. Kennedy* (Up Close). Viking Juvenile, 2007. ISBN 0670060666. 202 p. Grades 6–up.

This is a different biography from a lot of the ones kids read. For starters, it probably won't help you much to write a school report. It is not filled with all sorts of data or facts. What it is is a really good read about a man who was one of the most interesting men of the twentieth century—and probably one of the most controversial as well.

Bobby was a Kennedy, the son of Joseph and Rose Kennedy, and if you think it was easy being the kid of wealthy parents, you are definitely wrong. Money was never a problem in Bobby's life, but his family sure was. Bobby was the smallest of four boys in his family of nine children, and the family was very competitive, always fighting each other and playing killer sports. Bobby was always getting banged up by his older brothers, but in spite of that he loved and admired them, and they were a powerful influence on him all his life.

Bobby did not always get to choose what he wanted to do with his life. When his family needed him, he was there. When his brother Joe died in World War II, his dad decided that his next son, John, should be the first Catholic president of the United States, and Bobby's job was to help make that happen. Bobby became the person his brother depended on the most.

When John was assassinated, Bobby had to take a hard look at his own life. It took him a while, but he decided he wanted to be president himself—and he worked hard to make that happen. Unfortunately, his life was cut short.

This is an excellent true story, and you'll enjoy meeting Bobby Kennedy.

With Courage and Cloth: Winning the
Fight for a Woman's Right to Vote
by Ann Bausum.

Bausum, Ann. *With Courage and Cloth: Winning the Fight for a Woman's Right to Vote.* National Geographic, 2004. ISBN 0792276477. 112 p. Grades 5–8.

The American history that many people learn in school is mainly about men and battlefields and war. As Ann Bausum says, "That's a shame, because the history of how American women fought for and won their right to vote is one of the great stories about the growth of our nation. It is a tale of courage and adventure, challenge and skill, patience and hope. Countless women—and a few men too—fought campaigns not unlike those waged by an army at war. Although the fight was less bloody, it lasted much longer than any U.S. conflict" (p. 8).

Bausum chose her title because the women who finally won the long battle fought with homemade banners made of cloth. And the words they put on those banners made many men absolutely furious.

As early as the time of the Revolutionary War, a few American women, perhaps most notably Abigail Adams, were questioning why they were not considered equal to men. They could not vote, and everything they owned belonged to their husbands. They had few rights. By 1848, several women, led by Elizabeth Cady Stanton, had decided to do something about it. They held a women's rights convention in Seneca Falls, New York. Several men, including the former slave and prominent abolitionist Frederick Douglass, attended and supported the women. And they started working. They called themselves suffragists, which means people who are working to gain voting rights. Their job took them seventy-two years. Most men simply did not want to share their power.

They marched, they paraded, and they went to prison and held hunger strikes. The women wouldn't give up, no matter how slow the progress. They were nonviolent, although some of the things done to them were violent indeed.

This is a true story filled with drama and suspense—with a real cliffhanger at the last stage of their battle.

Show the picture on page 16 of how opponents of women's suffrage thought that women who were able to vote would dress and treat their men.

Where Washington Walked **by Raymond Bial.**

Bial, Raymond. *Where Washington Walked.* Walker & Company, 2004. ISBN 0802788998. 48 p. Grades 3–8.

If you are interested in George Washington, this book takes a different look at his life.

At least part of what makes all people unique is the places they lived and visited.

Raymond Bial gives us photographs of many of the places where Washington lived, visited, fought, and spent his life. Included on the endpapers are photographs of paintings of George, his wife Martha, and her children and grandchildren, all of whom George loved like a father. These pictures are worth a thousand words.

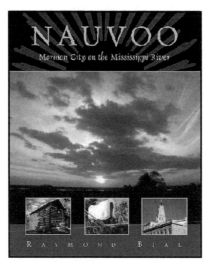

Nauvoo: Mormon City on the Mississippi River **by Raymond Bial.**

Bial, Raymond. *Nauvoo: Mormon City on the Mississippi River*. Houghton Mifflin, 2006. ISBN 0618396853. 48 p. Grades 4–8.

A young man named Joseph Smith had a vision near Palmyra, New York, in 1820, and between then and 1827 he had many more visions. Those visions led him to found a new religion called the Mormon Church, named after the father of the angel Moroni who had appeared to him. Moroni revealed to him *The Book of Mormon,* which Mormons believe to be a supplement to the Christian King James Bible. Joseph, along with five others, founded the church in 1830.

Most people did not think highly of the new religion. Smith's group left New York and moved to Ohio, where they were disliked and even hated. They fled to Missouri where they found their neighbors no more welcoming. The Missouri governor made a statement that "The Mormons must be treated as enemies and must be exterminated or driven from the state" (p. 14). One mob murdered eighteen men and boys.

Next they moved to Illinois, to a town they built and named Nauvoo, a Hebrew word meaning "the city beautiful." Now they hoped they could find a real home, a lasting home, one where they could remain.

This beautiful book tells us the story of the beautiful place that they created and populated. By 1846, seven years after they arrived, their city was the tenth largest in the United States—and about the same size as Chicago.

And then they had to leave it.

There are many fine photographs. You'll want to visit Nauvoo by the time you finish reading this book.

Bogaert, H. M. van den, with artwork by George O'Connor and color by Hilary Sycamore. *Journey Into Mohawk Country*. First Second, 2006. ISBN 1596431067. 144 p. Grades 5–up.

This is graphic nonfiction—*and* a primary source. How cool is that?

In 1634, a twenty-three-year-old Dutch trader set out with some friends on a dangerous mission. His job: go to the Iroquois Country, where the Mohawk Indians were beginning to trade their furs to the French rather than the Dutch. And his mission? He was to try to make friendships with the Indians, who hopefully would be friendly, as he left the southern tip of Manhattan Island on December 11. And he was to try to persuade those Indians (who it turned out had excellent reasons for trading with the French) to trade with the Dutch again.

It snowed. It got very cold. He saw ways of living he had never known before. And all of this is put into graphic format—and it provides an interesting look into early colonial America.

***Journeys for Freedom: A New Look at America's
Story* by Susan Buckley and Elspeth Leacock.**

Buckley, Susan, and Elspeth Leacock. *Journeys for Freedom: A New Look at America's Story.* Illustrations by Rodica Prato. Houghton Mifflin, 2006. ISBN 0618223231. 48 p. Grades 4–8.

Some of the first immigrants to come to what is now America were seeking freedom. They wanted freedom to worship in the way they chose.

Other people followed them. They wanted freedom in many different ways, but they were all willing to make long, difficult journeys to get it.

There are eighteen stories in this book, complete with maps and illustrations to show us what happened, that tell how people sought and eventually found freedom.

Read about:

- The prosperous, happy Acadians, all of French descent, who were forced to leave Canada with nothing when the British conquered their country. After years of wandering, many found homes in Louisiana.

- Deborah Sampson, who believed that the patriots were right to revolt against King George III and who, disguised as a man, enlisted in the colonial Army.

- Free Frank, an astonishing slave who managed to work hard and save enough money to buy himself and his entire family—and move them all to the North where slavery was illegal.

- The Chinese man Ah Goong, who moved to America for seven years to work on the railroad and make enough money to free his family in China from poverty.

• The migrant workers who marched 350 miles with Cesar Chavez to present their demands for fair treatment and wages to the governor of California.

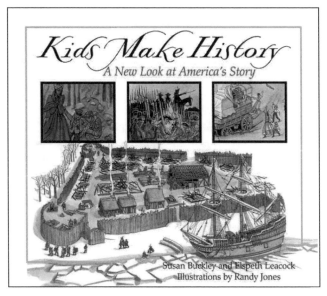

Kids Make History: A New Look at America's Story
by Susan Buckley and Elspeth Leacock.

Buckley, Susan, and Elspeth Leacock. *Kids Make History: A New Look at America's Story.* Illustrations by Randy Jones. Houghton Mifflin, 2006. ISBN 0618223290. 48 p. Grades 4–8.

Kids and young people have always been around, and if you look closely at many of the important events in American history, you will find that kids were there.

Each two-page spread in this book tells about a kid who was there. We learn some facts about them, and, if we follow the numbers, you can watch what happens to each one of them. But there are only two pages! You find out just enough to make you want to know more.

Read this book to learn about:

• A girl named Pocahontas. You probably know some of the things she did.

• A boy named Samuel Collier. He was one of the Jamestown settlers, and he was John Smith's servant. He met Pocahontas.

• The girls who accused so many people in Salem, Massachusetts, of being witches.

• Twelve-year-old Peter Williamson who was kidnapped and forced to come to the British colonies in America and sold as an indentured servant.

• A runaway slave named Eliza who carried her baby across the dangerous, breaking-up ice on the Ohio River to reach freedom and safety.

• Marty Myers, who was six years old when he started working with a blast furnace in an Iron Works in Pennsylvania.

Kathy's Top Ten American History Booktalking Favorites

- Armstrong, Jennifer. *The American Story: 100 True Tales from American History*. Knopf Books for Young Readers, 2006.

- Freedman, Russell. *Freedom Walkers: The Story of the Montgomery Bus Boycott*. Holiday House, 2006.

- Giblin, James Cross. *The Many Rides of Paul Revere*. Scholastic, 2007.

- Sullivan, George. *Helen Keller: Her Life In Pictures*. Scholastic Nonfiction, 2007.

- Cooper, Michael L. *Jamestown, 1607*. Holiday House, 2007.

- Schanzer, Rosalyn. *John Smith Escapes Again!* National Geographic, 2006.

- Walker, Paul Robert. *Remember Little Bighorn: Indians, Soldiers, and Scouts Tell Their Stories*. National Geographic, 2006.

- Bogaert, H. M. van den, with artwork by George O'Connor and color by Hilary Sycamore. *Journey into Mohawk Country*. First Second, 2006.

- Murphy, Claire Rudolf. *Children of Alcatraz: Growing Up on the Rock*. Walker & Company, 2006.

- Magaziner, Henry Jonas. *Our Liberty Bell*. Illustrated by John O'Brien. Holiday House, 2007.

From *Gotcha Good! Nonfiction Books to Get Kids Excited About Reading* by Kathleen A. Baxter and Marcia Agness Kochel. Westport, CT: Libraries Unlimited. Copyright © 2008.

- Al Nailling, who rode the orphan train with his two brothers to find a new home with new parents.

And that's just the beginning. You'll enjoy looking through this interesting book.

Colman, C. H. *The Bald Eagle's View of American History*. Illustrated by Joanne Friar. Charlesbridge, 2006. ISBN 1580893007. 48 p. Grades 4–6.

Do you like stamps? Do you like eagles? Do you like history?

Charlie Colman has collected stamps since he was five years old. He loves them. He also loves history. He decided to tell American history with stamps from the bald eagle's point of view.

Bald eagles were here before people were. They watched people come from Asia and settle on the land. They were free and could live wherever they chose.

But when European settlers came, they began to build towns and grow crops, and they didn't want eagles close to them. But they loved them anyway. When the American colonies started a revolution, the country's founders wanted to pick the country's national emblem. Benjamin Franklin wanted a turkey! But Thomas Jefferson wanted the bald eagle. Do you know who won?

At the beginning of each chapter, there is a picture of a United States postage stamp. Many of those stamps have an eagle on them. Through these stamps, and from the eagle's point of view, we learn a little bit of American history.

It has not always been easy for the eagle. Read this and find out why.

Cook, Peter. *You Wouldn't Want to Sail on the* Mayflower: *A Trip That Took Entirely Too Long.* Illustrated by Kevin Whelan. Created and designed by David Salariya. Franklin Watts, a Division of Scholastic, 2005. ISBN 053112391x. 32 p. Grades 3–6.

Today it takes a few hours to travel from the east coast of the United States to England. It's not a very long flight. Even in a crowded plane cabin, it is reasonably comfortable. The temperature is controlled, there is food and plenty of water, and there are private bathrooms. You can even watch a movie!

In 1620, the situation was entirely different. The *Mayflower,* the ship that brought the Pilgrims to what is now Massachusetts, was at sea for sixty-six days! Imagine how awful that must have been. The passengers were jammed into a fairly small space below deck, and families put up blankets to have a little privacy. It was smelly and dirty, and there was no fresh food. You went to the bathroom in something called the beakhead (show the picture on page 11), and you were out in the open. It was dangerous in bad weather.

There were 102 passengers and about 30 crew members on the small ship. Many people got ill; some died and were buried at sea. Even after land was spied, most people still lived on the ship, because there was no shelter at all on the land. And that first year was awful—about half of the people died in the first winter.

Pair this with *Eating the Plates* by Lucille Penner when booktalking about the Pilgrims.

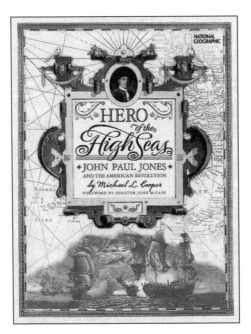

Hero of the High Seas: John Paul Jones and the American Revolution **by Michael Cooper.**

Cooper, Michael. *Hero of the High Seas: John Paul Jones and the American Revolution.* National Geographic, 2006. ISBN 079225547x. 128 p. Grades 5–8.

In 1773, John Paul got into big trouble when, at the age of twenty-six, he killed a man. He was told he would have to go to trial and face a jury that included several of the dead man's friends and relatives. He had been in trouble before. This was not the first man he had killed. He decided to flee to the American colonies and change his name. He changed it to John Paul Jones.

John Paul Jones was quite a guy. More than anything he wanted to be famous. He was born to a poor family in a two-room cottage in Scotland, and he left to go to sea and try to make his fortune. He got what he wanted. He is a big name in American history, and he has an elaborate tomb at the U.S. Naval Academy in Annapolis, Maryland.

When the American Revolution started, John joined up. He wanted to command a ship, and that is exactly what he did. He commanded several, as a matter of fact, and the most famous of them all was named after Ben Franklin. The ship was called the *Le Bonhomme Richard.* It had been a French ship, and Franklin was in France working for the American Revolution. The name of the ship was a French translation of Franklin's pen name, *Good Richard.*

Le Bonhomme Richard became famous for one of the greatest naval battles of all time, in which she sank a British warship, than she herself sank two days later. At the height of the battle, John Paul Jones *might* have said the words he became famous for, "I have not yet begun to fight!" Then again, he may never have said that. But the story of that battle is exciting, horrible, and makes for great reading.

This is a good book about a fascinating man. If you like history, or the ocean, or ships, you will enjoy reading it.

Cooper, Michael L. *Jamestown, 1607.* Holiday House, 2007. ISBN 0823419487. 98 p. Grades 5–8.

On April 26, 1607, three small sailing ships finally spotted land. Loaded on those ships were 105 colonists and 39 sailors, and they were all jammed together and thoroughly sick of it. The food was rotten, the water stank horribly, and it had taken them four months to get to their destination.

"The Englishmen had come to Chesapeake Bay to establish, or *plant,* as they said then, a *plantation,* or colony, in Virginia" (p. 6). They were late. Spaniards had been colonizing the Americas for some time, and England wanted a piece of the pie. They were sure there was lots of gold in the area, and they believed hopefully that they might be able to find a water route to the Pacific Ocean.

This is the story of the beginning of the Jamestown Colony, the terrible times the residents there went through with not enough supplies and not nearly enough food, and the relationships they established with the local Native Americans. Those were not the best either. Neither the colonists nor the natives trusted each other very much, and there was a good reason for that.

The colonists had a pretty good leader, John Smith, and the natives had an excellent one, the chief Powhatan, whose daughter Pocahontas became the most famous native American of her time.

Find out how our country got its first English settlement—the things that were good and the things that were bad. It's a good, true story.

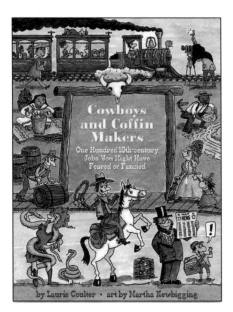

*Cowboys and Coffin Makers: One Hundred
19th-Century Jobs You Might Have Feared
or Fancied* **by Laurie Coulter.**

Coulter, Laurie. *Cowboys and Coffin Makers: One Hundred 19th-Century Jobs You Might
Have Feared or Fancied.* Art by Martha Newbigging. Annick Press, 2007. ISBN
1554510678. 96 p. Grades 4–8.

A lot of things were changing rapidly in the 1800s. One thing did not really
change much, though. Almost everyone, male, female, child, and adult, had to
work—unless the family was quite wealthy. Many of the jobs that were available re-
sulted from all of the changes that were happening. And some of those jobs were absolutely awful. Here are a few:

- Nightman: House owners and landlords paid this man money to empty out the
privies (or outhouses where people went to the bathroom). They could only
work at night because no one wanted to see them or accidentally run into them.

- Sandhogs worked underneath the water of the East River in New York City
building the Brooklyn Bridge. They worked inside a caisson filled with a lot of
compressed air. Their ears and head often ached, and a disease caused by coming up to the surface too quickly could have killed you. That disease is called
"the bends."

- Breaker boys had horrible jobs. They sat on benches and sorted out pieces of
rock from the coal coming up from the mines. It was filthy. It was too noisy to
talk. Their backs hurt all of the time. Their hands bled until they got toughened
up. Yuck.

- Field slaves led horrible lives. They barely were given enough to eat, and they
had to work from can to can't—can see the sun to can't see the sun. They were
often beaten, and the work was hard and horribly hot. Most of them worked with
cotton. Plus their families could be sold away from them. They had no freedom.

- Mill workers were often women. They worked twelve hours a day in dangerous conditions and deafening noise. The machinery wasn't safe, and they were exposed to many diseases.

And that's just a start. Take a look at this book with its fun illustrations and see if any of the jobs look good to you. Telegraph operator anyone? Snake charmer? Dinosaur hunter? Salt maker? You'll accidentally learn some amazing history.

***New York: The Empire State* by
Margery Facklam and Peggy Thomas.**

Facklam, Margery, and Peggy Thomas. *New York: The Empire State* (Welcome to the Empire State!). Illustrated by Jon Messer. Charlesbridge, 2007. ISBN 1570916608. 44 p. Grades 4–6.

When we say New York, a lot of us think of one city. It's a big and beautiful one, but it has a whole big state attached to it.

This book is filled with interesting facts and fun pictures. Here are a few fun things about New York State:

- Montauk Point Lighthouse on Long Island was ordered built by George Washington in 1792. It still works!

- In the Leatherstocking Region, you can take a boat on an underground lake in the Howe Caverns. You take an elevator to get there.

- The Erie Canal was one of the wonders of the world when it was built. Today it is mainly used by pleasure boats. It opened in 1825, and cannons boomed along the length of the canal, one at a time, to spread the news.

- Syracuse is called the "Salt City" because it was a great place to collect salt. Syracuse gets more snow than anyplace else in New York State.

- Adirondack Park is larger than Yellowstone, Grand Canyon, and Yosemite parks combined. It is more than six million acres!

- Buffalo used to be called the City of Light. Niagara Falls generated a lot of electricity.

And that's just the beginning. You will want to visit all these places when you read the book.

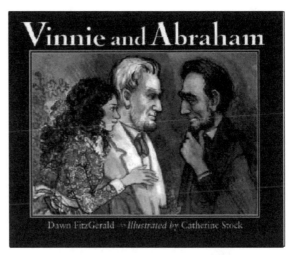

***Vinnie and Abraham* by Dawn FitzGerald.**

FitzGerald, Dawn. *Vinnie and Abraham.* Illustrated by Catherine Stock. Charlesbridge, 2007. ISBN 1570916586. Unpaged. Grades 3–5.

Vinnie Ream had a dream, one she was determined to make come true.

Vinnie loved to sculpt, and she was good at it. She made faces of her friends out of mud when she was growing up in the Wisconsin territory, but her family moved to Washington, D.C. when the Civil War broke out. There, she did something else unusual. She got a job in the dead letter office of the U.S. Post Office even though she was only fourteen years old. So many men were fighting that the post office actually had to hire females!

But Vinnie dreamed. After work, she went to graveyards and studied statues on tombstones. Eventually, she did something pretty scary and brave. She went to a famous sculptor and asked for a job making art. When he saw what she could do, he hired her. Vinnie achieved the biggest dream of her life, for eventually she sculpted the man she so admired: the president of the United States, Abraham Lincoln. And today her statue is famous. This is her story.

Fleming, Thomas. *Everybody's Revolution: A New Look at the People Who Won America's Freedom.* Scholastic Nonfiction, an imprint of Scholastic, A Byron Preiss Visual Publications, Book, 2006. ISBN 0439634040. 96 p. Grades 4–6.

So who were those guys who fought in the American Revolution? Weren't they all a bunch of English guys? I mean I know that some of them were born in the United States, but they all considered themselves English, didn't they?

Well, maybe not, and the author of this book is out to set the record straight. The American Revolution was not just a bunch of white English guys fighting each other. There were African Americans—some were still slaves—in that war. There were Native Americans fighting on both sides. There were people of German, Irish, Scottish,

French, Dutch, Polish, Jewish, Swedish, and Swiss backgrounds. Some people from those countries even came to the colonies to help, and they made huge differences.

And guess what? There were women too! Some of them even fought in battles. A few disguised themselves as men and joined the Continental Army. Another few served as spies. Many thousands did all sorts of work at home to help the army. One was sixteen-year-old Sybil Ludington, who made a nighttime ride longer than Paul Revere's to warn the people around Danbury, Connecticut, that the British were attacking. She was just a teenager, and many kids even younger than she fought and did other things to help the cause. One young trumpeter, a slave about twelve years old, fired a pistol at an attacking British officer's horse and saved the life of George Washington's brother.

Oneidas, who were Native Americans, stopped the British from capturing Lafayette, the young Frenchman who had volunteered to come to America to help the colonists fight for freedom. Thousands of British attacked a group of only about one hundred Americans, but when they sent in their cavalry, the Oneida let out a fierce war whoop and scared the heck out of the British. They pretty much fell apart, saving the day.

This book is loaded with stories like these. You will enjoy reading about the brave people from many different backgrounds who helped win freedom for Colonial America.

Show the picture of Sybil Ludington on page 80.

5,000 Miles to Freedom: Ellen and William Craft's Flight from Slavery **by Judith Bloom Fradin and Dennis Brindell Fradin.**

Fradin, Judith Bloom, and Dennis Brindell Fradin. *5,000 Miles to Freedom: Ellen and William Craft's Flight from Slavery.* National Geographic, 2006. ISBN 0792278852. 96 p. Grades 4–up.

It was December 1848, and two slaves in a cabin near Macon, Georgia, woke up and began the greatest adventure of their lives.

They planned to escape. Ellen was twenty-two years old, and her husband, William Craft, was twenty-five (although their marriage was a "slave" marriage, not legal according to law). They had a scary, courageous, and original plan.

Ellen looked like a white person. Her father had been white, and she did not look African American. Her husband was black. What the couple decided to do was disguise Ellen as a young white man—and William as that young white man's slave. Together they would travel more than a thousand miles to freedom in Pennsylvania.

William cut Ellen's hair, and she dressed herself in a man's suit and shoes. She tied a handkerchief around her chin and face to pretend that she had a toothache—and to hide the fact that she had no whiskers. She put her arm in a sling and told everyone she had rheumatism because she was afraid she might be asked to write something—and neither she nor William could read or write. Once she even pretended to be deaf when she did not want to answer a question.

The two of them bought train tickets. William, the young man's slave, did not get a seat. He had to ride in the baggage train.

Would they be able to escape? If they didn't make it, they would be tortured, beaten, maybe even killed. For sure, they would be separated and never see each other again.

Was it worth the risk?

This is one of the most incredible stories ever—and it's true. It is a great read!

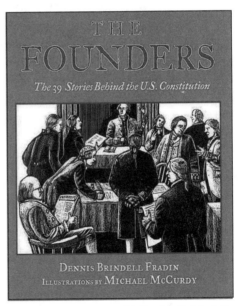

The Founders: The 39 Stories Behind the
U.S. Constitution **by Dennis Brindell Fradin.**

Fradin, Dennis Brindell. *The Founders: The 39 Stories Behind the U.S. Constitution.* Illustrations by Michael McCurdy. Walker & Company, 2005. ISBN 0802789722. 162 p. Grades 5–up.

After the Revolutionary War, some people called our country the united states—not capitalized. Each state name seemed more important than the country it belonged to.

The reason for that was pretty obvious. The states had always been more important than a unified country. The idea of a unified country with states in it was something new—and that new unified government had very little power.

Our founding fathers knew that would not work for long. The federal government had to have some authority and be able to govern this new country. So thirty-nine men, from twelve states (Rhode Island did not want a strong federal government and did not want to get involved in writing a constitution!), met in Philadelphia to write a constitution.

These are their stories. There are about three pages on each man who helped write the amazing U.S. Constitution, including portraits of them all based on real-life paintings. They are a fascinating group.

Once you start reading this book, you will have a hard time putting it down! Here are some of the facts you will learn:

- Between 1776 and 1787, the capital of the United States moved *nine* times! This country needed a new and permanent capital.

- John Dickinson of Delaware was the governor of two states at the same time—for two months. He was governor of both Delaware and Pennsylvania.

- Gunning Bedford Jr., also of Delaware, told the representatives of the big states that he did not trust them. He was afraid they would gang up on the small states.

- At the age of twelve, William Livingston of New Jersey went to spend a year living with a missionary with the Mohawk Indians. When he was older, he helped a homeless young man with good letters of introduction by putting him through school. That young man was Alexander Hamilton, who later also signed the Constitution.

- David Brearley, also of New Jersey, thought all the states should be the same size. He thought they should take a map, erase all of the borders, and create equal-sized new states.

- Nathaniel Gorham of Massachusetts thought the United States really needed a king. He wrote to Prince Henry of Prussia (which is now a part of Germany) asking him to consider the job.

This is a fine read.

Freedman, Russell. *Freedom Walkers: The Story of the Montgomery Bus Boycott.* Holiday House, 2006. ISBN 0823420310. 114 p. Grades 4–8.

In 1865 American slaves were freed. Most of them really had no place to go. With no money and no land and no education, most of them stayed in the South. Laws were soon passed to keep them "in their place," which was far away from equality. These laws were called "Jim Crow" laws, and one of them said that black people could ride in a public bus, but they had to sit in the back of the bus. White people could sit up front. If too many white people got on the bus, black people had to stand up and give away their seats.

This was a crazy law, and it constantly humiliated blacks. In many cities, they had to pay in the front of the bus and then get off and go in the back door to seat themselves. Sometimes the bus driver drove away before they could get in. But it was legal. African Americans had almost no rights.

By 1955, a few people had tried, unsuccessfully, to change that law. But in Montgomery, Alabama, a seamstress named Rosa Parks refused to get up and let a white person take her seat. She was arrested and taken to jail. She was released on bail, but the African American community decided it had had it. Rosa was arrested on December 1, a Thursday. All over the community, people began to organize a bus boycott. Almost all of the bus riders were African American. They figured if African Americans stopped riding the buses, the bus companies would realize how valuable their business was. So, on Monday, December 5, almost no black people rode the bus.

And that was the beginning of the freedom walkers.

For more than one year, people walked or car pooled or taxied or did whatever was necessary to get themselves to school and to work and to wherever else they needed to go. Some of them walked twenty miles a day! And a new, young minister in town emerged as a powerful, incredibly articulate leader. His name was Martin Luther King, Jr., and some of the speeches he made will take your breath away.

The city leaders, who were all white, did everything they could to stop that boycott, including arresting dozens of people for no good reason.

This is one of the most moving, compelling books you will ever read.

*The Silent Witness: A True Story of the
Civil War* by **Robin Friedman.**

Friedman, Robin. *The Silent Witness: A True Story of the Civil War.* Illustrated by Claire A. Nivola. Houghton Mifflin, 2005. ISBN 0618442308. Unpaged. Grades 1–3.

Lula McLean was only four years old when the Civil War started, but she was close to it. The first battle of the war, the Battle of Bull Run, as the Union called it, or Manassas, as the Confederates called it, took place in her yard. Her father, Wilmer McLean, let the Confederates use his home for their headquarters, but he hated being so close to the battle. After it was over, he moved to a tiny little town in southwestern Virginia—the town of Appomattox Courthouse.

In his home there, the Civil War ended. For General Grant of the Union and General Lee of the Confederacy met there, and Lee surrendered.

Lula's doll was there in that room when it happened.

This is a true story. It is a great introduction to the Civil War.

Fritz, Jean. *Who's Saying What in Jamestown, Thomas Savage?* Illustrations by Sally Wern Comport. G. P. Putnam's Sons, 2007. ISBN 0399246444. 64 p. Grades 4–6.

The first British colony in North America that survived was Jamestown, Virginia. A shipload of settlers, all male, arrived there in 1607, and one of them was a kid—a thirteen-year-old named Thomas Savage, who made a pretty astonishing life for himself in the New World. He wasn't wealthy, that was for sure. He was the cabin boy on the way over, but the captain of the ship really liked him, and so, it seemed, did a lot of other people. John Smith chose him to live with the Native Americans for a while and learn their language so he could translate. He even became a friend with Pocahontas, the daughter of the mighty chief.

Jamestown was not a very nice place at the beginning. A lot of the men did not want to work. They were gentlemen and considered hard work beneath them. Let other people do the hard stuff! They liked to sit around. But there was no food, and no place to live at first. If everyone didn't work hard, they were all going to freeze and starve—and a lot of them did exactly that.

Thomas was definitely one of the hard workers. And he ended up not poor at all. This is his amazing true story, and you'll enjoy reading about him.

Giblin, James Cross. *The Many Rides of Paul Revere.* Illustrated with Archival Photographs. Scholastic Press, 2007. ISBN 0439572908. 86 p. Grades 4–up.

If you have ever heard of Paul Revere, you probably know one thing for sure. He is famous for a horseback ride that led to the beginning of the American Revolution against Great Britain.

But exactly what happened on that ride? The reason so many people have heard about it is that a poet named Henry Wadsworth Longfellow wrote a poem called "The Midnight Ride of Paul Revere." Most people believe that the information he put in that poem is correct. And it is, partly.

But this is a book about more than one ride, and what it does tell us about that ride adds a lot of interesting new information. It also tells a lot more about the man himself, Paul Revere, a great American patriot who made a lot more than just one ride to help out the cause of the revolutionaries. He was riding a lot, for many reasons, during this time, and his own life was happening constantly in between.

It was an interesting life!

This book is loaded with lots of old illustrations, and, with them and the stories, we get a real feel for what this great man was like.

Alaska **by Shelley Gill.**

Gill, Shelley. *Alaska.* Photographs by Patrick J. Endres. Charlesbridge, 2007. ISBN 0881062928. Unpaged. Grades 2–5.

Have you been to Alaska? If not, have you ever wanted to visit it? If you say no, wait until you take a look at this beautiful book. You'll want to go immediately, for Alaska is a beautiful, beautiful place.

What is it like there? Well, it has all sorts of unusual things. In Barrow the sun doesn't come up for weeks between November and January—it is dark all of the time. But from most of May to July, the sun never sets there. It is always daylight! When it gets really cold, people's nose hair freezes and their spit shatters! In 1964 Alaska had the strongest earthquake ever recorded in North America—9.2 on the Richter scale. Alaska has the highest mountain in North America, Denali or Mount McKinley, and it does not have a lot of roads. Many people get around mainly in small planes.

A newcomer to Alaska is called a *cheechako,* and you will love reading some of the tips for cheechakos. Here are a few:

- "Don't eat yellow snow."

- "Don't ski on slopes where there are no trees."

- "Be careful where you step. Some mudflats are quicksand."

- "When Alaskans leave the state, they say they are 'going Outside'."

Greenwood, Barbara. *Factory Girl.* Kids Can Press, 2007. ISBN 1553376498. 136 p. Grades 5–9.

Times have changed. One of the ways in which they have changed for the better in much of the world is that most kids no longer have to work outside the home so that their families can eat. A hundred years ago, that was not the case. Poor people, especially immigrants to North America, had to work very hard just to stay alive. Their living conditions were often horrible. They had little free time and owned almost nothing. And the jobs they were able to find paid almost nothing and were in unsafe and unsanitary conditions.

This book takes the story of one girl, Emily Watson, who needs to find a job in 1912. The jobs that she can get are few, for she is too young to legally work. The places that will hire her will probably pay her less because of this. Emily gets a job sewing in a factory. Her father has gone west to earn a living and has stopped sending money to the family. Her mother has pawned her sewing machine to pay the rent, but now they have been forced to move into a slum, and any money at all that Emily can make is needed for food.

Mixed in with Emily's story are photographs and a lot of information about what it was like to be a kid and have to work. What was it like to live in a slum? Why would people do almost anything to hold on to their rotten, low-paying jobs? What was it like to be a newcomer in a land and not speak any English?

Perhaps most importantly, for the kids, was how were things going to change? What kind of help would they need to be able to stop having to do the things that were often killing them? Who would come to their rescue?

You will be glad you were not alive during the time that this book takes place.

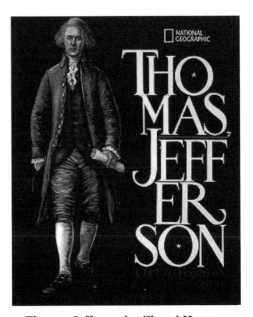

***Thomas Jefferson* by Cheryl Harness.**

Harness, Cheryl. *Thomas Jefferson*. National Geographic, 2004. ISBN 0792264967. 44 p. Grades 3–5.

Almost no one was more important to the colonies that became the United States of America than Thomas Jefferson. He wrote the Declaration of Independence, he was the third president, and he bought a huge amount of land, the Louisiana Purchase, which more than doubled the size of the country. After that, the United States didn't have just one ocean coast—it went from sea to shining sea, Atlantic to Pacific.

Jefferson was born in 1743 in Virginia, the state that he loved and which was his home for almost all of his life. He had a beloved best friend named Dabney Carr, as good an education as you could get in those days, and he fell in love with and married a beautiful young woman. Life seemed good, and it was, in many ways, but Jefferson had more than his share of sorrow. His beloved young wife died young, and he never remarried. Most of his children died before he did. He was never very good with money and usually owed a lot of it.

But he was brilliant, a man who envisioned the future and was delighted by so many of life's pleasures. He believed that every man had the right to life, liberty, and the pursuit of happiness, but yet he himself owned many slaves. Some of them may have been his own children.

Jefferson was a man of many contradictions, and this is a beautiful pictorial story of his life.

Show the picture of Jefferson with the globe and with his feet up on the title page.

The Tragic Tale of Narcissa Whitman and
a Faithful History of the Oregon Trail
by Cheryl Harness.

Harness, Cheryl. *The Tragic Tale of Narcissa Whitman and a Faithful History of the Oregon Trail* (A Cheryl Harness History). National Geographic, 2006. ISBN 0792259203. 144 p. Grades 4–8.

Narcissa Prentiss, born in western New York State in 1808, had a dream. When she was sixteen years old she wrote a letter to the American Board of Commissioners of Foreign Missions in which she said, "I frequently desired to go to the heathen … and [on] the first Monday of January 1824 … I felt to consecrate myself without reserve to the Missionary Work."

Narcissa did not have much chance of being a missionary. Not many single ladies were. She needed a husband, one who was a missionary, and a few years later she got one. Marcus Whitman was a physician (not very well trained, but none of them were at that time), and apparently she loved him.

With another missionary couple, Marcus and Narcissa were to embark upon one of the great adventures in American history. They were to head west and set up a mission in the Oregon territory—and Narcissa and Eliza Spalding were the first white women ever to make the trip.

It was a hard, hard trip, with no roads, not enough food, and frequently not enough water.

And at the end of it, Narcissa and her husband and family were living in a mission on land that belonged to the Indians, and they did not treat those Indians very well at all.

This is the true, compelling story of a real pioneer, who paid horribly for the way she treated those Indians.

***Delivering Justice: W. W. Law and the
Fight for Civil Rights* by Jim Haskins.**

Haskins, Jim. *Delivering Justice: W. W. Law and the Fight for Civil Rights.* Illustrated by Benny Andrews. Candlewick Press, 2006. ISBN 0763625922. Unpaged. Grades 2–5.

Westley Law grew up in a time when African Americans did not have the same rights as white people. In Savannah, Georgia, he only got to see his mother one day a week. She had to work for a white family the rest of the time. His grandma had a hard time buying things at stores. The clerk would wait on any white person first, even if African Americans had already been waiting for a long time. Westley was determined to help change things, and he started when he was a teenager. He helped black people register to vote. They had to pass tests that were set up to prevent them from voting. He helped them study for the test.

Next he became a mailman, and things really started to change—he was a big leader of that change. Read this book and find out what he did.

Haskins, James, and Kathleen Benson. *John Lewis in the Lead: A Story of the Civil Rights Movement.* Illustrations by Benny Andrews. Lee & Low Books, 2006. ISBN 158430250X. Unpaged. Grades 3–5.

John Lewis was born poor—really poor. His family were sharecroppers in Alabama and had almost no money. He was African American, born in 1940, and segregation was the law. No way were black people treated fairly or equally. And John wanted that to change.

He decided he was going to do something when he first heard a man named Dr. Martin Luther King, Jr. speaking on the radio. Dr. King was one of the leaders in the Montgomery, Alabama, bus boycott, sparked on the day Rosa Parks refused to give up her seat on the bus so a white person could sit. Dr. King believe in nonviolent change. And John Lewis went and applied for a card at the public library. He knew—and he was right—that the librarian would tell him the library was for white people only. It was the beginning of a life of trying to make changes for the better.

This is the true story of a brave, thoughtful man who put his own life on the line several times so that the world would be a better place. Today he is a U.S. congressman from Georgia.

Up Before Daybreak: Cotton and People in America
by Deborah Hopkinson.

Hopkinson, Deborah. *Up Before Daybreak: Cotton and People in America.* Scholastic Nonfiction, an imprint of Scholastic, 2006. ISBN 0439639018. 120 p. Grades 4–up.

People called it "King Cotton," and there was a reason for that. Cotton drove the economy of the southern United States for many years, and cotton also destroyed lives.

Long ago, people learned all over the world that cotton could be used to make cloth and clothing. The textile industry in Great Britain needed more cotton for its mills, and the land in the American South was perfect for growing the plant.

But cotton was labor-intensive. Workers had to plant the cotton, weed the cotton, and then pick the cotton. All of these were hard to do, but they paled in comparison to preparing the cotton plant for the market. For the cotton was full of seeds, seeds that were very difficult to get out—sort of like picking a burr out of your sock. Slaves took these out, slowly, painstakingly, one at a time, and many times their hands bled from the effort. Slaves also picked the cotton, pulling long, heavy sacks of the stuff, sometimes weighing one hundred pounds or more. The slaves were needed to make the growing and production of cotton cheap. They worked before the sun came up until after the sun came down, with little to eat, little clothing, poor treatment, and almost no time off.

When the cotton gin was invented to take out the seeds, it just meant slaves had to pick more cotton, for more cotton was able to be produced.

Then the cotton had to be turned into cloth, and mills in New England started up, hiring young women at low wages to work long hours.

And that is just part of the story. This book has excellent photographs, both of the people who worked with the cotton and of the plant itself. It has great and tragic stories of life under slavery and the people who worked with the plant.

Double Cheeseburgers, Quiche, and Vegetarian Burritos: American Cooking from the 1920s Through Today **by Loretta Frances Ichord.**

Ichord, Loretta Frances. *Double Cheeseburgers, Quiche, and Vegetarian Burritos: American Cooking from the 1920s Through Today* (Cooking Through Time). Illustrated by Jan Davey Ellis. Millbrook Press, 2007. ISBN 0822559692. 64 p. Grades 4–6.

Have you ever heard someone say, "That's the greatest thing since sliced bread!"? If you think about it, you might wonder why people say that. There is a good reason.

The first machine that sliced bread was invented in 1928. Now almost all the bread people buy comes sliced, and we think nothing of it, but it was a big deal back then, and we are still talking about it, even though we don't always know why.

This is a really interesting book that tells us what Americans ate starting in about 1900 and up until the present.

In 1900, making meals was hard and time-consuming work. Very few labor saving devices had been invented, and we learn that many women spent as long as forty-four hours a week working in the kitchen. Stoves were heated with wood or coal, and they were dirty, messy—and you could not really control the temperature. People had iceboxes to keep food cold, but no frozen food. No microwaves. No TV dinners. No fast food. Most food, in fact, took a long time to cook.

Look at the way it is now. Many women spend very little time preparing food. They even have dishwashers to do the cleaning up.

Take a walk through the last one hundred or so years and see all the changes that happened and all the different ways people started cooking. For instance, there was very little ethnic food available to most people—like Mexican or Chinese or Italian, which today we eat all the time (and love!). There were few cookbooks; now there are thousands. And that's just the beginning. You will love the information you find out in this interesting, colorful book.

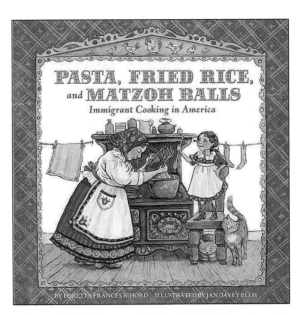

Pasta, Fried Rice, and Matzoh Balls: Immigrant Cooking in America **by Loretta Frances Ichord.**

Ichord, Loretta Frances. *Pasta, Fried Rice, and Matzoh Balls: Immigrant Cooking in America.* Illustrated by Jan Davey Ellis. Millbrook Press, 2006. ISBN 0761329137. 64 p. Grades 3–5.

Some people call the United States a melting pot. People came and are coming from all over the world to live there—and they all like to bring their favorite foods and recipes with them. America has some wonderfully exciting foods that came from all over the world.

The British brought their foods with them when they first settled the colonies, but Spanish people in the southwestern part of the United States adapted their own recipes to include foods inspired by the Mexicans and the Native Americans. French immigrants, especially in the Louisiana area, gave us Cajun and Creole food. Do you like French onion soup? Mayonnaise? French bread? The Dutch gave us doughnuts, coleslaw, and waffles!

Swedes gave us coffee parties, which Americans turned into coffee breaks. Then the Germans arrived with pretzels, wieners, and potato salad.

Italians, who started arriving around 1880, gave us perhaps the most popular foods of all—pizza, pasta, olive oil, macaroni, garlic bread—and more.

Eastern Europeans arrived with goulash, strudel, paprika, and Polish sausage. And when millions of Jewish emigrated, they, too, gave us great food. You will learn what kosher foods are and how the laws of *kashrut* (Jewish dietary laws of cleanliness) work.

Asians were much discriminated against, but their cooking conquered a lot of prejudice against them.

This book has lots of pictures and several recipes. Your mouth will be watering almost as soon as you start reading.

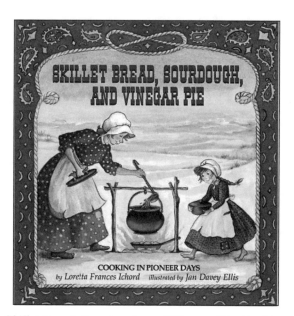

Skillet Bread, Sourdough, and Vinegar Pie: Cooking in Pioneer Days **by Loretta Frances Ichord.**

Ichord, Loretta Frances. *Skillet Bread, Sourdough, and Vinegar Pie: Cooking in Pioneer Days.* Illustrated by Jan Davey Ellis. Millbrook Press, 2003. ISBN 0761395210. 64 p. Grades 3–up.

Do you like to go camping? Do you think it is fun to cook your food over a fire? Is it fun to pick which foods you want to bring with you and to carry them? Do you like building fires?

Well, imagine that you were a pioneer, or a gold miner, or a cowboy. You got to camp out *a lot*. You might camp out as much as six months at a time. And building a fire, especially when you could not find any fuel, might not be any fun at all.

In the middle of the 1800s, many Americans decided to move west. They wanted more space and good land. "Their heads had been filled with tall tales of pigs waiting in Oregon Country, already cooked with forks and knives sticking in them, and pumpkins so big that a barn could be carved out of just one!" (p. 8).

But, oh, did they have to pack food—lots and lots of food. Read the list of what a person should have for provisions at the top of page 10. That food was heavy, and the further west they got, the harder it was to find clean water. The food that was available to buy was incredibly expensive.

One thing some of them ate was buffalo, if they could kill one. Here are some recipes they tried: Baked Buffalo Nose, Raw Buffalo Liver Sprinkled with Gall Bladder

Juice, and Buffalo Intestines filled with Grasses and Set in the Sun to Ferment. Sound good?

But some of the things they made *do* sound good, and this book includes the recipes for several of them.

The gold miners and the cowboys may have had it even worse. Most of them were not very good cooks, and they loved the thought of eating a woman's cooking. There were not many women in the west, and one way a woman could make a good living was by cooking and baking.

By the time you finish reading, you will have learned a lot about an interesting time in history—and you will probably be very happy that you never had to be a pioneer or a gold miner or even a cowboy.

Jacobson, Sid, and Ernie Colón. *The 9/11 Report: A Graphic Adaptation*. Hill and Wang, 2006. ISBN 9780809057382. 128 p. Grades 7–up.

Do you want to read a 600-page book explaining the terrorist attacks of September 11? Probably not. Luckily, Jacobson and Colón have taken the lengthy 9-11 Commission Report and put it into words and pictures, providing an effect that words alone could never achieve. It begins with the four airplanes that were hijacked and shows a timeline of the events of that day. Then it shows what the president and other officials were doing and how they handled the disaster. Then it goes back in time and shows how Osama bin Laden became the leader of Al Qaeda and how the nineteen hijackers came to be chosen and trained. In the end, it tells what the 9-11 Commission thinks the United States should be doing to fight terrorism. Unfortunately, the country has not been doing a good job of following the commission's recommendations. This is a fine comic book that is easy to read. If you want to understand September 11, it is the perfect book for you.

Jordan, Anne Devereaux, with Virginia Schomp. *Slavery and Resistance* (The Drama of African-American History). Marshall Cavendish Benchmark Books, 2006. ISBN 0761421785. 70 p. Grades 4–8.

Africans were captured and made into slaves before Columbus first came to America. What happened to them as they were shipped across the ocean was horrifying and savage. Only about one third of them survived the trip across the Atlantic Ocean.

The first slaves to arrive in an English settlement came to Jamestown in 1619. These people were at first not treated as slaves. They were treated as indentured servants. They worked for a period of years and then they were set free. But over the years that changed.

By the 1600s, settlers along the Chesapeake Bay needed more helpers to plant, grow, and cultivate their tobacco crops. They began to buy African slaves. Africans could not easily escape. White indentured servants could escape and blend into the population, but Africans were easy to find.

Then in South Carolina, more and more slaves were purchased for rice plantations. And after Eli Whitney invented the cotton gin (engine), more slaves were needed to produce what was the most profitable crop of them all: cotton.

As more slaves arrived, their rights began to vanish completely. Slaves had almost no rights at all. Their masters could do *anything* to them and not be punished for it. Some were freed, but their lives were not very good—better in the North than in the

South, but still far from equal. By the early 1800s, there were few slaves in the northern part of the country, but millions in the South.

Slaves hated being slaves, and no wonder. They tried to snatch every opportunity to escape and to fight back. They hoped that the Revolutionary War would bring them the freedom the colonists talked about all the time, but they were wrong. It did not. Some white people, such as Abigail Adams, supported their right to be free and many people became abolitionists, wanting to abolish slavery forever.

This is the story of what slaves did to fight back in all sorts of ways, and of how they got to be in the terrible institution of slavery. It is sad but fascinating.

O, Say Can You See? America's Symbols, Landmarks, and Inspiring Words **by Sheila Keenan.**

Keenan, Sheila. *O, Say Can You See? America's Symbols, Landmarks, and Inspiring Words*. Illustrated by Ann Boyajian. Scholastic Nonfiction, 2004. ISBN 043942450x. 64 p. Grades 3–6.

This book is filled with fun information about the United States of America. Did you know that:

- The Pilgrims never landed on Plymouth Rock? It wasn't believable that they ever did, but it made a good story, so people ran with it. Read the facts on pages 6–7.

- The White House has 132 rooms?

- The tallest building in Washington, D.C., is the Washington Monument?

- Mount Rushmore is the largest work of art in the world?

- Uncle Sam started out as a cartoon character in the 1880s?

- Ben Franklin wanted the turkey, not the bald eagle, to be our national bird?

And much, much more!

Krull, Kathleen. *Pocahontas: Princess of the New World.* Pictures by David Diaz. Walker & Company, 2007. ISBN 0802795552. Unpaged. Grades 2–5.

We do not know a whole lot about Pocahontas, but what we do know makes us very curious. She must have been quite a person! The first time we hear about her, she was about eleven years old. We know what her life was probably like before that, for we know how young girls were treated in her tribe. And we know she had a great fierce warrior for a father, Chief Powhatan—and that she was his favorite. That alone makes her special.

But in 1607, a group of Englishmen arrived in a small ship to found a colony in a place they called Virginia. "The men were exhausted, sick, smelly and crabby." And they weren't very good at what they were doing either. Within a few months, half of the men in the group were dead.

They didn't think it was important that the land already had people living on it. But one man, Captain John Smith, knew they needed to have good relationships with the natives who were there. And it turned out that he and Pocahontas ended up having a good relationship.

This is the story of that famous girl and young woman, the one who started out as a free and happy young Native American and ended up dying in England, married to an Englishman.

This is her story.

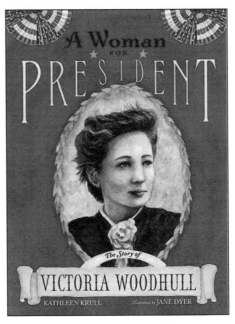

A Woman for President: the Story of Victoria Woodhull **by Kathleen Krull.**

Krull, Kathleen. *A Woman for President: The Story of Victoria Woodhull.* Illustrations by Jane Dyer. Walker & Company, 2004. ISBN 0802789080. Unpaged. Grades 3–5.

You might not know which candidate for president never even got to vote at all—and also got to spend Election Day in jail. After you read this book, you will.

Victoria Woodhull must be one of the most interesting Americans you'll ever meet. She was born in a shack in Homer, Ohio, and her name then was Victoria Claflin. She had nine brothers and sisters and a father who beat them. Sometimes the children had to beg for food.

By the time she was eight years old, she was a child preacher, and she and her sister, Tennessee, started leading séances, which helped people communicate with their relatives and friends who had died. Their earnings supported the entire family.

She married an alcoholic, unreliable husband, Canning Woodhull, when she was a young teenager, and she later left him. She went back to doing séances with her sister again, and this time they kept the richest man in America, Cornelius Vanderbilt, in touch with his dead mother. He rewarded them so well that Victoria became a millionaire.

And Victoria decided that things needed to change. Women in America in the mid-1800s had very few rights and they were not allowed to vote. She decided to challenge the laws that prevented that.

This is a fascinating story.

Lakin, Patricia. *Abigail Adams: First Lady of the American Revolution* (Ready-to-Read. Level 3). Illustrated by Bob Dacey and Debra Bandelin. Aladdin, 2006. ISBN 0689870329. 48 p. Grades 2–4.

Abigail Smith Adams would have been an amazing woman at any time, but in the late 1700s and early 1800s she was almost unbelievable. Not many people believed at that time that women should be educated—a lot of them did not feel that women even needed to learn how to read.

But Abigail was lucky. Her father wanted her to learn things and to read, and she just loved getting an education.

When she was a young woman, she fell in love with a man with whom she had a lot in common. He loved to read too, and his name was John Adams. Have you heard of him?

Well, helping the new country of the United States of America be born, getting involved in a revolution, and trying to get help in that war from other countries proved to be a lot of the work of his life. He had to be gone a lot to get that done.

Abigail had to keep things running at home, trying to make money and take care of their family—and she wrote him wonderful letters.

This is the true story of the second First Lady of the United States, and she was a great one!

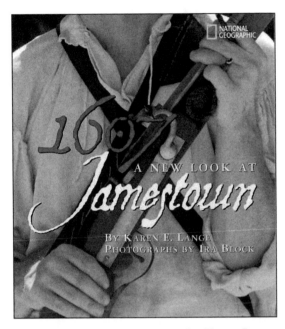

1607: A New Look at Jamestown by **Karen Lange.**

Lange, Karen. *1607: A New Look at Jamestown.* Photography by Ira Block. National Geographic, 2007. ISBN 1426300123. 48 p. Grades 4–7.

The first permanent English settlement in North America began thirteen years before the Pilgrims landed in New England. One hundred and four Englishmen arrived
on three ships. They had spent five months crossing the ocean, and they called the land
Virginia. They named the river they sailed up James, after their king.

They were most scared of the Spanish colonies and the Spanish ships, and they
wanted a place where they could keep watch. About thirty-six miles up the river, they
found it.

But, to put it mildly, the site they chose had problems. And those problems in addition to some of their own creating, were to make the first few years of that settlement
disastrous.

It was low and it was marshy. The river water was salty. There was no freshwater
spring. When the settlers drank the water, many became ill. It was often contaminated
with bacteria, and people got sick from the salt in it.

Furthermore, the settlers and the natives did not get along well. The land they
wanted to settle already belonged to an Indian tribe. Historians now believe about
25,000 Indians lived in the region. The English were able to trade one thing the Indians valued highly: copper.

This is the true story of what happened during the first few years of the colony,
and of the archaeological expeditions that are happening there today. Researchers
want to find out what caused "the starving time" that killed so many of the settlers.
They want to understand what went on at the very beginning of the English settlement
of America.

If you like history and mysteries and trying to figure them out, you will love reading and looking through this book with its great photographs. Show the one of the
skull on page 27.

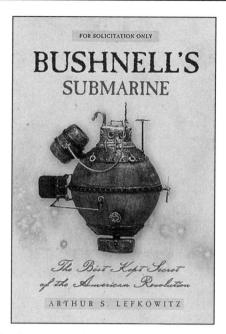

Bushnell's Submarine: The Best-Kept Secret of the
American Revolution **by Arthur S. Lefkowitz.**

Lefkowitz, Arthur S. *Bushnell's Submarine: The Best-Kept Secret of the American Revolution.* Scholastic Nonfiction, an imprint of Scholastic, 2006. ISBN 0439743524. 136 p. Grades 4–up.

The first submarine to actually sink an enemy ship was the *H.L. Hunley,* during the Civil War, but it wasn't the first submarine. That was built almost ninety years earlier during the American Revolution, and it came mighty close to sinking a ship.

The idea for building a ship that could travel underwater and blow up British ships came to a Connecticut farm boy who had gone to Yale. He was sure there had to be a way, a safe way, to glide underneath the water, attach a keg of gunpowder to a ship, and get out of the way successfully.

Look at the picture on the cover of the book. There it is. The barrel attached to the top of it is the gunpowder. It is attached to a screw. That screw was supposed to be screwed into the hull of a ship. The barrel would then detach and hang on to the ship, leaving enough time for the submarine to get out of the way. The ship would then blow up.

Well, that was the theory.

This tiny little ship came so close. But it had terrible flaws. The ship held only one person, the captain, who had to do everything in pitch dark. He could not see anything, inside or out. He was sitting partially in water. There were 150 pounds of gunpowder attached to him. And he had to supply all of the power to run the ship—no motors or engines.

This is a little-known story, and a fascinating one. You'll learn about the great inventor, David Bushnell, and about his newfangled machine.

Low, William. *Old Penn Station.* Henry Holt, 2007. ISBN 0805079254. Unpaged. Grades 2–5.

> The age of the railroad did not last all that long.
>
> The Pennsylvania Railroad Company was one of the biggest businesses in the United States in the 1890s, but it had a problem. It had no access to tunnels or bridges, and it could not get onto Manhattan Island, the heart of New York City. All of its passengers had to get out in New Jersey and board a ferry.
>
> The railroad company hired one of the most famous architectural firms in the world, McKim, Mead and White, to build a palace of a railway station and tunnels to get its passengers onto Manhattan. It hired hundreds of workers. What they built was staggeringly beautiful.
>
> Passengers could see the sky from the train platforms. There were shops and a fantastic restaurant. The waiting room was filled with sunlight. People loved to go there.
>
> And then people stopped taking so many trains. And the owners of Penn Station decided it had to go.
>
> This is a sad but beautiful book.

Maestro, Betsy. *Liberty or Death: The American Revolution: 1763–1783.* Illustrated by Giulio Maestro. HarperCollins, 2005. ISBN 0688088031. 64 p. Grades 3–6.

> In 1763, the French and Indian War ended in the American colonies. France at last agreed to leave many of its holdings, in Canada and east of the Mississippi River, in North America.
>
> But the war with the French had been very expensive for the rulers of the colonies, the British. They wanted the American colonials to pay for it, so in 1765 they created the Stamp Act, which would tax the Americans in a way those Americans felt was incredibly unfair.
>
> And that was the beginning of a disagreement that took more than twenty years to resolve.
>
> For the Stamp Act represented taxation without representation. The Colonists had no say in how they were governed or whether a tax was fair. They just had to pay it. And they did not want to and they started protesting. And it turned out they were very good at protesting.
>
> This is the step-by-step story of the American Revolutionary War, illustrated with lots of fine color pictures. How did it happen? What were some of the Americans' biggest successes and their worst failures? Who helped them? They could not have won a Revolution on their own.
>
> You'll meet some fascinating heroes, and a few rotten villains as well. This is an entertaining and very interesting look at the Revolution that created a brand-new country, dedicated to a theory that was pretty wild and crazy at the time—that all men were created equal and that they were entitled to life, liberty, and the pursuit of happiness.
>
> You will enjoy reading about it.

Magaziner, Henry Jonas. *Our Liberty Bell.* Illustrated by John O'Brien. Holiday House, 2007. ISBN 0823418928. 32 p. Grades 4–6.

Have you ever seen a picture of the Liberty Bell? If you have, you probably remember one thing for sure. It has a great big crack in it, and that means it does not ring anymore. But what is the Liberty Bell and why is it such a big deal?

This book tells its story.

The Liberty Bell had a hard history before it even got hung in the first place. It was first put up in 1752, in the Pennsylvania State House in Philadelphia. The Pennsylvania Colony guaranteed many liberties, including religious liberty, and the bell was made in England, brought to the colonies, and hung to celebrate the fiftieth anniversary of the colony.

It was a dud. It made a terrible noise, and then it cracked. The ship that brought it would not take it back. Two local bell makers decided to make a new one. They made a mold of the cracked bell then melted it. Out of that, and adding other materials, they made a new bell.

It was a dud, too. It did not crack, but it made a terrible noise, not a beautiful one like people want bells to make. So the same two guys repeated the whole process, and finally got it right. It was pretty, and it sounded good. And it stayed uncracked for a long time.

This is the story of the many times it rang, and the reasons it rang for liberty—and the story of how it got its famous crack. We can still see it today. Do you know where? This interesting book will answer all your questions.

McCarthy, Meghan. *Aliens are Coming: The True Account of the 1938 War of the Worlds Radio Broadcast.* Alfred A. Knopf, 2006. ISBN 0375835180. Unpaged. Grades 1–4.

In 1938, people loved to listen to the radio. They did not have TV yet, and they believed just about everything they heard on the news, even if it wasn't really the news.

It was the night before Halloween, October 30, and a young man named Orson Welles had created a special play. It was based on a famous book, *The War of the Worlds,* by H. G. Wells, and it described an alien invasion. The invaders were Martians, and they were killing people in New Jersey!

Even though the broadcast was interrupted a few times to alert people that it was only a play, a lot of people believed that Martians were really invading America—and those radio listeners were absolutely terrified!

Read all about it and find out why on earth they were so scared!

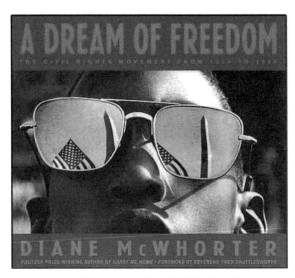

*A Dream of Freedom: The Civil Rights Movement
from 1954 to 1968* **by Diane McWhorter.**

McWhorter, Diane. *A Dream of Freedom: The Civil Rights Movement from 1954 to 1968*.
Foreword by Reverend Fred Shuttlesworth. Scholastic Nonfiction, 2004. ISBN
0439576784. 160 p. Grades 5–up.

In 1963, Diane McWhorter, the author of this book, was in sixth grade. She lived
in Birmingham, Alabama, and she was a white kid. She thought the phrase "civil
rights" was probably made up of bad words. She had no idea what African Americans
were suffering or enduring, and she was happy in her own little world. Birmingham
was considered the most segregated city in America.

In Birmingham that year, something terrible happened, as you may recall if you
have read *The Watsons Go to Birmingham, 1963* by Christopher Paul Curtis. But it
was just one of the many horrifying things that happened in the years covered in this
book, which tells us how the Civil Rights movement suddenly mushroomed, led by
the amazing Dr. Martin Luther King, Jr. and other activists, including the Reverend
Fred Shuttlesworth, who wrote the introduction to the book.

Segregation had been normal in many places in America, especially in the South,
almost since the end of the Civil War. "Black behavior under segregation was all
about 'knowing your place' and not acting 'uppity.' Your place was the back of the
bus, the balcony of the movie theater, and the colored waiting room. If you were trying
to get service in a store, all white people would be helped before you, even if they had
arrived after you. … It was dangerous to ignore the rules. During World War II, two
black soldiers were murdered in Mississippi by a group of white men to whom they
had said 'yes' instead of 'yes, sir' " (p. 15).

The injustices that African Americans had to endure are almost unbelievable.
They even had to pay taxes to be allowed to vote, and most of them could not afford it.
But a number of things happened that made change almost inevitable, and in a time
when heroes, male and female, were desperately needed, those heroes appeared. They
sometimes even gave their lives to the cause of civil rights.

This is an incredible book, illustrated with wonderful photographs.

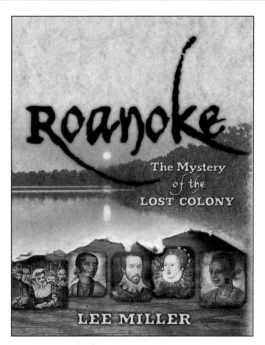

Roanoke: The Mystery of the Lost Colony
by Lee Todd Miller.

Miller, Lee Todd. *Roanoke: The Mystery of the Lost Colony*. Scholastic Nonfiction, 2007.
   ISBN 0439712661. 112 p. Grades 5–9.

   A lot of people love to read about real-life mysteries. The story of the Roanoke
Colony, a group of more than one hundred British people who settled in what is now
North Carolina in 1587, is one of the best. The colonists, who were left by the ships
that brought them there without enough food or supplies, were pretty much depending
on the Native Americans to feed them—and those people barely had enough to feed
themselves. Plus, the colonists were not on good terms with the natives. Relations between the two groups had always been strained. The governor of the colony, a fine artist named John White, went back to England to get help. When he returned three years
later, he could not find the colony or anyone who had been a member of it. One of
those members was his own daughter, her husband, and their child, Virginia Dare.

   What happened to those colonists is one of the biggest mysteries in American history.

   Lee Miller wrote an adult book about her theories as to what happened to the colonists.

   Now she has written a book for kids, and you will have a fine time reading it. But
you may want to read more to find out what the experts think might have happened. A
lot of people would disagree with Miller. Would you? Read it and find out.

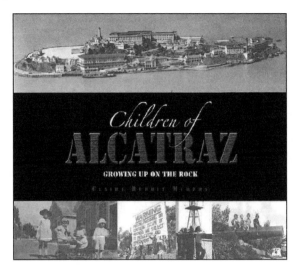

Children of Alcatraz: Growing Up on the Rock
by Claire Rudolf Murphy.

Murphy, Claire Rudolf. *Children of Alcatraz: Growing Up on the Rock.* Walker & Company, 2006. ISBN 0802795773. 64 p. Grades 4–7.

Do you know what Alcatraz is? It is an island located in San Francisco Bay. It has one of the greatest views in the world. It was named *La Isla de los Alcatraces,* which means the Island of the Pelicans, by Spanish sailors. They named it after the many pelicans that lived on the island.

It is unlikely anyone lived there in the beginning, for there was no fresh water, no wild animals, and no safe harbor. Native Americans called it Diamond Island.

In 1848 the island, now called Alcatraz, became the property of the United States—and in such a busy harbor, it was a great place to put a lighthouse, and then an army post, one designed to prevent the country from being invaded by sea.

Kids lived in the lighthouse and at the army post. The army post also had a military prison, and kids lived there, too. Some of them were even inmates in that prison.

But Alcatraz became world-famous in 1934 when it was turned into a maximum security federal penitentiary—the toughest one in the United States. The first shipment of federal prisoners included a really famous one, a gangster named Al Capone. Kids watched them arrive, because lots of kids lived on that island—children of the guards and the prison officers, lots of them. Sometimes, when they crossed the Bay to go to school in San Francisco, people did not believe them when they said they lived on Alcatraz, but they did.

This is their story. What do *you* think it would be like to live on an island from which you could not escape, surrounded by dangerous criminals? Find out in this book!

Quiet Hero: The Ira Hayes Story
by S. D. Nelson.

Nelson, S. D. *Quiet Hero: The Ira Hayes Story.* Lee & Low Books, 2006. ISBN 1584302631. Unpaged. Grades 2–6.

Ira Hayes never really wanted a lot of attention. His people, known as Pima Indians, lived on a reservation in Sacaton, Arizona. He was the oldest of four boys, and his family was so poor that they sent him to a government-run boarding school for Native Americans when he was a teenager. There he was shy and lonely. He missed his family horribly.

Then, in 1941, the Japanese bombed Pearl Harbor and the United States entered World War II. Ira joined the Marines, and there he found a place where he belonged. Native Americans were thought of as fierce fighters, so Ira was not put in a segregated unit. The guys he met became his best buddies, and early in 1943 the group headed into the war in the Pacific Ocean, where intense battles were being waged.

In 1945, his battalion was sent to Iwo Jima to fight one of the most fierce battles of the war. If you saw the movie *Flags of Our Fathers,* you may know quite a bit about it. That is when perhaps the most exciting and saddest event in his life happened. For Ira was one of the six men who raised the American flag at Iwo Jima, and the photograph a man named Joe Rosenthal took of them doing it became one of the most famous pictures in history. There is even a huge bronze statue of it in Washington, D.C.

Suddenly Ira was famous. Suddenly he was separated from his friends. Suddenly he really did not know what to do to cope with all of the attention.

This is the true story of a quiet hero.

Nobleman, Marc Tyler. *The Sinking of the USS* Indianapolis (We the People). Compass Point Books, 2007. ISBN 0756520312. 48 p. Grades 4–6.

The USS *Indianapolis* was already thirteen years old in 1945, but it was given a special mission anyway—one that was absolutely top secret. It carried parts for the first atomic bomb to a tiny island in the Pacific Ocean.

After it made that delivery, it sailed to Guam and then set off for the Philippine island of Leyte. The ship was going to participate in the invasion of Japan, but it never reached its destination.

The *Indianapolis* did not have the power to detect submarines, and the captain requested that a destroyer, which had that power, accompany the ship. This was common practice. But the superior of the ship's captain, Charles McVay, denied that request.

McVay left for Leyte unaware that there were Japanese submarines in the area and that his ship was in grave danger. And one of those submarines saw his ship and hit it with two torpedoes. The *Indianapolis* started sinking, fast.

And this was just the beginning of the nightmare. About three hundred men died quickly, and about nine hundred had to jump into the ocean and hope they could stay alive and not be eaten by sharks or die of thirst or starvation or exposure. They were three hundred miles from the nearest land.

This is a true horror story, and a classic story of injustice as well.

O'Connor, Jane. *If the Walls Could Talk: Family Life at the White House*. Illustrated by Gary Hovland. A Paula Wiseman Book/Simon and Schuster Books for Young Readers, 2004. ISBN 0689868634. Unpaged. Grades 4–6.

If you enjoy bits of odd information and fun facts (and who doesn't?), you'll enjoy reading this book about the White House and the presidents and their families. It is full of good stuff, such as:

- George Washington was the only president who never lived there. It wasn't finished yet when he left the presidency.

- Andrew Jackson had an open house celebration. Anyone could come and meet the president. It got out of hand—20,000 people showed up and made a terrible mess. Jackson ended up going out and staying in a hotel.

- The person who was president for the shortest time was William Henry Harrison. He only lived for thirty days after he took office. The longest time? Franklin Roosevelt, twelve years.

- Grover Cleveland was the only president to be married in the White House (so far) and his wife gave birth to the only child of a president who was born in the White House.

- Teddy Roosevelt officially named the building "The White House."

And there is much, much more, and a lot of fun illustrations.

Patent, Dorothy Hinshaw. *The Buffalo and the Indians: A Shared Destiny*. Photographs by William Munoz. Clarion Books, 2006. ISBN 0618485708. 85 p. Grades 4–8.

The animal that most of us call the buffalo, but some call the bison, has been living in North America for at least 129,000 years. There were several different types of bison, and about 8,500 years ago the native hunters found a good way to kill a small species of the animal. They would startle them into stampeding, and then drive them over a cliff. Below the cliff, they could kill any that survived—and get a lot of meat fairly simply. This technique worked for thousands of years.

The author tells us that the natives used every single part of the buffalo that they killed, and they treated the buffalo with great reverence. There are many stories about the buffalo and about how the buffalo and the natives worked together, and Hinshaw tells us one of those stories at the beginning of each chapter.

Even buffalo that were once considered fairly small are big by today's standards. A mature bull can measure as high as six feet tall at the shoulders and weigh as much as a ton. There are some wonderful photos of the animals.

The fate of the natives and the buffalo did seem related. When the Spaniards brought horses to North America in the 1500s, Indians soon learned to catch and ride them, and that made buffalo hunting very different—it was much easier to kill an individual or even several buffalo.

But what really caused the end of the buffalo was the coming of the pioneers. It became a government policy to kill buffalo, for the government knew that without buffalo, the Native Americans and their culture could not survive. If they could not get enough to eat, they would be forced to adopt American ways.

This is a good read. Show the pictures of the buffalos on pages 6 and 7.

Pringle, Laurence. *American Slave, American Hero: York of the Lewis and Clark Expedition.* Illustrations by Cornelius Van Wright and Ying-Hwa Hu. Calkins Creek Books, 2006. ISBN 1597782828. 40 p. Grades 2–5.

For about 250 years there were slaves in America. If you were a slave, you were usually of African descent and someone owned you. You had no rights at all. Your owner could do anything he or she wanted with you, and it was legal. It was an awful way to live.

One man did something no other slave got to do. More than fifty years before slavery ended, he got to vote. And his vote counted the same as all the other people who were voting. This was astonishing!

This slave was York, and he belonged to William Clark, one of the two leaders of the Lewis and Clark expedition. Clark decided to bring him along on that expedition, and this meant that Clark likely had a very high opinion of him. He must have been right, because, apparently, everybody liked York.

This is his story. We wish we knew more about him, but this excellent book tells us what we do know and also what is probably true.

Show the picture of York scaring the Native American children on page 19 and of him dancing on page 21.

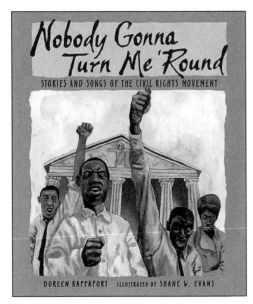

*Nobody Gonna Turn Me 'Round: Stories and Songs
of the Civil Rights Movement* by **Doreen Rappaport.**

Rappaport, Doreen. *Nobody Gonna Turn Me 'Round: Stories and Songs of the Civil Rights Movement.* Illustrated by Shane W. Evans. Candlewick, 2006. ISBN 0763619272. 64 p. Grades 4–7.

By the 1950s, African Americans were sick and tired of being treated as people with no rights at all, abused and exploited. Things needed to change. Many had been working for change for decades, but in the fifties major things started happening.

The Supreme Court declared that the separate but equal doctrine in education was against the law. African American schools might have been separate, but they certainly were not equal. Laws began to change.

In Greensboro, North Carolina, a group of students held a sit-in at a local Woolworth's store. Many restaurants would not serve African Americans. All of the students who took part were determined not to be violent, no matter what violence was done to them. Change, they believed, would come only through nonviolent behavior. They prepared to defend themselves as best they could, nonviolently (see the picture on page 27). It was a start.

They fought segregation on buses, inequality in voting tests, and discrimination wherever they found it, which was almost everywhere. Many paid for their protests with their lives, and more were badly beaten.

And through it all, many sang—songs like "We Shall Overcome" and "Keep Your Eyes on the Prize."

This book, with its beautiful illustrations, gives us the words and music for those songs, and tells us the story of the civil rights movement.

Reef, Catherine. *Alone in the World: Orphans and Orphanages in America.* Clarion Books, 2005. ISBN 0618356703. 136 p. Grades 4–up.

We surely all know that to be an orphan is not a good thing, but read this book and you will be wildly grateful that you never had to be one more than 75 years ago.

Orphans back then had it *really* bad. A lot of them were not real orphans, just kids whose parents were so poor that they couldn't keep them anymore, for a variety of reasons, including the fact that they could not afford a babysitter. There were a lot of kids like that, especially in New York City, which was filled with poor immigrants living in terrible conditions and horrible poverty. Many of them spent all their money just getting to the United States, where competition for jobs, most of which paid almost nothing, was fierce. At first, people who could not support themselves were sometimes put in poorhouses, where they were packed in tightly. Mentally ill people were often chained. Food tasted terrible, and there was never enough.

Gradually, orphan asylums opened up. By 1860 there were 124 of them in America. Women took care of the kids, but men were in charge. Most did not allow children who were not white. Most made the parent, or parents, give up all rights to ever see their children again. Some asylums took care of children orphaned by wars, such as the Civil War. As in workhouses, the food was often skimpy and of poor quality, children were disciplined heavily and beaten for no good reason, and they often had to be silent almost all day long. Some were also sexually abused.

Orphaned kids who got into trouble were sent into prisons with hardened criminals.

By the 1850s, the Children's Aid Society was sending orphans and homeless kids to the country, some on trains headed west. The trains would stop at towns along the railroad track, the children would get out and be exhibited, and people could take them home if they wanted them.

This is a compelling account of how bad things can be if you are a kid. Show the before-and-after pictures on page 89 of Mary Ellen Wilson, who was chained and beaten before she was rescued by a missionary.

Haym Salomon: American Patriot
by Susan Goldman Rubin.

Rubin, Susan Goldman. *Haym Salomon: American Patriot*. Illustrated by David Slonim. Abrams Books for Young Readers, 2007. ISBN 081091087X. Unpaged. Grades 3–5.

Haym Salomon came to America in the 1770s as a Jewish immigrant from Poland. He had a lot of experience working in banks, he understood money, and he could speak a lot of languages. His business in New York included loaning and exchanging money, and people like him. His business did well.

He arrived in this country at a time when all sorts of things were happening. The American colonies had decided to revolt against Great Britain, and their government and their leaders were new at the job and not very well organized. They needed someone who understood how to raise money to help out the revolution.

In Haym Salomon they found the man they needed.

He believed in freedom and was willing to put his life in danger for it. He spent much time in prison, accused of being a rebel (which he was). He gave help to the soldiers and to the brand-new country at a time when help was desperately needed, and in the process he suffered horribly himself.

This is the story of an amazing human being.

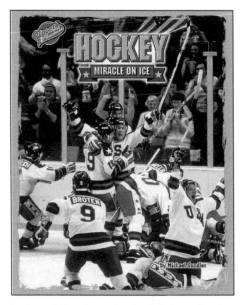

Hockey: Miracle on Ice by Michael Sandler.

Sandler, Michael. *Hockey: Miracle on Ice* (Upsets & Comebacks). Bearport, 2006. ISBN 1597161683. 32 p. Grades 2–4.

One of the greatest moments in American Olympic history happened in Lake Placid, New York, in 1980. It seemed like a miracle to the people who were watching it. Do you know what it was?

The U.S. team won the gold medal in hockey. Why would that be a miracle?

Well, everyone believed, and had good reason for believing, that the Soviet Union would win the gold medal. They were *really* good, and the guys on their team had played together for years. They had won twenty-seven of their last twenty-eight Olympic games. They had won gold medals in the last four Olympics.

The American team was a bunch of young men from all over the United States. Most of them didn't even know each other before they were selected for the team. They had to get to know how to play with and understand each other before they could even think of winning. At the beginning, hardly anybody, even the guys on the team, thought they had a chance except the coach. His name was Herb Brooks, and he believed his kids could pull it off—win the big one. And this is the story, with a lot of good information about hockey, of how it all happened.

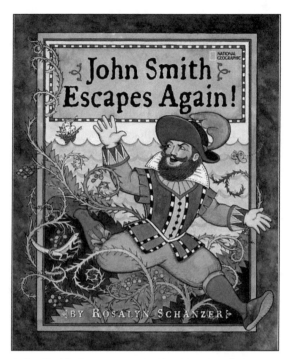

John Smith Escapes Again! **by Rosalyn Schanzer.**

Schanzer, Rosalyn. *John Smith Escapes Again!* National Geographic, 2006. ISBN 0792259300. 64 p. Grades 3–6.

He really isn't as famous as he ought to be, considering what an important person he was in the beginning of colonial America, but there is no doubt about it. John Smith was one interesting fellow.

He was born in England in 1580, and almost from the first he wanted to have adventures. And, boy, did his wish come true! John was always getting into some kind of trouble, and somehow or other he almost always came out of it just fine—even if there were times when it did not look like the outcome was going to be good for John. So John Smith is well known for all of the times that he escaped!

He escaped from being a farmer. He escaped from a shipwreck when he was nineteen years old. He escaped from some thieves who stole everything he had. When he was about twenty-two years old, he was caught in what is now Austria by enemy soldiers, and they sold him as a slave. He spent many miserable months in slavery wearing an iron collar around his neck with his head and beard shaved wearing only a smelly, itchy hair coat.

Then one day, when his master started beating him for no reason, John fought back. He killed his master and escaped from slavery!

And then he decided to come to Virginia to help found a colony. Even on board the ship carrying the colonists, John got into trouble and was put in chains. Many of the other passengers wanted to hang him, but John escaped again.

And that's just the beginning. Do you know what John's most famous escape was? And do you know who helped him?

This is a good read with great illustrations.

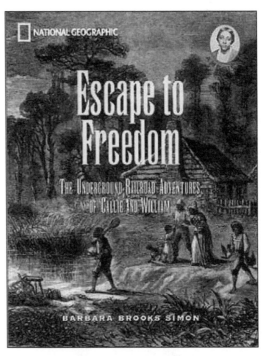

Escape to Freedom: the Underground Railroad
Adventures of Callie and William
by Barbara Brooks Simon.

Simon, Barbara Brooks. *Escape to Freedom: The Underground Railroad Adventures of Callie and William.* National Geographic, 2004. ISBN 0792265513. 40 p. Grades 4–7.

The Underground Railroad was not a place, it was a route. It had helpers along the way, people who would help escaping slaves get out of slave territory and into the free states, and often into Canada, where freedom was a guarantee. No slave catcher could come to get an escaped slave in Canada.

To be a traveler on the Underground Railroad was a terrifying thing. Maps were not well defined, and dangers lurked everywhere. There were big rewards for catching escaped slaves and terrible punishments awaiting the ones who were caught.

But slavery was evil, and to be a slave was to have no rights at all—and run a constant risk of being separated from the people you loved. Many chose to escape and take their chances.

This is the story of two slaves, teenagers Callie and William, who realize they are likely to be sold and decide that escape is the only answer. They do not know each other until they meet while escaping, and their life experiences are different. Each tells his or her own story of the journey to freedom and of the people they meet along the way.

There are lots of illustrations here, including some of famous escapes.

If you are interested in adventure and justice, you will be fascinated by this book.

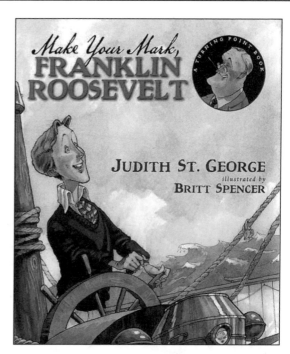

Make Your Mark, Franklin Roosevelt
by Judith St. George.

St. George, Judith. *Make Your Mark, Franklin Roosevelt* (Turning Point Books). Illustrated by Britt Spencer. Philomel Books, 2007. ISBN 0399241752. Unpaged. Grades 2–4.

Franklin Roosevelt wasn't poor, ever. But he had problems, just like everyone else—and some of them were big problems. Nevertheless, most people believe he was one of our greatest presidents.

Franklin was his mother's only child, and she adored him. She made him wear dresses and long hair and called him "Baby" until he was three years old. But when he was six, he had had enough. He had his hair cut at last.

Both his mother and his father were wealthy, and they had three fancy homes. Franklin did not go to school. Instead he had governesses, who taught him at home until he was fourteen years old. Then he went off to boarding school, which was really pretty awful. Most of the other boys had been there since they were twelve, and he didn't fit in. It took him a long time to become part of the gang.

He had one big hero—his fifth cousin, a guy named Theodore Roosevelt. Franklin wanted to be just like Teddy in many ways. Teddy even became president of the United States. But Franklin's mother (who was pretty much a control freak) didn't want him to go into politics. After all, he was too good to be a politician. He should be a country gentleman, just like his father.

But Franklin had other ideas. This is the true story of his childhood and growing up, and how his ideas helped him become one of our greatest Americans.

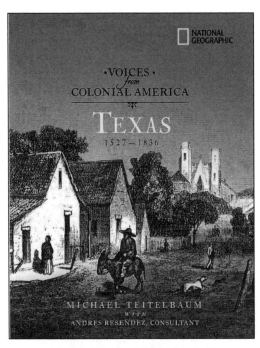

Texas, 1527–1836 **by Michael Teitelbaum.**

Teitelbaum, Michael. *Texas, 1527–1836* (Voices from Colonial America). National Geographic, 2005. ISBN 09792263871. 109 p. Grades 4–up.

Texas entered the Union in perhaps the most unusual way of all the fifty states. It was already an independent country when it was annexed by the United States of America in 1845—and it *wanted* to be a state. Even its president, Sam Houston, wanted it to become a state.

But Texas had a long and colorful history. Spaniards arrived there in 1528 but decided not to settle it yet. Spain got interested again when the French decided to settle at the mouth of the Mississippi River. The Spanish did not want France to get ahead of them when it came to colonizing the New World, so they decided to do some investigating. They decided that France was not a threat, but they could focus their efforts on spreading Christianity to the Native Americans in the area, so they began building missions and sending out missionaries. Thus began the permanent settlement by Europeans. The Caddo Indians in the area welcomed the new arrivals, and the Spaniards learned a new word from them. That word, *tejas,* meant "friend" or "ally," and the Spaniards began using the word when describing the area. Later the word was Americanized to one we all know: Texas. Later, the most prominent mission in the area was established: San Antonio de Valero, in San Antonio. That mission became the Alamo.

There are many interesting facts in the book:

- Colonists from the Canary Islands arrived in San Antonio in 1731. The Spanish king had paid for their journey, and they immediately started causing trouble. They wanted everything *their* way, and they proved pretty good at getting it. An ongoing crisis in the history of the area was that people born in Spain and of full Spanish heritage were privileged, and were usually in charge of everyone else. Almost everyone else lived in terrible poverty.

- Comanche and Apache Indians refused to be colonized or become Christian.

- By 1810, a revolution, led by a priest, began. The settlers in the area wanted to get rid of Spanish rule. It took many battles and much loss of life, but the area became independent in 1821.

- Then American settlers started to come, and they wanted things *their* way.

Remember Little Bighorn: Indians, Soldiers, and Scouts Tell Their Stories **by Paul Robert Walker.**

Walker, Paul Robert. *Remember Little Bighorn: Indians, Soldiers, and Scouts Tell Their Stories.* National Geographic, 2006. ISBN 0792255216. 64 p. Grades 4–9.

For hundreds of years, the American settlers had treated the natives as though they were entitled to almost nothing. Wherever the new people wanted to live, they made the natives leave. The Indians would sign treaties agreeing to turn over some land to the settlers, but then they were frequently asked to turn over more and more. Their own way of life was disappearing rapidly. The Plains Indians, who relied on the buffalo for so much, watched the new people kill almost all of those animals.

Now the white people wanted to take over a sacred place, the Black Hills.

In 1874, Lieutenant Colonel George Custer led an expedition into those hills. What happened on that expedition changed the future. His men discovered small bits of gold, and suddenly the Gold Rush was on! White people were moving like crazy onto Indian land, and, after this had begun, no one did much to try and stop them. Relations between the American government, its army, and the natives deteriorated. All of this led up to what became one of the most famous battles of all time: the one many still call Custer's Last Stand, or, more properly, The Battle of Little Bighorn.

What happened? How could a reasonably well-equipped U.S. Army be so utterly defeated by the Indians?

This book tells us the story of what actually happened, and there is a lot of interesting information here. Here are a few facts:

- George Armstrong Custer was not the only Custer killed in the battle. Two of his brothers, his brother-in-law, and his nephew were also killed.

- Indians could ride horseback and shoot a lot better than soldiers. They could actually stay on a horse without holding on to it, which freed up both of their hands. Hardly any soldiers could do that.

- Although the day of the battle was a glorious one for the Indians, they suffered mightily for it later.

This is an excellent read with a lot of pictures.

Weitzman, David. *A Subway for New York*. Farrar, Straus & Giroux, 2005. ISBN 0374372845. Unpaged. Grades 3–5.

In 1900 New York City was the second largest city in the world, after London. "Buildings were getting so tall—over twenty stories—that people worried that the island of Manhattan might tip over into the river."

The city and its streets were jammed with people trying to get from place to place. Other cities had figured out a way to move them: London's subway system opened in 1863, followed by other cities, including Boston, in 1898. New York City decided to build one, too.

This is the amazing story of how it was constructed. Some interesting facts are:

- Almost every single sewer line in Manhattan had to be removed and replaced!

- There were no maps of what was under the streets. What *was* under there was all jumbled up, mainly cables and pipes.

- Workers dug up prehistoric mastodon bones.

- The men who did the tunneling were called "sandhogs," and their work was extremely dangerous. They had to work under high air pressure and could get very sick and even die from it.

- The subway proved enormously popular right away when it opened in 1904. One hundred fifty thousand riders tried it out on the first day.

If you have ever ridden in the New York subway or would like to try it some time, you will enjoy this book.

Chapter 2

People to Know

Athletes. Artists. Explorers. Photographers. Magicians. Astronauts. Scientists. Architects. For many readers (including children, teens, and adults), there is nothing more interesting than the lives of real people. Here you will find a smorgasbord of fascinating people brought to life by some of the best writers currently writing for children.

Adler, David A. *Campy: The Story of Roy Campanella*. Illustrated by Gordon James. Viking, 2007. ISBN 0670060410. Unpaged. Grades 2–5.

Roy Campanella was used to hard work and making the best of things. His father was Italian American and his mother was African American, and he lived in a time when segregation and discrimination were common. But his parents lived in a mixed neighborhood in Philadelphia, and he helped his dad deliver groceries before he got his own job delivering milk. He was twelve years old and had to get up at 2 A.M.

Roy loved baseball. He loved to watch Major League games for free, sitting on the roof of a house near the stadium. He practiced and practiced and became so good that by the time he was fifteen, he started playing with the Negro League. And when he was sixteen, he quit school to do that full time. He was so good that he joined the Brooklyn Dodgers shortly after Jackie Robinson did. Their job was to desegregate baseball, and they did a great job of it.

It seemed like Roy's life was going well. He was a popular, successful baseball player. And then he had an accident, one that would have destroyed most people's lives, but not Roy's.

You will enjoy reading about this great guy who kept up his good spirits and his love of life despite everything that happened to him.

Adler, David A. *Satchel Paige: Don't Look Back*. Illustrated by Terry Widener. Harcourt, 2006. ISBN 0152055851. Unpaged. Grades 1–4.

Some of the greatest baseball players of all time said he was the best. He thought he was, too! He said, "Only one person can pitch like me. I could nip frosting off a cake with my fast ball."

He was Satchel Paige. His real name was Leroy, but when he was seven years old, he started carrying bags and satchels for the passengers at a train depot. He rigged up a contraption with a pole and a rope. That way he could carry several bags at one time. Someone said he looked like a "walking satchel tree," and people started calling him Satchel.

He got in big trouble when he was a kid and spent five years in a reform school. He didn't think it was all that bad. He played baseball there, and the coach thought he was pretty good.

The coach was right. Satchel was great. But he had a terrible handicap—he was African American at a time when African Americans could not play in the major leagues. He wanted to be in the major leagues, and he knew he was good enough for it.

Read this interesting story to find out what happened.

Bardoe, Cheryl. *Gregor Mendel: The Friar who Grew Peas*. Illustrated by Jos. A. Smith. Published in association with the Field Museum, Abrams Books for Young Readers, 2006. ISBN 0810954753. Unpaged. Grades 2–4.

You can come from a small town and you can come from a poor family, but if you work hard and persevere, you can accomplish amazing things.

Gregor Mendel grew up in a tiny town in what is now the Czech Republic. He loved to learn and go to school, and when he had finished all the school he could get in his hometown, he wanted more. His parents managed to find enough money to send him to school and pay for his bed and for half of his food. He was hungry. But he decided to feed his mind rather than his stomach.

Things got even worse. He could not afford to get the education he yearned for. He decided to become a friar, which is like a monk, because in the abbey where he lived, he got enough to eat, the opportunity to do good works, the chance to get a lot of education, and, above all, the opportunity to do some research and make a contribution of his own.

Gregor went on to make one of the most important scientific discoveries of all time. Read all about it in this interesting book.

Bolden, Tonya. *Maritcha: A Nineteenth-Century American Girl*. Harry N. Abrams, 2005. ISBN 0810950456. 48 p. Grades 4–8.

When you look at the picture on the cover of this book, you may find it hard to believe that Maritcha was a real person, a girl who lived more than 150 years ago. She is so beautiful that she looks like an actress or a model playing a part.

But Maritcha was real. She was an African American, and she was comparatively lucky, for she was never a slave. She lived most of her childhood in New York City, where her family operated various businesses, including a boarding house. Her family were victims in one of the most famous riots in New York City history—the riots against the Draft Acts, which basically meant that rich people could pay someone else to fight in the Civil War, but poor people had to go and fight. Also, poor white people believed that poor black people were trying to get their jobs. Maritcha's home was completely trashed during these riots, and almost burned, but the family was at least lucky to get out alive.

Maritcha's story is also the story of what life was like in that time, and it is a fascinating picture, graced with many wonderful illustrations and photographs.

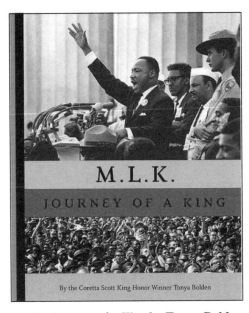

M.L.K.: Journey of a King **by Tonya Bolden.**

Bolden, Tonya. *M.L.K.: Journey of a King.* Abrams Books for Young Readers, 2007. ISBN 0810954761. 128 p. Grades 5–8.

Martin Luther King told his congregation at Ebenezer Baptist Church in Atlanta what he wanted said at his funeral. He often thought about his death, although he was only thirty-nine years old. "I'd like," he said, "somebody to mention that day that Martin Luther King, Jr. tried to give his life serving others. I'd like for somebody to say that day that Martin Luther King, Jr., tried to love somebody" (p. 101).

Reverend King did not know that he would only live a few more weeks before he was assassinated.

Martin was a brilliant man, a fascinating man, and like every other human being, flawed. But he was one of the greatest leaders the United States has ever seen, and today his birthday is a national holiday. He was one of the most important leaders, probably *the* most important leader, in the Civil Rights movement, and he was willing to suffer mightily for what he believed.

His first name was originally Michael, but his father changed his own name to Martin Luther King, Sr., and his son's name to Martin Luther King, Jr. when he was five years old. Some of his friends called him Mike all of his life.

His father was a Baptist minister, and Martin Jr. chose that same calling. He became famous at only twenty-six years old when he was named the new minister at the Dexter Avenue Baptist Church in Montgomery, Alabama.

Something important happened in Montgomery. A woman named Rosa Parks was arrested because she would not give up her seat so a white person could sit while she stood on the bus. The black community was galvanized and started a city bus boy-cott. They needed a leader, and they found they had a brilliant one: Martin Luther King, Jr. Some of the things he said give you goose bumps just reading them.

Martin believed that no matter how violent white people were to blacks, black people should not be violent in return, and this philosophy helped change the laws of our country.

This is an excellent introduction to the life of an amazing man—one who even won the Nobel Peace Prize and who also spent a lot of time in prison.

The Other Mozart: The Life of the Famous Chevalier de Saint George by Hugh Brewster.

Brewster, Hugh. *The Other Mozart: The Life of the Famous Chevalier de Saint George*. Illustrated by Eric Velasquez. Abrams Books for Young Readers, 2006. ISBN 0810957205. 48 p. Grades 4–7.

Joseph was born a slave on an island called Guadeloupe in the West Indies. He had nothing in the way of possessions, but he had two great things going for him. His father owned the plantation where he and his mother were slaves, and his father loved him. More importantly, perhaps, he was an amazingly talented and brilliant man. He was an extraordinary man for any time.

Joseph was born in 1845, and when he was eight years old his father decided to sell his plantation and return to his original home in France. Both Joseph and his mother were to come along and be slaves no more. Slavery was illegal in France. Joseph already knew how to read and write in French, had learned from his father how to fence a little, and had also had some violin lessons. All of these things would be very useful in his new life in Paris.

Joseph's father wanted people to accept his talented son, and one way he could do this was by making sure his son had a title, the Chevalier de Saint George, which was equivalent to a knight in England. And he sent his son to a fine school, where Joseph soon became the best fencer in the school. Everyone loved to see him fight with a sword.

And that was just the beginning. Joseph went on to lead an amazing life, even spending over a year in prison in danger of being beheaded during the French Revolution.

This is an excellent read.

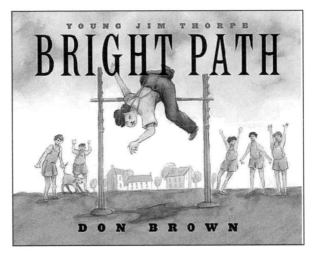

Bright Path: Young Jim Thorpe **by Don Brown.**

Brown, Don. *Bright Path: Young Jim Thorpe.* Roaring Brook Press, 2006. ISBN 1596430419. Unpaged. Grades 2–4.

When he was born in 1888, they named him Wa-tho-huck, which means Bright Path, but almost all of his life, people knew him as Jim Thorpe. Jim grew up in Oklahoma, and his tribe was the Sac and Fox Indians. He loved games, and he loved hunting, but he also had to do a lot of work around his parents' farm.

At age six his parents enrolled him in an Indian school. He had to dress and act differently. He hated it. He often ran away. So his parents sent him to a school even further away. He left that school too, but he ended up at one so far away that it was pointless to run. There Jim made a discovery that changed his life: he was an incredible athlete, one of the best of all time. And that was the beginning of his bright path.

This is a true story. Readers who ever felt like they didn't belong will be able to relate to Jim Thorpe.

Burleigh, Robert. *Stealing Home: Jackie Robinson: Against the Odds.* Illustrated by Mike Wimmer. A Paula Wiseman Book/Simon & Schuster Books for Young Readers, 2007. ISBN 0689862768. Unpaged. Grades 1–5.

All you have to do to sell this book to an eager audience is read the picture book text. You can skip the sidebars, which contain the meaty explanation and the facts about Jackie Robinson stealing home plate. But let students watch him actually *do* it and watch the spectators explode with joy, and you will have your audience dying to read the facts about this historic, astonishing man.

Here are just a few facts:

• If Jackie Robinson had not been black, he probably would have been picked by the NFL and gone on to become one of the best football players of all time.

- Jackie Robinson stole home base 27 times, most famously in the 1955 World Series.

- How can you steal home plate and score a run when the pitcher's pitch takes only a second and the run to home base from third base takes at least three seconds? You'll find out how.

This is a spectacular book.

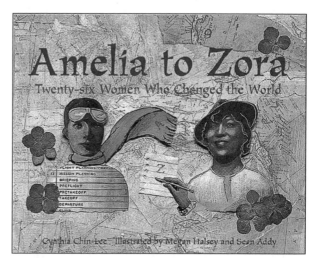

***Amelia to Zora: Twenty-Six Women Who Changed the World* by Cynthia Chin-Lee.**

Chin-Lee, Cynthia. *Amelia to Zora: Twenty-Six Women Who Changed the World.* Illustrated by Megan Halsey and Sean Addy. Charlesbridge, 2005. ISBN 1570915229. 32 p. Grades 1–5.

The author of this book loves to read biographies, she tells us, and she wanted to give us an unusual one. So she picked twenty-six women, all of whom lived most of their lives in the past one hundred years, and she wrote a page about each one—with a quote from the woman.

The pictures are wonderful, and the quotes are great!

"You gain strength, courage, and confidence by every experience in which you really stop to look fear in the face." (Eleanor Roosevelt, p. 9)

"Humans are allergic to change. They love to say 'We've always done it that way.' I try to fight that. That's why I have a clock on my wall that runs counterclockwise." (Grace Hopper, p. 10)

"We have a choice to use the gift of our life to make the world a better place—or to not bother." (Jane Goodall, p.13)

Are these the women *you* would pick for an alphabet book?

Jump! From the Life of Michael Jordan
by Floyd Cooper.

Cooper, Floyd. *Jump! From the Life of Michael Jordan.* Philomel Books, 2004. ISBN 0399242309. Unpaged. Grades 1–4.

The greatest basketball player of them all didn't start out as the greatest basketball player of them all. He had to work for it, and he worked darn hard.

Michael grew up as one of five kids, but the one he competed with was his older brother Larry. It seemed like Larry was better than Michael at just about everything. One of the things the boys did all of the time was to throw basketballs in the hoop their dad had put up in the backyard. No doubt about it, Larry was bigger and better than Michael.

So what could Michael do to beat his brother? He figured the only thing he *could* do would be to practice more, practice harder. But he must not have been practicing hard enough. He did not even make the high school varsity basketball team.

You'll have to read the book to find out what happens next.

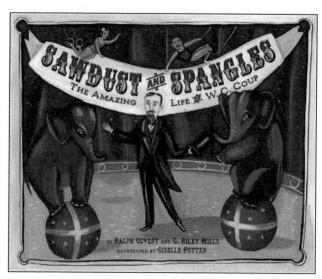

Sawdust and Spangles: The Amazing Life of W. C. Coup
by Ralph Covert and G. Riley Mills.

Covert, Ralph, and G. Riley Mills. *Sawdust and Spangles: The Amazing Life of W. C. Coup*. Illustrated by Giselle Potter. Abrams Books for Young Readers, 2007. ISBN 0810993511. Unpaged. Grades 2–4.

William Coup was a kid who got sick of taking out the garbage and sweeping the floors in his father's tavern in a small town in Indiana. He wanted adventure and excitement.

And one day, more than a hundred years ago, he knew he had found what he was looking for when a circus came to town. He liked it so much that he ran away with it!

It was hard work, but things were always happening there. Horse-drawn wagons pulled the whole circus from one town to another. By the time he grew into a young man, Coup knew he wanted to have his very own circus. He wanted to hire the best and most famous attractions, and he wanted to catch fantastic animals in Africa and show them wherever he went.

And that was not the end of what he dreamed—and what he got.

Read this true story of an amazing man who had an amazing dream—and made it come true.

Debon, Nicolas. *The Strongest Man in the World: Louis Cyr*. Groundwood Books, 2007. ISBN 0888997310. 28 p. Grades 3–5.

Emiliana is worried. In 1900 she sees a doctor leaving the little circus cart in which she and her father live, and she rushes in to find out what is wrong.

Her father tells her. He has a lot of health problems, and he is very overweight—about 360 pounds. He is too sick to keep on working, and the doctor tells him he must retire.

But what is his job? What must he retire from?

In this graphic novel we learn the story of Louis Cyr, who was the strongest man in the world—and could prove it. He beat anyone who tried to show that he was stronger. He grew up in Canada with a grandfather who urged him to use and develop his strength. And then things began to happen.

This is the incredible story of a man who would not be beaten.

Engle, Margarita. *The Poet Slave of Cuba: A Biography of Juan Francisco Manzano.* Art by Sean Qualls. Henry Holt, 2006. ISBN 0805077065. 183 p. Grades 5–up.

Juan Manzano was brilliant. He wrote amazing poetry, describing the world around him and his life, beautifully and painfully.

Juan was a slave with a horrible life story. His gifts and intelligence were obvious even when he was a small child, but his owners treated him with horrible brutality. They never allowed him to be educated, and he had to pick up anything he could on his own—and he did just that.

In lovely poetry, this tells the story of his life and the people who controlled him. It is a heartbreaking book.

Fleming, Candace. *Our Eleanor: A Scrapbook Look at Eleanor Roosevelt's Remarkable Life.* An Anne Schwartz Book/Atheneum Books for Young Readers, 2005. ISBN 0689865449. 192 p. Grades 5–up.

Eleanor Roosevelt was definitely one of the most amazing women who ever lived. She broke almost all of the rules for the wife of a president, and many, many people loved her for it. A large number hated her, too!

Candace Fleming tells us her story in an unusual way. She calls it a scrapbook. What the scrapbook does is give us glimpses into different parts of Roosevelt's life and personality, with photographs, quotations from people who knew her or wrote about her, and information about her life.

She was a miserable little girl. She was not pretty. Her mother was disappointed in that and belittled her because of it. Her mother died when she was only eight years old. She adored her father, but he was sick with alcoholism and killed himself when she was ten. Her mean-spirited grandmother raised her, but, mercifully, sent her to school in England when she was fifteen—and there she was happy and accepted and loved.

When she came back she ran into a distant relative, her fifth cousin, Franklin, and he fell in love first, asked her to marry him—and she accepted. But life with Franklin was not what she expected. His control freak mother tried to run every aspect of his life, and of Eleanor's, too. No one who knew her up to that time would ever have dreamed that she would turn out to be a brilliant, passionate, articulate fighter for human rights and poor people who railed against injustice.

When Franklin was elected president of the United States in 1932, Eleanor became First Lady and really came into her own.

This is a wonderful book, loaded with fun facts as well as great stories. Here is one: Eleanor refused to be guarded by the Secret Service. Franklin bought her a gun and sent her to the FBI firing range to learn how to shoot. The FBI director, J. Edgar Hoover, told the president "Mr. President, if there is one person in the U.S. who should not carry a gun, it is your good wife. She cannot hit a barn door" (p. 71).

Fradin, Dennis Brindell, and Judith Bloom Fradin. *Jane Addams: Champion of Democracy.* Clarion Books, 2006. ISBN 0618504362. 216 p. Grades 5–up.

She thought she was an ugly little girl, but she wasn't. All you have to do is look at her picture on page 12 and you will know that is not true. She was definitely an intelligent little girl, which was difficult in the tiny town of Cedarville, Illinois, in 1860 when a lot of people did not believe that women should be educated. When Jane graduated from high school, she desperately wanted to go to a real college—one like Vassar or Smith that granted degrees—but her father wanted her to be closer to home and allowed her to go to a college in nearby Rockford.

Her father, whom she loved, died when she was young, and he left her a lot of money. She wasn't at all sure what she wanted to do with her life. She was depressed a lot, ill a lot, and traveled to Europe a lot.

When she was twenty-seven years old, Jane found what she wanted to do. She was impressed with a place called a "settlement house" in London. A settlement house provided education and social services for people who lived in poverty. Jane knew that in Chicago there were a lot of poor people, especially immigrants, who lived in horrible homes and worked horrible jobs—and Jane decided that helping them would be the purpose of her life.

She was incredible. She met a person who owned a big house in a poor neighborhood and got that lady to donate her house, called Hull House, to the new project. Then she started recruiting educated people to help with her settlement house. And it worked! People gave money, time, and donations of all sorts, and the settlement house became a lifesaver for many people in Chicago.

Jane dedicated her life to making the world a better place. She even won the Nobel Peace Prize!

You will enjoy reading about this amazing woman.

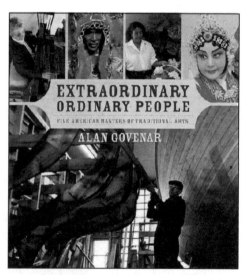

Extraordinary Ordinary People: Five American
Masters of Traditional Arts **by Alan B. Govenar.**

Govenar, Alan B. *Extraordinary Ordinary People: Five American Masters of Traditional Arts*. Candlewick Press, 2006. ISBN 0763620475. 85 p. Grades 4–8.

In Japan, a few extremely fine artists and craftspeople are designated as living national treasures. The people in this book are living national treasures in the United States. Each one of them has received the National Heritage Fellowship, which is given "by the National Endowment for the Arts to recognize the ongoing ingenuity of individuals who have mastered different culturally defined art forms" (page viii).

This book is loaded with photographs of these five outstanding people. First is Qi Shu Fang, a Chinese immigrant who has mastered the performance and production of the Beijing Opera. Other Chinese immigrants who perform in this tradition find her, and together they are creating the performances in a country very different from the one in which they were born and grew up.

Another is Ralph W. Stanley, who makes by hand beautiful boats in an oceanside village in Maine, and Eva Castellanoz, now living in Oregon, who makes gorgeous flowers with paper and wax and forms them into coronas, or crowns, a Mexican tradition. Dorothy Trumpold weaves rugs in the Amana colonies in Iowa, and Allison "Tootie" Montana creates over-the-top Mardi Gras Indian costumes in New Orleans. These people all have one important thing in common: they absolutely love what they do! You will enjoy reading about them.

Hampton, Wilborn. *Elvis Presley: A Twentieth Century Life* (Up Close). Viking, 2007. ISBN 9780670061662. 197 p. Grades 5–up.

Can you imagine a time when rock-and-roll didn't exist? When there was no such thing as popular music just for teenagers? This book makes it easy to understand how poor, small-town Elvis developed a new kind of music and was catapulted into unbelievable fame. Elvis started out as a shy kid who played guitar and liked gospel and hillbilly music. He had a pleasant voice that could be sweet or edgy, and he could make girls scream just by moving his hips. He quickly became incredibly famous, and later became—let's face it—pretty weird. He wore purple velvet suits, bought numerous guns, and asked President Nixon if he could be an undercover narcotics agent. Read this book to find out how fame changed Elvis into a different person and eventually led to addiction and an early death. Reading this book may help you understand why some people are still so interested in Elvis.

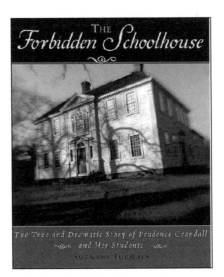

The Forbidden Schoolhouse: the True and
Dramatic Story of Prudence Crandall and Her
Students **by Suzanne Jurmain.**

Jurmain, Suzanne. *The Forbidden Schoolhouse: The True and Dramatic Story of Prudence Crandall and Her Students.* Houghton Mifflin, 2005. ISBN 0618473025. 150 p. Grades 4–up.

By anyone's standards, Prudence Crandall was an extraordinary woman. In 1831 at age twenty-eight, when few women had much education, she was opening her own school for girls.

Prudence had taught at two village schools in Connecticut, but now she wanted to do things *her* way. She bought a house in the little town of Canterbury, Connecticut, and opened a school. It looked like it would be a wonderful success.

And then something happened.

A free black girl named Sarah Harris stopped in to see Prudence in September 1832. She wanted to attend the school. She wanted to get more education so that she could teach black children.

Prudence knew that this would not be a good thing for the school. Most African Americans were slaves, and the ones who were free, like Sarah, faced incredible discrimination.

Prudence started thinking about it, and she made a big, scary decision. She decided to turn her school into a school *only* for African American females.

And when she did, her troubles really began.

This was almost thirty years before the Civil War, which ended slavery, began. This was more than one hundred years before African Americans were promised equal rights with white people. And a lot of people in that time and place did not want African Americans being educated in their little town.

This is the story of a very courageous woman and the horrors she and her students went through.

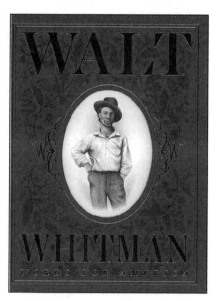

Walt Whitman: Words for America
by Barbara Kerley.

Kerley, Barbara. *Walt Whitman: Words for America.* Illustrated by Brian Selznick. Scholastic Press, 2004. ISBN 0439357918. Unpaged. Grades 4–8.

Walt Whitman loved words in every way possible. He loved to write them, to speak them, to read them, and to print them. He started out as a printer's apprentice, working on typesetting newspaper articles when he was only twelve years old. Within two years, he was writing newspaper articles himself. Within five more, he was publishing his own newspaper, *The Long Islander.*

He loved to walk, especially in Manhattan, right across the river from his home in Brooklyn, and he loved the country as well. He loved ordinary people, watching them and admiring them.

And then he started to write poems, many of them about those people. His dream was to become the voice of America. His poems were strange and different, unlike poems that had been written before. Some of the critics hated them. But Walt did his own thing and followed his own dream. When the War Between the States broke out, Walt was too old to fight, but he wrote poems to promote the Union cause and then visited wounded veterans—staying with them, being with them, watching them die—in the hospitals. He went to a battlefield to find his wounded brother.

His most famous poems were written about the death of Abraham Lincoln.

This beautiful book tells us his story. Be sure to read the pages at the end, for they tell a great deal about both Whitman and the creators of this book.

Kirkpatrick, Katherine. *The Snow Baby: The Arctic Childhood of Robert E. Peary's Daring Daughter.* Holiday House, 2007. ISBN 0823419738. 50 p. Grades 4–7.

On September 12, 1893, Marie Ahnighito Peary was born in an unusual place. Her parents were middle-class Americans, and a two-room tarpaper covered house in Greenland wasn't the kind of place most Americans considered an appropriate home for babies. But Marie's mother, Josephine Peary, felt she wanted to be with her husband. And her husband was Robert E. Peary, a man with a dream. He wanted to be the first human being to set foot on the North Pole.

The natives of Greenland, the Inuit, had never seen a baby with such white skin before, and they called Marie the snow baby. When the dark winter ended a few months after she was born, she played with rays of light as though they were toys!

Marie spent her childhood years partly in cold, remote areas, accompanying or trying to locate her father and even being stuck in ice in a ship one whole winter, and partly back in the more-or-less normal life in the United States, where the Pearys sometimes brought along Inuit friends. She always loved to have adventures, and she loved the Inuit and the land where they lived.

It took her father many years to realize his dream, and her life then changed dramatically.

This is an excellent read with a lot of wonderful photographs.

Author Profile: Kathleen Krull

Kathleen Krull, author of A Woman for President *as well as many other biographies for children, is nosy enough to dig into the juicy details of famous people's lives. She has spent the past twenty years writing children's nonfiction, often featuring heroes that children may not know about.*

What made you start to write nonfiction for kids?

My background is as an editor for children's books, and after I left publishing, I started noticing some gaps on the bookshelves. For example, I noticed that a lot of the biographies out there were old-fashioned—I couldn't picture kids picking them up and persisting reading the whole thing. When I got the idea for *Lives of the Musicians*, it was because I noticed that the biographies of famous composers that were already out there were really dated, and I thought there was room for improvement. I was a music minor in college, and that's why a lot of my books have to do with music. *Lives of the Musicians* is a collection of the twenty composers who have meant the most to me in my life. We didn't really know it was going to be the start of a series, but the book did well, so we followed it up with other books. One of the future books in that series will be *Lives of the Pirates*.

How do you do your research?

I do all my research at the library. I see what else is out there on the topic I'm writing about and I try to read everything there is, especially the most scholarly academic books I can find. Then I take a lot of notes and I try to distill those big heavy books into something that kids would want to read. I'm not doing original primary research, I'm using the most reliable secondary sources that I can find.

Have you had any research moments that stand out in your mind?

When I was doing the *Lives of the Musicians,* I started with Beethoven because there was so much material. Everybody who ever met him wrote a book about him. One day I ran into the fact that his favorite food was macaroni and cheese. That was a big day for me because it gave me a way to focus the rest of my research. I thought kids could relate to that, and I started looking for things like that fact. I'll always remember the mac-and-cheese moment.

You are unique in that your biographies tend to dig into juicy, gossipy parts of people's lives. How did you find this niche?

It's hard to pinpoint it exactly. I am really nosy. I always like to know juicy things about people's lives. I don't think I'm the only one who's like that. With the "Lives of" books, I started thinking in terms of what you would have noticed about these famous people if you were their neighbors. I turned my personal nosiness into a more philosophical approach where I wanted to show what these people were like as human beings.

How do you choose the books you will spend your time on?

I look for people who are really, really interesting to me, especially people who haven't had a lot done about them for kids. I look for famous, but often neglected heroes. Wilma Rudolph is a good example. She was somebody who most kids don't really know about. Her life story was incredibly dramatic, and I thought it would make a good picture book. Cesar Chavez is another example. He is someone I remember as a hero in the 1960s, but I don't think most kids have any idea who he was, and that really bothered me.

Other than being a writer, what jobs have you done?

When I was young I played the organ in my church. I also worked in a bakery, and I worked in a library, where I got fired for reading too many books instead of doing my job. After college I went right into publishing and worked as a children's book editor and I've stayed in books ever since. One of my first projects was editing the Trixie Belden series of mystery books.

What would you be doing if you were not writing for young people?

If I weren't a writer, I would still work with books. I would probably be a librarian if they would have me.

Visit Kathleen Krull online at http://www.kathleenkrull.com.

Isaac Newton **by Kathleen Krull.**

Krull, Kathleen. *Isaac Newton* (Giants of Science). Illustrated by Boris Kulikov. Viking, 2006. ISBN 0670059218. 126 p. Grades 5–9.

Isaac Newton was weird. *Really* weird, not just a little eccentric. He couldn't get along with people, he hated anyone who disagreed with him or whom he though was getting unfair attention, and his diet and living habits were strange, to say the least.

But, in spite of the fact that most of us probably wouldn't have wanted to be around him, he changed the world. Or at least he changed the way we look at the world and our knowledge of the universe. Albert Einstein, who was no slouch, said Newton was the greatest scientist ever.

Newton was British, born in the middle of a terrible civil war in 1642. He was the son of a prosperous farmer who soon died, and Isaac went to live with his grandparents when his mother remarried. He didn't much like any of them, and he didn't do very well at school either. But he had an aptitude for learning that led him to enroll in Cambridge University. There he had to wait on wealthier students—serving at tables, even emptying their chamber pots—to make enough money to live on. It wasn't much fun, and he worried about money a lot.

His thinking was so extraordinary that he was asked to stay on at Cambridge and teach, which he did. In his spare time, he started doing all sorts of experimenting. He had an amazing year in 1666, for the college closed because of the Plague. He went back to the farm and made some of the most amazing scientific discoveries of all time—you probably have heard the one about the apple.

You'll learn a lot about this exasperating, difficult, untidy genius—as well as what some of his greatest discoveries were and why he was so obnoxious to anyone who disagreed with him—when you read this wonderful book.

Krull, Kathleen. *Marie Curie* (Giants of Science). Illustrated by Boris Kulikov. Viking, 2007. ISBN 9780670058945. 139 p. Grades 5–9.

Marie Curie was only four years old when she taught herself to read. Then she started helping her older brothers and sisters with their math homework. Clearly she was something special. She was from Poland, but in the late 1800s a girl had no hope of pursuing scientific research there. So she went to Paris to pursue her education, and she eventually became the first woman in France to be awarded a doctorate degree. She went on to discover two elements and to invent the word "radioactivity." She fell in love with another scientist, Pierre Curie, and together they won the Nobel Prize for their discoveries. (He gave up his work to help her, and it paid off for them both.)

This is not just a dry book about a famous scientist. Kathleen Krull always makes sure to find the tantalizing details that make a person's life interesting. Find out about Curie's scandalous romance (this happened after Pierre died), her courageous work during World War I, and the success of her daughter Iréne, who also won a Nobel Prize. This is an intriguing, easy-to-read biography.

Sigmund Freud **by Kathleen Krull.**

Krull, Kathleen. *Sigmund Freud* (Giants of Science). Illustrated by Boris Kulikov. Viking, 2006. ISBN 0670058920. 144 p. Grades 5–9.

Kathleen Krull knows how to tell a story—and she is fantastic at writing true stories. Listen to the opening of this book.

"The brain has not always gotten respect. When turning a corpse into a mummy, the ancient Egyptians used a small hook to scrape brain matter out through the nostrils. Then they threw it away. After all, the brain did so little—everyone knew that intelligence and emotions arose from the heart, which *was* carefully preserved" (p. 8).

And that is just the beginning. It took thousands of years for scientists to recognize what the brain actually does, and it was not until the 1880s that physicians began to believe that diseases of the mind could be treated.

The man who made the biggest breakthroughs in that field was Sigmund Freud, born in 1852, the son of a poor family, but a kid whose mother always thought he was wonderful.

And he was pretty wonderful. He thought so himself. He was intelligent, curious, and arrogant. When he married, at a fairly late age because he did not have enough money to support a family, he took a typical nineteenth century view. Krull says, "He was going to support Martha, and in return she would obey and take care of him. The end" (p. 42). Although Freud was Jewish, he was an atheist and forbade Martha to practice her religion. She obeyed him but started right up all over again the day after he died.

What Freud believed was that people might be able to relieve their mental problems by talking about them. He wrote down what happened in his case studies, and he was a wonderful writer. It was almost like reading a mystery. He had an office in Vienna where his patients would lie on a couch and he would sit in a place they could not see, and they would talk. And he would listen. And he became world famous.

This is a fascinating, interesting book that gives you a lot to think about.

Up Close: Rachel Carson by Ellen Levine.

Levine, Ellen. *Up Close: Rachel Carson* (Up Close). Viking, 2007. ISBN 0670062200. 224 p. Grades 5–up.

Rachel Carson made a lot of choices in her life that other people could not understand. She was born in 1907, and her beloved mother taught her to appreciate and really see nature and the animals around her. She became interested in writing as well as the natural world.

She started writing when she was just in grade school and eventually had a story published in the most popular children's magazine of the time. This was very encouraging to her! Although her family never had much money, Rachel was able to go to college, and there she decided to be a scientist rather than a writer.

This was unusual at that time. There were almost no women scientists. Scientists were supposed to be men. Rachel suffered because so many people felt that way. At a very young age, she became financially responsible for most of her family, including her brother and her sister, and money was always a worry. There was never enough for all the things that were needed, and Rachel had to make sacrifices in her career plans to support them all.

Rachel may have decided not to pursue writing as a career, but it turned out that she could be a writer and a scientist as well. She started writing brochures, magazine articles, and eventually a book that became a big bestseller, *The Sea around Us.* All of a sudden Rachel had some money, although she also had health problems.

But the years of her greatest fame and influence were still ahead of her. She wrote a book called *The Silent Spring,* which many people feel is a book that changed the world. Read all about her, her choices, and the sad way in which women were treated not so long ago in this compelling biography.

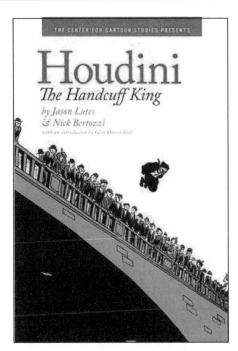

Houdini: The Handcuff King **by Jason
Lutes and Nick Bertozzi.**

Lutes, Jason, and Nick Bertozzi. *Houdini: The Handcuff King.* Hyperion, 2007. ISBN
0786839023. 89 p. Grades 4–up.

On May 1, 1908, Harry Houdini, the world-famous magician, who said (and
proved) that he could escape from anything, performed a death-defying stunt.

Handcuffed and chained, on a chilly morning in Cambridge, Massachusetts, he
jumped into the river from the bridge above it (it is still there!) and somehow escaped.
He reappeared in the water one minute and nineteen seconds after he jumped in.

This is a graphic book, so we can see the pictures of what is happening above and
below the water.

We also learn what Harry Houdini did to prepare for his trick—and, maybe, just
possibly, how he actually pulled it off.

This is an amazing story. You won't be able to put it down!

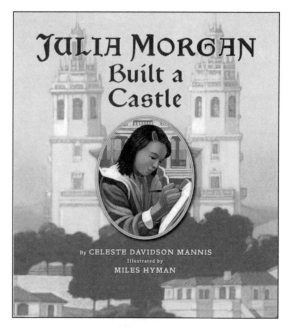

Julia Morgan Built a Castle
by Celeste Davidson Mannis.

Mannis, Celeste Davidson. *Julia Morgan Built a Castle.* Illustrated by Miles Hyman. Viking, 2006. ISBN 0670059641. Unpaged. Grades 2–5.

Julia Morgan was born in Oakland, California, in 1872, a time when not all jobs were open to women. Her father was an engineer, and he loved to look at buildings and construction sites; so did his daughter.

Julia wanted to be an architect. She began her college education by studying engineering. She was the only woman in her class. One of her teachers hired her after she graduated and she realized that engineering was not enough—she needed to study architecture. She wanted to go to Paris and study at the most famous architectural school of them all, Ecole des Beaux-Arts.

But that school did not take women, and its leaders made Julia wait and wait before they would even let her take their entrance exam. Eventually she won. She was accepted and became the first woman in the history of the school to receive a certificate in architecture.

By 1904 she was back in California opening her own office. When the San Francisco earthquake struck, every building she had built stayed up!

She later met a man with a big idea and a lot of money. And he wanted to build a castle. His name was William Randolph Hearst.

This is Julia's almost unbelievable story. You'll enjoy reading it.

Marx, Trish. *Jeanette Rankin: First Lady of Congress.* Illustrated by Dan Andreasen. Margaret K. McElderry Books, 2006. ISBN 0689862903. Unpaged. Grades 3–5.

Jeanette Rankin, born in Montana in 1880, accomplished an amazing first in American history. She was the first woman to be elected to the United States Congress in 1916. She was a congresswoman before there was a ladies' restroom for the Congress. She was a congresswoman before women could vote in national elections! And she stuck to her guns. She never voted for what was popular or what other people thought she should do. She always voted for what she thought was right, and that got her in big trouble.

Jeanette believed in helping people who needed help and got a lot of experience doing just that. She went to the slums and saw how people had to live there and vowed to make their lives better. She worried about children, who had almost no legal rights. She thought women should be paid the same as men when the work they were doing was the same.

She helped make changes. When she made a decision that cost her her place in Congress, one that many people hated her for, her brother told her that Montana was 110 percent against her. Jeanette told a friend "I have nothing left except my integrity."

Read the book to find out what that decision was and whether you agree with it.

Different Like Coco by Elizabeth Matthews.

Matthews, Elizabeth. *Different Like Coco.* Candlewick, 2007. ISBN 0763625485. Unpaged. Grades 1–5.

Coco Chanel was a poor and skinny little girl who had five brothers and sisters, a sickly mother, and a father who was a street merchant. When her mother died when Coco was twelve, she and her two sisters were sent to an orphanage run by nuns. There she learned to sew and began making beautiful dolls.

Coco knew she was going to be *somebody* someday, and she told all sorts of lies about her life. She watched the wealthy young women in the schools she went to and copied them. She wanted to be wealthy, too.

After she finished her schooling, she started sewing in a tailor's shop and watched her dreams begin to come true. When she opened her own shop, all of a sudden everyone wanted to be like Coco—everyone wanted to look like her and wear the clothes she wore. "Everyone loved Coco. And she was always different."

McCarthy, Meghan. *Strong Man: The Story of Charles Atlas.* Alfred A. Knopf, 2007. ISBN 0375829407. Unpaged. Grades 1–3.

A little immigrant boy from Italy named Angelo Siciliano came to New York more than one hundred years ago. He lived in a tough neighborhood in Brooklyn, and he was small for his age. He got picked on all the time.

As he grew older, it didn't get better. One day a bully kicked sand in his face—in front of his girlfriend. Angelo decided he had to do something. On a trip to a museum, he saw a statue of Hercules, and he decided he wanted his body to look like the body in the statue. How could he make that happen?

His teacher suggested lifting weights. Angelo tried making his own, but they did not work very well. Then he developed a new routine, and it worked. His body looked great! Some friends, who already called him Charlie, suggested he take the name Atlas, after the Greek God who carried the world on his shoulders. Charlie went for it.

And Charlie became the most famous bodybuilder of all time—and that is just the beginning of his story.

Read it! You'll have a grand time learning about this determined, handsome fellow.

McCully, Emily. *Marvelous Mattie: How Margaret E. Knight Became an Inventor.* Farrar, Straus & Giroux, 2006. ISBN 0374348103. Unpaged. Grades 2–5.

Mattie Knight grew up with her widowed mother and her older brothers, Charlie and Jim. The whole family was poor, but Mattie had a gift. She had her father's toolbox, and using that, she created all sorts of wonderful things that she described in a notebook labeled *My Inventions.*

Mattie made a foot warmer for her mother, a really cool kite and sleds for her brothers (some other boys paid her to make ones for them, too!), and other neat things.

But when she was eleven, the family moved so that her mother and her two brothers could work in the textile mills. When Mattie turned twelve, she started working, too—and when a terrible accident happened, she invented something that stopped that same accident from ever happening again.

Then Mattie went on to bigger and better things. She invented something that just about everybody today uses.

Read this book to find out what it was!

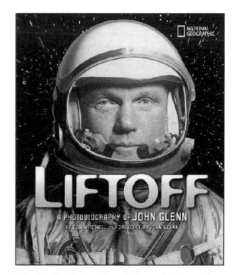

Liftoff: A Photobiography of John Glenn
by Don Mitchell.

Mitchell, Don. *Liftoff: A Photobiography of John Glenn.* National Geographic, 2006. ISBN 0792258991. 64 p. Grades 4–8.

John Glenn was born in 1921, just eighteen years after Wilbur and Orville Wright managed to invent a plane that actually worked. When he was six years old, he, like the rest of the world, was fascinated by the story of Charles Lindbergh, the first man to fly across the Atlantic Ocean. When he was eight, his father paid for John and himself to take a ride in an old plane, the first time he was ever able to fly. He was completely hooked! He wanted to fly, no matter what. He built model airplanes, and when he was old enough, he took government-sponsored flight training. He had his pilot's license before he was twenty. Then Japan attacked Pearl Harbor. John dropped out of college to join the Navy.

In 1943, he married a girl he had known all his life—they even shared the same playpen at family get-togethers when they were little. Her name was Annie.

John became a war hero, and, still wild for flying, he followed his dreams and became one of the first seven American astronauts.

As if this were not enough, John became the first American to orbit the earth, a successful businessman, a United States senator, and the oldest person ever to fly into space, when he was seventy-six years old.

This is an amazing story, illustrated with great photographs.

Author Profile: Ken Mochizuki

Ken Mochizuki has been writing for children for more than sixteen years. His first nonfiction book was Passage to Freedom: The Sugihara Story, *which is about a Japanese diplomat who saved thousands of lives during the Holocaust. His newest nonfiction title,* Be Water, My Friend, *focuses on another unique subject, Bruce Lee's early years.*

What made you start to write nonfiction for kids?

In 1994 my editor at Lee & Low Books called me and asked if I knew the story of a Japanese diplomat who saved 10,000 people in the Holocaust. I said yes, but I didn't know any details. Sugihara's son and wife were in the United States showing their family photo collection, and it was arranged for me to meet Hiroki, the son. Their story is better than any fiction you could come up with. It was probably one of the easiest books I've written. I just had to follow the facts.

How did you sell your first children's book?

I was lucky. The publisher of Lee & Low Books contacted me in the summer of 1991. He called me out of the blue. He was going through the country trying to find all the children's book authors and illustrators of color that he could find because that was going to be the focus of his children's book company. He asked if I wanted to do a book. Then he sent me an article about playing baseball in the internment camps in World War II, and that became *Baseball Saved Us*, which is historical fiction. I was lucky that the publisher came to me first, but I wouldn't say it was all luck. I was ready in the sense that I had been studying that subject for a long time before then and I was working in journalism and learning how to write, so when the time came, as the publisher said, it was the perfect storm.

Your books are all inspirational. Is that a conscious decision on your part?

If it's going to be for young readers, there has to be something positive to convey in the story, but I wouldn't say that's really my whole intent. My intent is to tell a good story, and if any messages come out of that, that's fine.

How do you do the research for your books?

For fiction you research that whole period of time. When I worked with a newspaper, I had been researching Japanese internment camps for a good six years, so I knew all the facts before I wrote *Baseball Saved Us*. With *Passage to Freedom,* I was lucky. I thought I would have to spend hours and days at dusty archives and libraries since there was very little written about Sugihara at the time. Then luckily Hiroki Sugihara, the son, pretty much put all the research in my hands. He gave me his self-published book of his mother's memoirs. I combined that with talking to Hiroki in person to get the story more from his point of view. So that was pretty much the research. The Bruce Lee book was a lot tougher. There wasn't too much on his earlier days. Luckily for us, Bruce Lee was a very prolific writer, and he wrote down a lot of what he remembered of his childhood days, so I was able to piece that story together.

How did you choose Bruce Lee as a subject?

In fall 2003, there was an exhibit of everything Bruce Lee in Seattle, and my publisher asked me to check it out. My initial reaction was, "Why him? He's just a stereotype or a perpetuator of one that we all know martial arts." I found all these things I didn't know about him before—that he was a child actor, that he was into ballroom dancing before martial arts, that he was Hong Kong's cha-cha dance champion. I wanted so badly to get that into the book, but I lost that battle with the editor. When I saw the photo of him sitting in front of his own personal library of 2,500 books, I became convinced that I should do a book about him because people should know about this. Everyone knows this super-human fighting machine. They don't know the spiritual and philosophical side of Bruce Lee. That was a good reason for me to do the book. He read all the time. Even as an adult he carried a book with him wherever he went whether he had time to read or not. I thought people should know that the man who was considered the most macho man around was also a voracious reader.

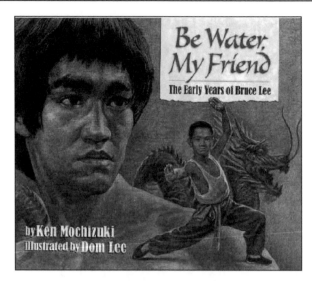

*Be Water, My Friend: The Early Years of
Bruce Lee* by Ken Mochizuki.

Mochizuki, Ken. *Be Water, My Friend: The Early Years of Bruce Lee*. Illustrated by Dom
  Lee. Lee & Low Books, 2006. ISBN 1584302658. Unpaged. Grades 2–5.

  Bruce Lee was only three months old when he was in his first movie. His father
was a performer, and he put Bruce in a movie, and then more movies. Bruce was acro-
batic and always moving around. His family called him Mo Si Tung, which means
"never sits still." One thing only could keep him quiet—books. He loved to read.

  But he wasn't good at school and often skipped it. He was sure he was going to be
a famous movie star. He had to wear thick glasses all the time, and not everyone believed that he would succeed.

  He got interested in the martial arts and started learning the moves. He took
classes from a master named Yip Man, who told him that there was gentleness in the
martial arts—and Bruce had a hard time understanding that.

  When he became a boxing champion, he did it by doing something he learned in
martial arts. And when he became a movie star, it was because of that training.

  This is his story.

Murphy, Frank. *Babe Ruth Saves Baseball* (Step Into Reading 2). Illustrated by Richard
  Walz. Random House, 2005. ISBN 0375830480. 48 p. Grades 1–3.

  The most famous baseball player of all time was a guy named George Herman
Ruth, but everybody called him Babe. He could pitch, he could hit, and he really liked
kids.

  But the most important thing he ever did, this book tells us, is that he saved baseball. He had been playing baseball, mostly pitching, for five years when a terrible
scandal almost ruined the professional sport. One of the teams in the World Series
cheated—they would intentionally lose the game, and gamblers would make money.
Everyone was so disappointed that people stopped going to games until Babe Ruth
started hitting.

  Everyone loved to watch Babe Ruth bat. How many home runs could he make?
People started going back to the game because they wanted to see.

  You'll enjoy reading this true story about the early days of major league baseball.

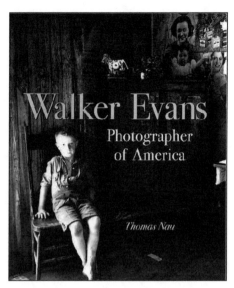

Walker Evans: Photographer of America
by Thomas Nau.

Nau, Thomas. *Walker Evans: Photographer of America.* A Neal Porter Book/Roaring Brook Press, 2007. ISBN 159643225X. 64 p. Grades 5–8.

Walker Evans wanted to write. He didn't do very well at school, but he just loved to read, and he thought that writing was something he would be good at. His first real job was in the New York Public Library, delivering maps to people who requested them. He had a friend who was a painter, and together in 1925 they headed for Paris where many talented young Americans were studying and working. He was twenty-two years old.

He brought along a camera.

That camera led Walker Evans to his life's work. By 1928 he was living in Brooklyn. He loved to take photographs of his neighborhood and the Brooklyn Bridge, which his apartment overlooked. He met a poet, Hart Crane, who loved the photos and started showing them to everyone, telling them about his friend the photographer. Walker met other photographers and became especially influenced by those who took pictures of ordinary people and places. He decided that taking those kinds of pictures was what he wanted to do—and he was going to do what he wanted to do even if no one would pay him money for it.

Perhaps his most famous photographs were taken in the middle of the Great Depression. He and the writer James Agee lived with and photographed a tenant farm family in Alabama and showed how terrible poverty can be. A lot of good readers may recognize one of the photos Walker took of that family—it is on the dust jacket of Karen Hesse's Newbery Medal winning book *Out of the Dust.*

This is an interesting book with a lot of great photographs in it.

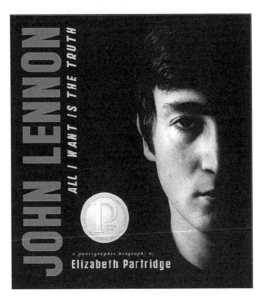

John Lennon: All I Want Is the Truth
by Elizabeth Partridge.

Partridge, Elizabeth. *John Lennon: All I Want Is the Truth.* Viking, 2005. ISBN 0670059544. 232 p. Grades 8–up.

Has anybody *not* heard of the Beatles, almost certainly the most famous and most influential musical group of all time?

It all started—and pretty much ended—with one man, John Lennon, who was a miserably unhappy kid whose parents pretty much weren't around. He lived with his aunt and uncle, whom he loved, but it wasn't the same as having your mom and dad in the same house with you.

He was smart, though, and he loved reading and music. By the time he was a teenager, he was nuts about American music, especially Elvis Presley. When he first heard Elvis Presley's recording of *Heartbreak Hotel,* he said "After that, nothing was the same for me" (p. 26). He decided that he, too, wanted to perform, to be a musician, and some of his friends joined him in forming a group. They called themselves *The Quarry Men.* Nobody else you ever heard of was in that original group, but in July 1957, *The Quarry Men* performed at a celebration, and another teenager named Paul McCartney saw them. When Paul played a borrowed guitar, John was amazed. Paul was really good, even though he was two years younger. A few weeks later he joined the group.

The road to worldwide fame was bumpy, but it did not take as long as you might expect. Over the next few years, George Harrison and Ringo Starr joined the Beatles, and other, less brilliant, performers left. The Beatles became more popular, John famously said, than Jesus. Their lives were crazy, out of control, but people were mad about them and their music—and John was not happy.

And then he met Yoko Ono.

John Lennon was a fascinating, brilliant, troubled man, who died way too young when he was murdered by a gunman in front of the apartment building in which he lived.

This book is compelling reading. Start it and you won't be able to stop. It's an amazing story.

Poole, Josephine. *Anne Frank.* Illustrated by Angela Barrett. Alfred A. Knopf, 2005. ISBN 0375832424. Unpaged. Grades 3–up.

Anne Frank was an ordinary, popular, pretty little girl, but she was Jewish in a time and place where being Jewish made your life horrible. The Nazis, under Adolf Hitler, invaded Anne's country, the Netherlands, and blamed the Jews for everything. By the time Anne was thirteen, she could not go to the movies or the park or to swimming pools. She had to wear a gold star all the time that said "Jude" (Jew) on it.

Anne's father was afraid for his family, and in 1942, he moved them into a hiding place he had prepared. There they lived, crowded in with others, trying to be quiet so that no one would know they were there. They lived in terror that the Nazis would find them and that they would die.

Anne did something special there. She kept a diary, one that told what life was like for a family afraid and in hiding.

This is her story.

John's Secret Dreams **by Doreen Rappaport.**

Rappaport, Doreen. *John's Secret Dreams.* Illustrated by Bryan Collier. Hyperion Books for Children, 2004. ISBN 0786808179. Unpaged. Grades 3–up.

John Lennon was one of the Beatles, probably the most famous musical group ever. He grew up in England, and when he was only five years old, his mother wanted out. She took him to live with an aunt and uncle. He always felt sad about that. His aunt and uncle were loving but strict, and he had to keep his dreams of what he wanted to do and be to himself.

What John dreamed of was becoming a poet or an artist—and then he got interested in music and met Paul McCartney. Together they formed a band, and history was made.

John *did* become a poet, and many of his most famous words are included in this beautiful book.

Ray, Deborah Kogan. *Down the Colorado: John Wesley Powell, the One-Armed Explorer.* Frances Foster Books/Farrar, Straus & Giroux, 2007. ISBN 0374318387. Unpaged. Grades 3–5.

John Wesley Powell was only seven years old when his parents decided he would not go to school anymore. The year was 1841, and they lived in Ohio. His father was an abolitionist, a man who was opposed to slavery, and other kids attacked John Wesley because of it.

It turned out to be a good thing for him. One of his neighbors was a naturalist, a man who loved nature, and he taught young Wes to love and respect it in every way. He helped Wes find what his life's work would be.

When he grew older, he married and became a schoolteacher and started taking college classes in all sorts of things, especially natural history.

When the Civil War started in 1861, he enlisted on the side of the Union, and in 1862 he lost his arm after he was wounded in the Battle of Shiloh.

A lot of people would have given up many of their dreams at that point, but not Wes. In 1867 he traveled to the Rocky Mountains to collect specimens and decided the next year to explore a river—one then called the Grand River, but now called the Colorado River. How could a one-armed man do such a dangerous thing in such terrifyingly rapid water?

This is the story of an amazing person in American history. You'll enjoy learning about him.

Ray, Deborah Kogan. *To Go Singing Through the World: The Childhood of Pablo Neruda.* Frances Foster Books/Farrar, Straus & Giroux, 2006. ISBN 0374376271. Unpaged. Grades 3–5.

Pablo Neruda was born in Chile in 1904. He was a shy little boy who was afraid of other people, almost afraid of talking. He liked to be alone and to explore the rain forest around Temuco, the town where he lived near the southern tip of South America, a rather wild frontier town blown about by Antarctic winds.

Who knows what might have happened to him or become of him? Lots of people are shy, and maybe a lot of them never get over it. But Pablo had something unique and special within him. He observed himself, observed everything about him, and wrote about all of that—and then wrote poems about everything he observed.

He won the Nobel Prize for Literature in 1971, which is the greatest prize any writer can win. Not only had he won an outstanding award for his poetry, but he also became politically active in his own country.

This is the story of his beginnings, and of the amazing woman, Gabriela Mistral, who helped him grow into himself. The illustrations are lovely.

The Longest Season: The Story of the Orioles'
1988 Losing Streak **by Cal Ripkin.**

Ripken, Cal. *The Longest Season: The Story of the Orioles' 1988 Losing Streak.* Illustrated
by Ron Mazellan. Philomel, 2007. ISBN 0399244921. Unpaged. Grades 2–5.

Cal Ripken, Jr. is one of baseball's all-time greatest players. He is a legend. He
played in 2,632 games, more than any player in history, and he was named the Most
Valuable Player of the American League in 1983, the year his team, the Baltimore
Orioles, won the World Series. Everything looked good. His team was good. Cal was
good.

1988 looked like it was going to be a fantastic year, especially for Cal. His own
father was the manager of the Orioles, and his brother was starting on second base.
Three guys from the same family were on one team. How could it get better than this?

Well, it did not get better. It got much worse.

The season started with high hopes. And they went to heck. They lost the first
game of the year, never a good sign. Then they lost the second, and the third, and the
fourth, and you get the picture. The Orioles, this fine team, couldn't win a game. Cal's
dad, the manager, got fired! Nothing they did seemed to work or make it better. Everyone was making fun of them, even the hometown newspapers. When would they ever
break the worst losing streak they had ever had?

This is the story of that streak and also of the day it finally broke—on the
twenty-second game of the season! Even the best and most talented people sometimes
have a hard time of it.

This is a good read with excellent illustrations. You'll feel for Cal and the
Orioles.

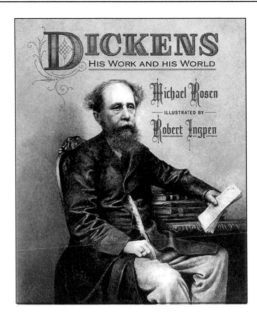

Dickens: His Work and His World
by Michael Rosen.

Rosen, Michael. *Dickens: His Work and His World.* Illustrated by Robert Ingpen. Candlewick Press, 2005. ISBN 0763627526. 96 p. Grades 4–up.

Charles Dickens. It is a name probably most of us have heard before. If we are not sure where, we might be reminded when we hear about some of the stories he wrote and some of the characters he created. Do you know what a Scrooge is? Scrooge was the name of a mean, money-hungry old man in what is perhaps the most famous Charles Dickens story of all, *A Christmas Carol.* Have you ever heard of the story of *Oliver Twist,* the sad little orphan who got into big trouble by asking for more food?

Charles Dickens has been dead since 1870, a long time ago. But the stories he wrote are more popular than ever. People are always making movies and plays and TV shows out of his stories.

Why? Because they are *really* good stories, filled with great characters with interesting names, and people who have the same human problems that people everywhere seem to have.

And Charles Dickens had those problems, too. He was born in 1812, and his father spent more than he earned, finally ending up in prison for owing so much money. Charles had to help out, making money on his own. Right after his twelfth birthday, he went to work in a blacking factory, a filthy, smelly, rotten factory where they made black boot polish. Charles hated absolutely every minute of it. He worked ten hours a day, six days a week, and he had to walk three miles each way to work. It was not all bad—he told stories to the other workers, something he was very good at, and when he was thirteen years old he was able to go to school again.

Sometimes he felt he would never get ahead in the world, but Charles was a determined and brilliant young man, and he ended up being one of the most famous people in the world.

He is still beloved and famous today. This beautiful book tells us why, and also how he got from where he was at the beginning to where he was at the end.

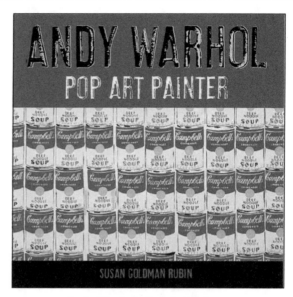

Andy Warhol: Pop Art Painter
by Susan Goldman Rubin.

Rubin, Susan Goldman. *Andy Warhol: Pop Art Painter*. Abrams Books for Young Readers, 2006. ISBN 081095477X. 48 p. Grades 4–8.

When he was a kid in Pittsburgh, Andy Warhola (Warhol's birthname was Warhola) loved to draw. He had two older brothers, and parents who were immigrants from Slovakia. His mother, too, was an artist and created lovely things. But his parents were blue-collar workers in America and did not have much money.

Andy said one of the best things that happened to him when he was eight (in 1936) was getting sick. He got to draw and read comic books and spend a lot of time doing the things he wanted to do. He was too sick for school but not for fun.

In college everyone was sure he had an enormous amount of talent and would one day be famous. Leonard Kessler, who later wrote and illustrated many children's books with his wife Ethel, said, "All of us knew there was something so incredibly special about him. We recognized that he was a genius" (page 9).

Andy showed them they were right. He went to New York City and almost immediately got a job illustrating shoes—a job that led to many other things. Soon Andy was a successful artist, making good money—and one of the main leaders of the new Pop Art movement.

This book, loaded with photographs and Warhol pictures, tells us the story of his early years.

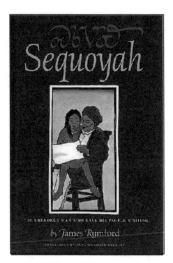

Sequoyah: The Cherokee Man Who Gave His People Writing **by James Rumford.**

Rumford, James. *Sequoyah: The Cherokee Man Who Gave His People Writing*. Houghton Mifflin, 2004. ISBN 0618369473. Unpaged. Grades 1–4.

"For much of his life, Sequoyah was nobody famous. He was a metalworker who could turn iron into chisels and drills and Georgia silver into forks and spoons."

But he loved his people. His mother was Cherokee, and his father was a white man he never knew. He wanted the Cherokee people to be proud and to not disappear from the earth. He felt called to preserve their language, and to do that he needed to create a Cherokee alphabet.

In the early 1800s, he did just that. This is his story, written in English *and* in Cherokee, the language, which is still in use today, thanks mostly to Sequoyah.

Show the table of the Cherokee alphabet on the last two-page spread.

Bethany Hamilton: Follow Your Dreams! **by Michael Sandler.**

Sandler, Michael. *Bethany Hamilton: Follow Your Dreams!* (Defining Moments). Bearport, 2007. ISBN 1597162701. 32 p. Grades 3–7.

Thirteen-year-old Bethany Hamilton was one of the top surfers in her age group in the United States. Everyone in her family surfed—her parents even moved to Hawaii because the surfing was so good there.

On Halloween 2003, Brittany lay on her surfboard, waiting for a wave, letting her left arm dangle in the water. All of a sudden she felt a tug.

A tiger shark had just bitten off her arm!

It was a race to get to her best friend's father and then to the hospital, which was nearly an hour away. Brittany lost a lot of blood. Everyone was afraid she would die on the way.

But she didn't. She survived, and her positive attitude and decision to surf again (she's still really good at it, even with only one arm!) make for a compelling story. Take a look at all of the great photos.

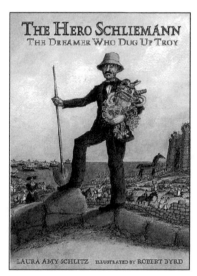

The Hero Schliemann: The Dreamer who Dug for Troy **by Laura Amy Schlitz.**

Schlitz, Laura Amy. *The Hero Schliemann: The Dreamer who Dug for Troy.* Illustrated by Robert Byrd. Candlewick Press, 2006. ISBN 0763622834. 72 p. Grades 3–5.

A little German boy growing up in the early 1800s loved the story of the Trojan War. "His last name was Schliemann, and in the center of that German name is the English word **lie.** Perhaps now is as good a time as any to consider the subject of lying, because the boy Heinrich did not grow up to be a truthful man.

Few people are entirely honest. Many people lie once in a while. Heinrich Schliemann lied more often than that" (page 2).

Maybe he grew up loving the story, maybe not.

He was a poor boy with no prospects. His first job was being a stock boy in a grocery store. He dreamed of being rich and finding treasures, but he had a long way to go. Heinrich's luck changed after, of all things, a shipwreck in which he was one of only three survivors. He became a wealthy businessman, got married, and definitely started loving the story of the Trojan War.

A lot of experts didn't believe that Troy ever existed. It was like a fairytale. It was like Rapunzel's tower, or the witch's cottage in Hansel and Gretel. What was the point of looking for something that might not be there?

Schliemann was *sure* it was there, and he was pretty sure where to start looking.

This is an incredible story of a man with a dream—and how he managed to make that dream come true—even if he did have to lie more than a little.

Shea, Pegi Deitz. *Patience Wright: American Sculptor and Revolutionary Spy*. Illustrated by Bethanne Andersen. Henry Holt, 2007. ISBN 0805067701. Unpaged. Grades 3–5.

Patience Wright was something else! She was born in 1725, while America still belonged to the British. She was a Quaker, raised in a different fashion from many. Quakers believed that women should be educated, which was unusual, and her family did not eat meat or wear leather.

When she was a child, she discovered that she and her sisters had a talent for sculpting. That became her life's work after she married, was widowed, and left to support her children.

She went into business with her sister Rachel, and they started making wax sculptures of people. Wax sculptures were hugely popular, and people loved to have images of themselves made, usually wearing their own clothes. Everyone was pleased when others thought the wax figure was real.

But Patience's great claim to fame came during the American Revolution, when she was living in England. She sculpted famous people, including government leaders, and found out what was going on in the war with the colonies. Anything she found she immediately shipped back to America—sometimes in the head of a sculpture!

You will enjoy reading about this extraordinary woman.

Show the picture of the head of Benjamin Franklin (secret message inside) in a box.

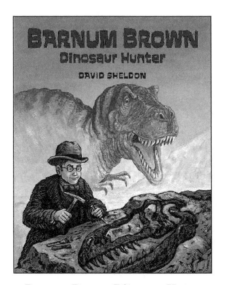

Barnum Brown, Dinosaur Hunter
by David Sheldon.

Sheldon, David. *Barnum Brown, Dinosaur Hunter*. Walker & Company, 2006. ISBN 0802796036. Unpaged. Grades 1–4.

Barnum got his first name from a very famous man, P. T. Barnum, whose circus happened to be playing in his hometown of Carbondale, Kansas, when he was born in 1873.

From the time he was young, Barnum loved fossils. He was a lucky kid! The area around his parents' farm had once been an ocean, and there were lots of fossils waiting to be found. The whole world, it seemed, was excited about dinosaurs and dinosaur fossils. Dinosaur hunters were almost fighting over them.

Barnum knew what he wanted to do when he grew up. He wanted to find a lot of dinosaur fossils, and that is exactly what he did. He got a job working for the American Museum of Natural History in New York City, and his job was to search for dinosaur fossils. Imagine! He got paid for doing the thing he loved the most.

You will enjoy reading about this famous (and very successful) fossil hunter. Show any of the excellent illustrations showing Barnum digging.

Siegel, Siena Cherson. *To Dance: A Ballerina's Graphic Novel*. Artwork by Mark Siegel. Atheneum/Richard Jackson Books, 2006. ISBN 978-06898674776. 64 p. Grades 3–7.

Have you ever dreamed of performing on stage? This beautiful graphic novel is the autobiography of a girl who dreamed of being a ballerina. The author, from Puerto Rico, moved to New York City as a girl to attend the School of American Ballet. She spent years there learning, performing, and working incredibly hard. You will learn about her successes and failures, and the problems going on in her family. Most of all you will see the passion that it takes to be a dancer. It's a graphic novel, and the artwork shows the freedom and joy of dance as seen through young Siena's eyes. Girls who like to dance (or who dream of dancing) will love it!

Sis, Peter. *Play, Mozart, Play*. Greenwillow Books, an imprint of HarperCollins, 2006. ISBN 0061121819. Unpaged. Grades K–3.

Have you ever heard of Mozart? He was one of the greatest composers of music in the history of the world—and he started making music when he was a little kid. His father was very proud of him and took him all over Europe so he and his sister could perform and show off their talent.

Mozart played and played and played the harpsichord, but he didn't get to play much with other kids because he had to practice all the time.

"Wolfgang Amadeus Mozart lived a long time ago, but he gave us beautiful music. The whole world is listening still. Bravo!"

Play a piece of Mozart's most joyful music for your audience.

Stauffacher, Sue. *Nothing but Trouble: The Story of Althea Gibson*. Illustrated by Greg Couch. Alfred A. Knopf, 2007. ISBN 0375834087. Unpaged. Grades 2–4.

"Althea Gibson was the tallest, wildest tomboy in the history of Harlem. Everybody said so." That girl could run. And play ball. She loved basketball, stickball. and running.

One night a musician watched her play paddle tennis, and he saw a lot of possibilities in her.

His name was Buddy Walker, and he decided he would try to help Althea be all that she could be. He bought her an old tennis racket and convinced a tennis pro to give her lessons.

They also had to teach her how to behave! She was not very polite or professional at the beginning, but she was a fast learner. Althea accomplished something no African American had ever done before. The whole world was watching and excited.

Read this neat book to find out what it was.

Sullivan, George. *Berenice Abbott, Photographer: An Independent Vision.* Clarion Books, 2006. ISBN 0618440267. 170 p. Grades 5–up.

Lots of people take photographs of New York City, but not many people have done it the way Berenice Abbott did. She devoted several years of her life taking meticulous photographs of the city as it was in the 1930s. Today they are classics, and people love them. A few years ago there was even a book that a modern photographer had put together. He went to many of the places where Berenice had taken photos and took photographs in the exact same place where she once stood—and thus the viewer could compare the way the city had changed.

But Berenice did not always want to be a photographer. Growing up in Ohio, she wasn't sure what she wanted to be at all except that she knew she wanted to be different, to follow her own dreams and go her own way, no matter what.

And that is exactly what Berenice Abbott did.

As a young woman she went to Paris and got a job as an assistant to a famous photographer and artist named Man Ray. Soon she became his competitor. People wanted *her* to take photographs of them, not him. He fired her.

She went back to New York and started taking photographs there. But times were hard. In the Great Depression, she could barely find enough work to feed herself. She taught classes in photography, invented cameras and accessories for photography, and somehow made it through, reinventing herself in the 1950s as a great science photographer. Always she remembered who she was and what was most important to her.

This is an interesting read.

Show some of Abbott's photographs. One of the most famous is *Night View* on page 78 and on the back cover.

Sullivan, George. *Helen Keller: Her Life In Pictures.* Scholastic Nonfiction, 2007. ISBN 0439918154. 80 p. Grades 3–8.

One of the most interesting people who ever lived was Helen Keller.

She was born in 1880 in Tuscumbia, Alabama, and was a healthy baby until she was nineteen months old. Then she became ill. No one is sure what illness she actually had, but at the end of it, she was completely blind and completely deaf. She could not communicate. No one could communicate with her. Although her parents loved her and took good care of her, she was a terrible problem for them.

And then a miracle occurred. The Kellers hired a young woman named Annie Sullivan to work with Helen. Mr. Keller wrote a letter to the Perkins Institution for the Blind in Boston, asking for a teacher who could come to Alabama to work with their daughter.

Annie Sullivan was exactly what they needed. She was twenty years old, very intelligent and creative—and patient and determined.

Annie spelled out shapes of letters in the palm of Helen's hand. Helen did it back, but she did not understand that those shapes were spelling words and that words were the names of things—until one day, pumping water in the backyard of the Keller home, when she realized that the word Annie was spelling in her hand, the letters w-a-t-e-r spelled something—and *meant* something!

And Helen started learning as much as she could, doing things no one believed anyone deaf and blind could do, and she became world famous.

This is her story, illustrated with dozens of wonderful photos.

Wallner, Alexandra. *Lucy Maud Montgomery: The Author of Anne of Green Gables.* Holiday House, 2006. ISBN 082341549X. Unpaged. Grades 1–3.

Lucy Maud Montgomery was born on Prince Edward Island in Canada. Before she was even two years old, her mother died, and a few years later her father moved west, leaving her alone with her mother's strict parents.

Maud was a lonely little girl. Living with two old people could be very difficult, but Maud's books kept her company. But she felt her best friend was nature—being outside on beautiful Prince Edward Island.

She started keeping a journal and making up stories and poems. "She pretended that two people were living behind the glass of her grandmother's china cabinet: a little girl to share secrets with and a lady to tell her sad stories. Maud had a good imagination. She used everything she heard and saw to make up her own stories and poems."

Maud's life was not always happy, but she always worked hard and had dreams. Then one day, her dreams began to come true. Her most famous stories were about a girl who was much like Maud—lonely and full of dreams, and living with two beloved older people. Her name was Anne Shirley, and the first book about her was *Anne of Green Gables.*

You will enjoy reading about one of the most beloved writers of all time.

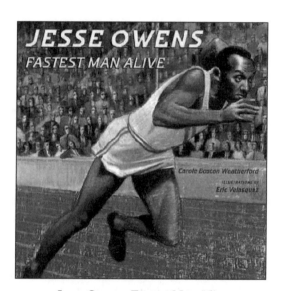

Jesse Owens: Fastest Man Alive
by Carole Boston Weatherford.

Weatherford, Carole Boston. *Jesse Owens: Fastest Man Alive.* Illustrations by Eric Velasquez. Walker & Company, 2007. ISBN 080279551X. Unpaged. Grades 2–5.

In 1936 Jesse Owens, an African American from a poor family, could run faster than anyone anywhere. And he got a chance to show the world.

It was an Olympic year, and the games were held in Berlin, Germany. The leader of the country was a man named Adolf Hitler, and he believed that only white people, especially German and non-Jewish white people, would and should win everything. He considered the games a great opportunity to show off his country and to prove his racial theories.

Jesse Owens proved him wrong.

Filled with beautiful illustrations, this book tells us the story of Jesse Owens and his gold medals—he won four—in the 1936 Olympics, and of the ticker-tape parade he got in Harlem when he came back to the United States.

He deserved that parade and those medals. It took twenty-five years for someone to beat the records he set.

This is an amazing true story.

Winter, Jonah. *Diego*. Concept and Illustrations by Jeanette Winter. Translated from the English into Spanish by Amy Prince. Alfred A. Knopf, 1991, reissued 2007. ISBN 0679819878. Unpaged. Grades 2–4.

Diego Rivera had a twin who died before he was two years old. When Diego became ill too, his parents sent him away from their town to live with an Indian healer in a hut in the mountains. He got better, and he learned to love the jungle and the smell of the healer's herbs and the interesting things in her home.

When he returned to his parents, they gave him some colored chalk, and Diego started drawing everywhere he could find a place. He never really stopped. He loved art and he loved Mexico and became, perhaps, its most famous artist.

This is his story, told in both English and Spanish.

Dizzy **by Jonah Winter.**

Winter, Jonah. *Dizzy*. Illustrated by Sean Qualls. Arthur A. Levine Books, an Imprint of Scholastic, 2006. ISBN 0439507375. Unpaged. Grades 1–4.

"This is the story of one real cool cat who must have been born with a horn in his hands. ... But, to tell you the truth, he wasn't born with a horn in his hands. He was born very poor and very tough."

His name was Dizzy Gillespie, and he was mad all of the time when he was a kid. His dad beat him up, so he beat up other kids, and bullied them, too.

One day his music teacher gave him a trumpet, and he was able to blast all of his anger right out of a horn. And his life started to change.

This is the really neat true story of how a tough kid became one of the world's greatest musicians—and how he invented a new kind of music.

Read the first three double-page spreads aloud.

The Perfect Wizard: Hans Christian Andersen **by Jane Yolen.**

Yolen, Jane. *The Perfect Wizard: Hans Christian Andersen*. Illustrated by Dennis Nolan. Dutton Children's Books, 2005. ISBN 0525469559. Unpaged. Grades 2–5.

As a child, Hans Christian Andersen was ugly and weird looking, to say the least. He said so himself. His looks didn't get much better as he got older either.

He was also strange. For a long time he was about the only person who believed he was a genius. He loved stories, and his father read him lots of them. His father also made him a toy theater, which is how his desire to perform was born.

Hans completely believed in himself, always. No matter what anyone else said or thought, he knew he would be successful. This is his story, illustrated with color illustrations and filled with quotes from his many books—and from the stories he wrote that we all know today, such as *Thumbelina* and *The Ugly Duckling*.

Sixteen Years in Sixteen Seconds: The Sammy Lee Story **by Paula Yoo.**

Yoo, Paula. *Sixteen Years in Sixteen Seconds: The Sammy Lee Story*. Illustrations by Dom Lee. Lee & Low Books, 2005. ISBN 158430247X. Unpaged. Grades 3–5.

In 1932 Sammy Lee was twelve years old. He loved to swim, but he did not get to do much of it. He was Korean American, and no one who was not white was allowed in the community swimming pool except for one day of the week. He longed to learn how to dive, but it was not going to be easy.

Slowly but surely he became a superb diver, in spite of the fact that his father, who wanted him to become a doctor, was opposed to him spending so much time on the sport. He was the first non-white student elected student body president in his high school, and his classmates voted him the most likely to succeed.

They knew what they were doing! Sammy showed everybody. This is the amazing story of Sammy Lee, who won gold medals for diving at two Olympics.

Show any of the pictures of Sammy diving and also the photograph of him on the back of the book jacket.

Chapter 3

Around the World and Through the Ages

Did you know that the creator of Curious George narrowly missed being killed during the Holocaust? Or that there were 144 public toilets in ancient Rome? Or that way back when there were Chinese pirates? These seem like unrelated facts, but they're examples of how nonfiction books can pique readers' interest in world cultures and history. Don't let these books languish on a library shelf—booktalk them and tell students some of the fascinating details within. This chapter contains the best of many recent books from around the globe and throughout time. Dig in!

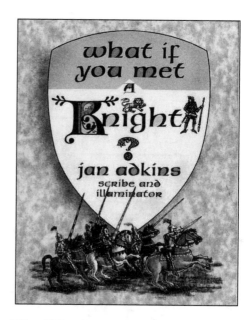

***What If You Met a Knight?* by Jan Adkins.**

Adkins, Jan. *What If You Met a Knight?* Roaring Brook Press, 2006. ISBN 1596431482. 32 p. Grades 4–6.

Most of us think we know all about knights. We've seen TV shows and movies and maybe read some books. But Jan Adkins lets us know what we probably *don't* know about knights, and that includes some really interesting stuff.

Take a look on pages 2 and 3 at the picture of the knights of the round table. They were quite a crew. You'll probably learn some things you did not know about them in this book.

We take a good look at Sir Guy of Wareham. He's a knight, alright, and it costs a lot of money being a knight. Sir Guy frequently worries about it. He has a lot of land, and he has to take good care of the peasants who live on it, but also make sure that he pays enough and makes enough money to pay off his warlord, to whom he is accountable.

Did Sir Guy know King Arthur? Probably not, because King Arthur probably never existed, and he certainly didn't have a fancy castle. If he did exist, his castle would have looked more like the one on pages 8–9.

We learn all the different jobs Sir Guy had to do and what living in a medieval castle was like. "The light in your refrigerator is brighter than anything castle folk ever had" (page 20). On page 21, take a look at what it was like going to the bathroom in a castle. Yuck!

You'll learn about war and weapons and suits of armor. (Knights went to the bathroom *before* they put on their armor!) You'll learn a little bit about the Crusades and about some of the most famous knights of all, plus there are a lot of fine pictures.

If you are interested in knights at all, this is the book for you.

Taj Mahal **by Caroline Arnold and
Madeleine Comora.**

Arnold, Caroline, and Madeleine Comora. *Taj Mahal.* Illustrated by Rahul Bhushan.
Carolrhoda Books, 2007. ISBN 076132609X. Unpaged. Grades 4–6.

In 1592 in India, a Mughal prince was born. His name was Khurram, and when he
was fifteen, he fell in love—hard. He had to wait six years to marry the girl, who took
the name Mumtaz Mahal, Jewel of the Palace, on her wedding day.

They lived a wondrously happy life together, but, alas, Mumtaz Mahal died when
she was only thirty-nine years old. Her husband, now the Shah Jahan, the ruler of the
land, decided to build a tomb for his wife that would make their love immortal. All
through the ages, people would admire its beauty.

He built a building so wonderful that many people think it is the most beautiful
building in the world.

This is a beautiful book with lovely illustrations that show us the Shah and his
love, and show us the building as it was being built. The Shah originally wanted a
tomb for himself across a pool from the Taj Mahal, but he spent the last years of his
life as a prisoner, and that never came to be.

Much of the truth is now legend. We are not sure exactly what really happened,
but you will enjoy reading the story of a great love and a beautiful building.

The World Made New: Why the Age of Exploration Happened & How It Changed the World **by Marc Aronson and John W. Glenn.**

Aronson, Marc, and John W. Glenn. *The World Made New: Why the Age of Exploration Happened & How It Changed the World* (Timelines of American History). National Geographic, 2007. ISBN 0792264541. 64 p. Grades 5–8.

Fourteen ninety-two was the big year. It was the year when two different kinds of advanced civilizations first met. Christopher Columbus was determined to find another route to the Far East. Muslims controlled all of the normal routes, and prices, especially for the spices the Europeans valued so highly, were extremely expensive.

Columbus was not the first man to explore and travel extensively. The first one we know of for sure was Chinese—the amazing admiral Zheng He, who explored Africa and Asia with a big fleet of ships. The Chinese might have ruled the seas—and the world would have taken a different shape—if the Chinese emperor had not decided it was too expensive and the explorations stopped.

Columbus went to several courts trying to get funding for his idea. The Spanish king and queen took a chance on him, and Spain ended up winning big. Columbus claimed all of the lands he found for Spain. He didn't care that advanced civilizations were already living in and owning that land. And the New World's discovery by the Old World was, in many ways, a catastrophe for the people already living in the Americas.

This is the fascinating story of how everything worked together to produce the world we know today.

Here is just one example: "In 1491, not one person in Italy had ever seen a tomato, nor was there a single potato in Ireland, a chili pepper in all of Asia, or a kernel of corn in Africa. In turn, no living American had ever ridden a horse, milked a cow, or eaten a bowl of rice" (p. 38). This is mind-boggling information.

If you are interested in history or how things change, you will enjoy reading this book with its great color illustrations.

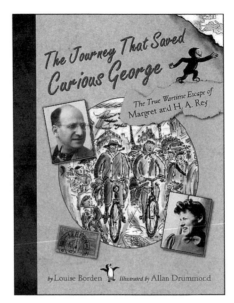

***The Journey That Saved Curious George: The
True Wartime Escape of Margret and H. A. Rey
by Louise Borden.***

Borden, Louise. *The Journey That Saved Curious George: The True Wartime Escape of Margret and H. A. Rey.* Illustrated by Allan Drummond. Houghton Mifflin, 2005. ISBN 0618339248. 73 p. Grades 2–5.

When the Nazis invaded France in 1940, two people escaped on bicycles. In doing so, they saved the character they would write about so brilliantly, Curious George. H. A. and Margret Rey had an exciting, breathless adventure, just steps ahead of an almost certain death. Colorful pictures highlight the text.

Buller, Laura. *History Dudes: Vikings.* Illustrated by Rich Cando. DK, 2007. ISBN 9780756629403. 64 p. Grades 4–8.

If you like cartoons, and if you know enough about the Vikings to realize that they were really interesting guys, this may be a book for you.

It is filled with sometimes sort of disgusting information about these powerful warriors, who basically scared just about anyone who came in contact with them for about three hundred years.

They got their reputation in 793, when they raided the calm and quiet Lindisfarne monastery on an English island. They killed a lot of the monks and captured the rest to be their slaves. They stole all the beautiful, historic treasure. That was the beginning.

But the Vikings were not just warriors and raiders and thieves. They also had an advanced civilization and traded all around Europe and some of Asia. You will learn what it means to "go berserk," how the Vikings dressed, what kinds of weapons they used, what kind of funerals they had, how they sailed first to Iceland, and then to Greenland, and then to Vinland, which it turned out was North America (way before Columbus!), what kind of games and ships they had and the stories of some of their most famous leaders, as well as a lot of other good information.

Show your audience the picture of the Viking longship on pages 6 and 7.

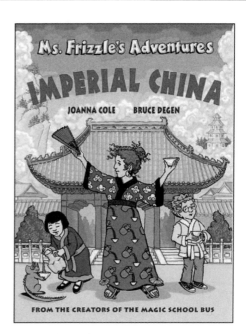

Ms. Frizzle's Adventures: Imperial China **by
Joanna Cole.**

Cole, Joanna. *Ms. Frizzle's Adventures: Imperial China.* Illustrated by Bruce Degen.
Scholastic Press, 2005. ISBN 0590108220. 40 p. Grades 1–5.

Ms. Frizzle is going to spend Chinese New Year's Eve eating dinner with the
family of Wanda, one of her favorite students. As they stroll around Chinatown looking at the holiday lights, they run into another student, Arnold, on his way to kung fu
lessons. As Wanda, her older brother Henry, Arnold, and Ms. Frizzle duck under a
cloth dragon, they are suddenly magically transported back to Imperial China about a
thousand years ago, and there they learn all sorts of interesting things. Ms. Frizzle, of
course, has packed her small bag full of all sorts of useful things that will save the day
more than once!

Well, you know by now that everyone who travels with Ms. Frizzle gets to have
an adventure, and you won't be disappointed in this one. Along the way, you'll learn
how to use chopsticks, how to grow rice, and many other things.

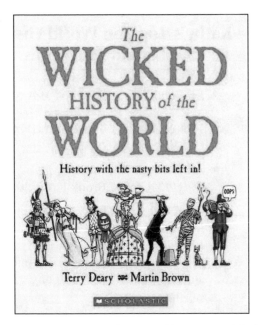

The Wicked History of the World: History with the Nasty Bits Left In! **by Terry Deary and Martin**

Deary, Terry, and Martin Brown. *The Wicked History of the World: History with the Nasty Bits Left In!* Scholastic Nonfiction, an imprint of Scholastic, 2006. ISBN 0439877865. 97 p. Grades 4–up.

This is a really disgusting book. The nasty bits are absolutely awful. Much of what is nasty in history is about people hurting and killing other people in horrible ways—some you can barely even imagine.

But if you like to know all sorts of interesting things, and you like looking at books that look a lot like comic books, you might want to take a good look at this one. Here are a few facts you will learn:

- Alexander the Great would not let his soldiers wear beards because enemies could grab them in fights.

- In A.D. 315 there were 144 public toilets in ancient Rome. There were jars on the corner of the streets where men could pee. The pee was useful: it was used in laundries to clean clothes—and it worked very well!

- El Cid, the great Spanish knight, dreamed that he would die in 30 days. He ordered his men to put his corpse on a warhorse so that he could lead them into battle even though he was dead. It worked. He died thirty days later and his dead body scared the enemies so much that they ran away—and his side won!

There's a good quiz on pages 44–45. See if you can figure out what is wrong in this picture—or, rather, how many things are wrong. Some of them may surprise you.

Kathy's Top Ten World History Booktalking Favorites

- Schlitz, Laura Amy. *Good Masters! Sweet Ladies! Voices from a Medieval Village.* Illustrated by Robert Byrd. Candlewick, 2007.

- Adkins, Jan. *What If You Met a Knight?* Roaring Brook Press, 2006.

- Lauber, Patricia. *What You Never Knew About Beds, Bedrooms, & Pajamas* (Around the House History). Illustrated by John Manders. Simon and Schuster Books for Young Readers, 2006.

- O'Brien, Patrick. *The Mutiny on the Bounty.* Walker & Company, 2007.

- Hama, Larry. *The Battle of Iwo Jima: Guerrilla Warfare in the Pacific* (Graphic Battles of World War II). Illustrated by Anthony Williams. Rosen Publishing's Rosen Central, 2007.

- Steele, Philip. *The Medieval World.* Kingfisher, 2006.

- Shoveller, Herb. *Ryan and Jimmy: And the Well in Africa That Brought Them Together.* Kids Can Press, 2006.

- Buller, Laura. *History Dudes: Vikings.* Illustrated by Rich Cando. DK, 2007.

- *Piratepedia.* DK, 2006.

- Malam, John. *How to Be a Pirate.* Illustrated by Dave Antram. National Geographic, 2005.

Desaix, Deborah Durland, and Karen Gray Ruelle. *Hidden on the Mountain: Stories of Children Sheltered from the Nazis in Le Chambon.* Holiday House, 2007. ISBN 0823419282. 275 p. Grades 5–up.

When Adolf Hitler came to power in Germany, one of his major goals was to destroy every Jewish person. Although he did not succeed at doing that, he was successful at killing about six million Jewish people. Of course, he did not do it alone. He had help—and not nearly enough people resisted what he wanted to do.

There was one place in all of Europe that was unique. It was a small French village called Le Chambon. It was isolated, surrounded by even more isolated farms and hard to travel to in the winter. The people who lived there were almost all Protestants, whose ancestors had been persecuted for their religion. They remembered stories told of what it was like, and they knew it was wrong. They decided their village should be a place where Jewish people, especially young ones, could come and be safe. And they did it.

"For the four years of the Nazi occupation of France, almost the entire population of 8,000 people worked actively toward the same goal: saving Jews from destruction. Not a single inhabitant … ever betrayed any of the refugees. By the end of the war, they had saved at least three thousand five hundred Jews, as well as about one thousand five hundred other refugees" (p. 241–242).

This book tells us the stories of several of the young people who were saviors and of those who were saved by the people of Le Chambon. The authors spent four years finding and interviewing survivors of the Holocaust who were still alive to tell their own stories.

There are many photographs of the kids and teenagers, and in their own words, they tell us what it was like—usually to be all alone and uncertain as to where their parents were and even if they were dead or alive. It's an excellent look at a terrifying time. Think what would have happened if all of the people in Europe had reacted to Hitler's plan the way the villagers of Le Chambon did.

Doeden, Matt. *The Sinking of the Titanic* (Graphic Library: Graphic History). Illustrated by Charles Barnett III and Phil Miller. Capstone Press, 2005. ISBN 0736838341. 32 p. Grades 3–8.

If you don't already know about the night the *Titanic* sank and you like comic books, you might want to try this book. It shows us what happened on April 14 and 15, 1912, when the supposedly safest, biggest passenger ship in the world, loaded with passengers and on its first voyage anywhere, ran into an iceberg and sank, killing almost two-thirds of the people onboard. It's a story that still intrigues everyone.

There are numerous fine books about the *Titanic* that fly off the shelves after a booktalk. When booktalking about shipwrecks or the *Titanic,* be sure to include this one for less-than-eager readers.

The Adventures of Marco Polo
by Russell Freedman.

Freedman, Russell. *The Adventures of Marco Polo.* With illustrations by Bagram Ibatoulline accompanied by archival, period artwork. Arthur A. Levine Books, an Imprint of Scholastic, 2006. ISBN 043952394X. 64 p. Grades 4–8.

Have you ever heard of Marco Polo? Do you know who he was? Do you know about the stories that he told more than seven hundred years ago?

People are still fascinated by his stories, although some people don't believe they are true. But some people think they are. Even the experts disagree.

We do know this much for sure. In 1298, he was captured while commanding a Venetian war galley. Venice was his home, and he was willing to fight for it in a war. But the city of Genoa imprisoned him. The good news for the world was that he was not in solitary confinement. No, he had a cellmate, a guy named Rustichello of Pisa, who had also been captured in battle. Rustichello wrote books of stories, mostly about chivalry. Marco told his cellmate his story, and Rustichello wrote it down. When they were released from prison, Rustichello started selling the story.

Here is the problem. Printing hadn't been invented yet. All the copies of a book had to be printed by hand. And sometimes the copier added some of his own stuff to the story, changed it, or couldn't read the writing—you get the general idea. There are in existence about 150 versions of the original story. So how do we know what is true and what isn't? And more important, what did Marco Polo really say in the first place?

This book tells us what Russell Freedman believes he said, although he, like everybody else, isn't sure. Still, this is a really good read of some of the most incredible adventures in the history of the world. Marco said he went all the way from Venice to China and saw incredible, amazing things. Some, we can figure out what they were. Others have us scratching our heads.

The pictures in the book are just stunning. You will have a good time reading all about it.

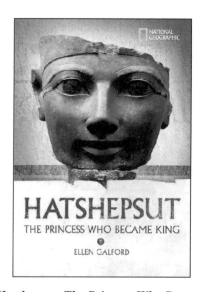

Hatshepsut: The Princess Who Became King **by Ellen Galford.**

Galford, Ellen. *Hatshepsut: The Princess Who Became King*. National Geographic, 2005. ISBN 0792236459. 64 p. Grades 4–up.

She was a woman in ancient Egypt, about 3,500 years ago, and yet she became a king—a Pharaoh. She was a real pharaoh, and she wore a fake beard, and she must have had a lot of people who supported her, or she could never have ruled for the twenty years that she did.

Her story has intrigued historians ever since they found out about it.

Hatshepsut was the daughter of a pharaoh, so she had no hopes of becoming the ruler of her country. But, as was the tradition, she married one of her half-brothers. He died about fifteen years after becoming the pharaoh. Historians believe that she, as the senior member of the pharaoh's household, became regent for her husband's son, but somehow she took over.

This book is filled with interesting information.

• Egyptian children did not wear clothing, except for special occasions.

- Egyptian toilets were low, wooden stools with large holes cut in the seats. Underneath the seat was a box of sand, much like kitty litter.

- Archaeologists have found the mummy of the man they believe was Hatshepsut's husband. There is a picture of it on page 44.

- Twenty years after Hatshepsut died, someone tried to erase every piece of evidence that showed she ever existed. Her images were destroyed, and her name was crossed out. Historians still do not know why this happened.

She must have been quite a woman!

Hall, Martin, and Rebecca Stefoff. *Great Zimbabwe* (Digging for the Past). Oxford University Press, 2006. ISBN 0195157737. 48 p. Grades 5–8.

Imagine a big, beautiful city right in the heart of Africa. Most of the cities in Africa are near the coast. This one is in the heart of a country that was named after it—the country of Zimbabwe.

European traders had heard legends of a city, but they did not know where or what it was. They thought it might have gold. Europeans were always looking for gold. They thought that if a big city did exist, it was probably an ancient city, maybe one mentioned in the Bible. Maybe it was a city that was once ruled by the Queen of Sheba.

They were wrong, and they stayed wrong for a long time. The first white man who wrote about it was a German geologist named Karl Mauch. He was sure that it was the biblical city of Ophir. People liked that theory, because he was sure that white people had built the city. There was so much prejudice at the time that historians and archaeologists did not believe African people were enlightened enough to build such a beautiful place.

As other archaeologists worked there, they spent more time destroying than examining carefully. It took a woman, Gertrude Caton-Thompson, working in the 1920s, to realize that it was a completely African city, made by Africans, and it was not nearly as old as any city in the Bible. It was built between 1300 and 1450.

This is the story of an amazing place in an unlikely spot and the people who lived there and are studying it. If you like history or archaeology, you will enjoy reading it.

Hama, Larry. *The Battle of Iwo Jima: Guerrilla Warfare in the Pacific* (Graphic Battles of World War II). Illustrated by Anthony Williams. Rosen Publishing's Rosen Central, 2007. ISBN 1404207813. 48 p. Grades 4–up.

On February 19, 1945, one of the hardest-fought battles of World War II began. The American forces landed on the beaches of the tiny Japanese island of Iwo Jima. The United States was getting closer and closer to Japan, taking island by island, and the Japanese were completely determined that they would not get this one. The Japanese commander there, General Kuribayashi, was brilliant, and he knew that he and his men had no chance to win. All they could do was kill as many Americans as possible. Every Japanese soldier vowed to kill ten Americans before dying himself. It was hard for Kuribayashi, for he had been to the United States, and he liked Americans.

The Americans themselves expected to win in four or five days. Little did they know it would take thirty-six days; at the end of it, 6,821 Americans were dead and

19,217 were wounded. Of the Japanese, about 20,000 died and only 1,083 survived to be taken prisoner.

This is the true story, told in graphic novel format, of this horrifying battle, and of the brave men on both sides.

In the Trenches in World War I
by Adam Hibbert.

Hibbert, Adam. *In the Trenches in World War I* (On the Front Line). Raintree, 2006. ISBN 1410914666. 48 p. Grades 5–8.

World War I became known as "The Great War," because it was the first war in history that involved many different countries all over the world. It was hugely different from any war before it, partly because of the great numbers of soldiers involved, and partly because the weapons of war were so different—poisonous gas, powerful guns, and newly invented machines.

The war started in August 1914, and by December the Germans had dug five hundred miles of trenches in which their soldiers could defend their positions. The Allied soldiers, which included Britain and France, built their own trenches. In between the trenches was an area called "No Man's Land," which was a terrible and dangerous place, littered with dead bodies and devoid of grass or any other vegetation.

The Germans built trenches that had at least some comforts in them—they made warm, dry rooms where soldiers could gather when not on duty—but the Allied trenches were horrible. They were all zigzag rows dug in the dirt, with a step here and there where soldiers would climb up to see what was going on and to fire at the enemy. They were cold and filthy, often full of mud, and usually open to the weather. The soldiers who had to live in them had horrible lives, with poor food, not enough water, and lots of vermin, both in the trenches and on their bodies.

This is the story of life in those trenches, and of individual men who toughed it out. You will be very happy you never had to be in the trenches when you start reading this interesting book.

Kraske, Robert. *Marooned: The Strange but True Adventures of Alexander Selkirk, the Real Robinson Crusoe*. Illustrated by Robert Andrew Parker. Clarion Books, 2005. ISBN 0618568433. 120 p. Grades 4–8.

Have you ever heard of Robinson Crusoe? A lot of people have. There have been movies about him, and there was a very famous book about him by a man named Daniel Defoe. Robinson Crusoe was marooned—or left alone—on an island with very little to eat and almost no supplies. He had to figure out how to stay alive and find food and build shelter.

It's a great story, but Daniel Defoe, who wrote it, didn't make up the whole thing. There was a real man named Alexander Selkirk who got into an argument with the captain of his ship in 1704, and he was marooned on Juan Fernandez Island in the Pacific Ocean. There were no other people on the island, and he was alone for over four years, eating whatever he could find and kill or grow.

He missed other people horribly, but on the whole he was pretty happy.

This is the story of how he got into trouble, how he managed to survive, and how he was discovered and came back to his home. It's an excellent read.

Memories of Survival **by Esther Nisenthal Krinitz and Bernice Steinhardt.**

Krinitz, Esther Nisenthal, and Bernice Steinhardt. *Memories of Survival*. Hyperion Books for Children, 2005. ISBN 0786851260. 64 p. Grades 4–up.

Esther Nisenthal Krinitz grew up in a tiny village in central Poland. She loved her family and her life there, but in 1939 when she was twelve years old, everything changed.

Nazi soldiers arrived in September that year. As they entered the town, they stopped in front of her grandparents' house, then roughed up her grandfather and cut off his beard. Her grandmother screamed, but it was only the beginning of a series of horrors that ended in death for almost everyone in Esther's family.

Everyone, even the children, had to work for the Nazis, and some of the people were imprisoned in labor camps, and later killed. Life became harder and harder, as the persecution of the Jews became more and more outrageous.

In October 1942 the Gestapo ordered all of the Jews to leave their homes and walk to the Krasnik railroad station and then to their deaths.

Esther fled with her younger sister Mania, and they somehow managed to survive the war. In 1949 she came to America, and when she was older, she embroidered a series of pictures that showed what her life was like before and during the war. Her daughter Bernice assembled these works of art into a story—it is beautiful and horrible and fascinating.

Lewin, Ted. *How Much? Visiting Markets Around the World.* HarperCollins, 2006. ISBN 0688175538. 32 p. Grades 1–4.

Do you have a market in your hometown? Maybe a farmer's market, where farmers sell the things that they grow? Maybe a flea market, where dealers sell things that they hope others will want to buy?

Yours may be like the one in New Jersey pictured on pages 24–27, but here Ted Lewin shows us markets all over the world and the things they sell.

Would you like to buy a *durian* (what the heck is that?) in Thailand? Or pay for flowers by their weight in India? Maybe a poncho in Peru? How about a camel in Egypt?

You'll enjoy reading about these interesting places and looking at the great pictures.

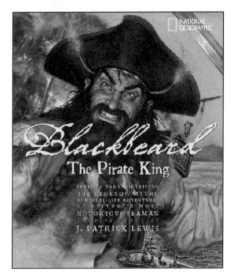

Blackbeard the Pirate King: Several Yarns
Detailing the Legends, Myths, and Real-Life
Adventures of History's Most Notorious Seaman
by J. Patrick Lewis.

Lewis, J. Patrick. *Blackbeard the Pirate King: Several Yarns Detailing the Legends, Myths, and Real-Life Adventures of History's Most Notorious Seaman.* National Geographic, 2006. ISBN 0792255852. Unpaged. Grades 3–7.

Just like the book says, Blackbeard is probably the most famous seaman, let alone pirate, who ever lived.

What do you know about him? You know one thing, right? He had a black beard!

The truth is that nobody really knows much about him—not even his real name. Most people think that was Edward Teach, but it might have been Thatch or Tach.

But there are a lot of stories.

Blackbeard was born probably in 1680, but we do not know where. He became a pirate of the Caribbean (bet you heard of another pirate of the Caribbean) and did all sorts of exciting, horrifying, and interesting things. It is said that he shot his first mate in the knee just to show him who was the boss. We know for sure when he died, in 1718, because a British ship fought him and his crew, killed him, cut off his head and attached in to the bowsprit of their ship. They say his headless body still swims in the waters, looking for its head.

This book is filled with poems about Blackbeard, other information about him, and pictures of him created from 1730 to the present.

If you like pirates, you'll love reading this book.

Show the frontispiece picture to your audience.

Limke, Jeff. *Isis & Osiris: To the Ends of the Earth: An Egyptian Myth*. Pencils and inks by David Witt. Graphic Universe, 2007. ISBN 0822530864. 48 p. Grades 4–8.

Some of the best stories ever are thousands of years old. They *have* to be good or they would not have lasted. The story of Isis and Osiris is one of those old, old stories, and it was told long ago by the ancient Egyptians. Isis and Osiris were gods, but Osiris was the king of Egypt, and he had a brother, Set, who hated him. Set wanted to be the king himself, and he set up a terrible game at a party to get his brother good—and he did just that. Isis wanted her beloved husband back.

This is a graphic version, or comic book, of that story. Find out what happened and why the story has lasted so long.

Hidden World of the Aztec by Peter Lourie.

Lourie, Peter. *Hidden World of the Aztec* (Ancient Civilizations of the Americas). Boyds Mills Press, 2006. ISBN 1590780698. 48 p. Grades 4–8.

If you go to Mexico City, you will see a huge metropolitan area with many modern buildings and a beautiful cathedral. That is what is on top.

Underneath there are many amazing and astounding things. Mexico City was built on top of the capital of the Aztec Empire, which was a beautiful city called Tenochtitlan. When the Spaniards arrived in 1519, they were stunned at its beauty. And then they destroyed it—they certainly must have hoped forever. On top of the great Aztec temple they built the cathedral. Surely they must have thought, it was gone forever.

But nothing really goes away forever.

Peter Lourie, who loves adventure and treasure and traveling, tells us the story of all of the wondrous Aztec treasures now hidden underneath that city and all around it. He tells us of the treasures that archaeologists are slowly, carefully discovering every day. He tells us of their patient, painstaking work and gives us photographs of some of their wonderful finds. Take a look at the head of the God of Death, as found buried on page 27, and as now reassembled on page 28.

Archaeologists and readers alike can learn a lot about this ancient, great civilization.

How to Be a Pirate by John Malam.

Malam, John. *How to Be a Pirate*. Illustrated by Dave Antram. National Geographic, 2005. ISBN 0792274482. 32 p. Grades 4–8.

Johnny Depp looks very cool in *Pirates of the Caribbean*. He clearly made an extremely interesting career choice in choosing that role. What do you think about piracy as a career? Does it sound fun or interesting? What on earth would you have to do to become a pirate?

This book takes an imaginary pirate ship called *The Dolphin* and tells us about its crew and their duties. *The Dolphin* is based in Port Royal, in the Caribbean, and is one of many ships in its quiet, safe harbor.

Here's what you'll need to do to get a job onboard:

• Be able to sew—sailcloth is always in need of mending.

• Be able to climb high on ropes.

• Be able to tie good knots.

• Be able to row and to fight with swords.

- Be a good cleaner. A lot of work is going to consist of keeping the ship clean.

- Be able to eat disgusting food—food rots quickly on board, and you have to eat anyway.

You will learn what a pirate ship does when it attacks another ship. Pirates are not noted for their kindness and mercy. It isn't a pretty sight.

And it is not a pretty sight when a pirate gets captured, either, or gets in trouble on his ship.

Read this book with its interesting colorful pictures to make a decision—is the life of a pirate a life you would enjoy?

The Parthenon: The Height of Greek Civilization
by Elizabeth Mann.

Mann, Elizabeth. *The Parthenon: The Height of Greek Civilization* (A Wonders of the World Book). With illustrations by Yuan Lee. Mikaya Press, 2006. ISBN 1931414157. 48 p. Grades 4–7.

In ancient Greece, the city of Athens was originally only a small settlement. Theseus, a great leader, organized some of the other areas around the city and it grew bigger and safer. By the 600s B.C.E., Athens no longer had kings. It had the beginnings of what would turn out to be the first democracy—government by the people—in the world.

Athens was dedicated to and named after a particular Greek goddess, Athena, the goddess of wisdom. There was a statue of her on top of the Acropolis, a high area that was once the city center. Every year the citizens had feast days in which they celebrated and honored her.

And things went very well in Athens. They won their battles and were prosperous and happy people. In the battle of Marathon in 490 B.C.E., the Athenians so outwitted their Persian enemies that they killed 6,400 of the Persians—and only 192 of their own men were killed.

They wanted to thank the goddess, for they felt they owed such a wonderful victory to her. How could they do this?

They decided to build a temple to Athena sunk deep into the Acropolis and made of the beautiful stone marble. And this is the story of how they built it—it is an amazing and interesting one.

If you enjoy history or architecture, you will enjoy reading this book.

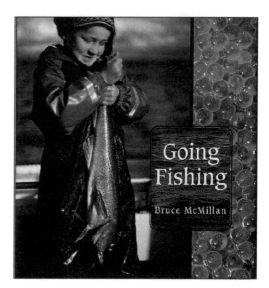

***Going Fishing* by Bruce McMillan.**

McMillan, Bruce. *Going Fishing.* Houghton Mifflin, 2005. ISBN 0618472010. 32 p. Grades K–3.

Fridrik, who lives in Reykjavik, Iceland, goes fishing with his grandfathers—one at a time. One fishes for cod; the other fishes for lumpfish, and Fridrik has a blast with them both.

Iceland, this book tells us, is the land of fish. Even the money and the stamps have fish on them! So the Icelandic people are experts at catching fish, and this shows us exactly how they go about doing it.

Bruce McMillan, the author and photographer of this book, gives us some wonderful color photographs that make anyone who sees them want to get on a boat and go fishing in Iceland.

Morris, Ann, and Heidi Larson. *Tsunami: Helping Each Other.* Millbrook Press, 2005. ISBN 0761395016. 32 p. Grades 2–5.

On December 26, 2004, one of the worst disasters *ever* happened. Under the sea near northern Indonesia a violent earthquake erupted, which caused massive waves to start shooting away from its center. When the waves hit land, tragedy came with them. More than 150,000 people were killed or disappeared in more than one dozen countries. The wall of water struck both the poor people who actually lived on the land and the usually wealthier tourists who were staying at some of the fancy hotels.

This is the true story of two brothers who went out to play that morning. Cahipreak and Chaiya were going to a beautiful beach. Their parents did not come with them, as both of them had errands to do.

They never saw their father again. He disappeared in the tsunami. They *did* find their mother near the ruins of what had been their home.

Then they had to try to survive, and eventually build a new life for their family.

There are many color photographs here and a lot of information about this horrible catastrophe.

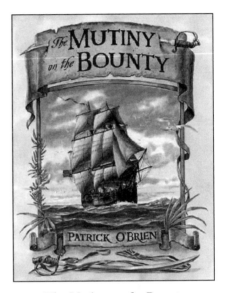

The Mutiny on the Bounty
by Patrick O'Brien.

O'Brien, Patrick. *The Mutiny on the Bounty.* Walker & Company, 2007. ISBN 0802795870. Unpaged. Grades 3–7.

If you know what the word "mutiny" means, you probably also know about the most famous mutiny in all of history.

In a mutiny, people under the command of another rise up and rebel. In 1788 that is what happened on the *Bounty,* a British ship that had just spent five months in what seemed like paradise—the island of Tahiti. Life onboard the ship had been hard during the ten months it took to get there, with rotten food and hard discipline.

Captain Bligh was not happy with the way some of his men were behaving when the ship re-embarked, now loaded with plants to take to the Caribbean, and he was particularly irritated by his second in command, a man named Fletcher Christian.

When Bligh and Christian started arguing, Christian decided he had had it. He led a mutiny! He took over the ship and put Bligh and the men who were still loyal to him on a rowboat, then set them adrift.

He knew what the penalty would be for leading a mutiny. He would be hanged—and so would all the men who were loyal to him. He had better hide as fast as he could!

This is the exciting true story of what happened—and where he went.

Pauketat, Timothy R., and Nancy Stone Bernard. *Cahokia Mounds* (Digging for the Past). Oxford University Press, 2004. ISBN 0195158105. 48 p. Grades 5–up.

"Between 1000 and 1350 C.E., long before Europeans landed in the Americas, as many as 16,000 Native Americans lived in Cahokia, with thousands more living in outlying villages" (p. 8).

This was the biggest city north of what is now Mexico. By the standards of that time, it was colossal. And yet hardly anyone who doesn't live nearby it has ever heard of it.

It is in what today is East Saint Louis, Illinois, and that is one of the major problems. For East Saint Louis, like many American cities, is both growing and sprawling, using up more and more space for housing and roads. The need for roads and new houses seems to be a lot more important than the need to preserve an amazing piece of our heritage as Americans.

Where Cahokia once was, there are now mounds. Monks Mound is as big as the Great Pyramid of Egypt. There are many mounds in Cahokia, and they are filled with pottery, bodies, and all sorts of artifacts of this once thriving civilization.

This book, with lots of interesting color pictures, tells us about those mounds and about the artifacts—including bows, arrowheads, stone axes, and game pieces—that archaeologists are finding. It is hard, for they often have to work too quickly, because a new construction is going to wipe out the site.

That we have such a place in America is wonderful. Read all about it in this interesting book.

We Gather Together: Celebrating the Harvest Season by **Wendy Pfeffer.**

Pfeffer, Wendy. *We Gather Together: Celebrating the Harvest Season.* Illustrated by Linda Bleck. Dutton Children's Books, 2006. ISBN 0525476695. Unpaged. Grades 1–3.

In North America, animals get ready for winter in early autumn. They gather and store food and some eat a lot to get fat.

People used to have to store food for winter, too, but now food comes to them from all over the world.

This book explains why autumn happens and what happens during that season—and it also tells of how people learned to plant seeds and grow food, and how happy they were to have that food for the long winters ahead. They celebrated. All around the world they celebrated the harvest time after the long planting and growing seasons. They ate the harvest and had parties and festivals—and this shows you what some of the parties and festivals around the world are like. Can you name any besides Thanksgiving?

This has lots of fun information. Do you know why the full moon nearest to the first day of autumn is called the harvest moon? It is because it was so bright that people could harvest their crops at night.

Piratepedia. DK, 2006. ISBN 9780756626600. 125 p. Grades 4–8.

If you like pirates, as well as lots of good pictures and all sorts of bits of fascinating information, this may be just the book you are looking for. You will learn some great information about pirates throughout history. Here's a sample:

- Many pirates did not spend much time at sea. Instead, they attacked towns and took treasure and captured the inhabitants to sell as slaves.

- Look at the picture of the barbarous barbs on page 33. These were sharp, pointed pieces of iron that stuck out in different directions. When pirates attacked, they might throw these on the deck of the ship they were trying to capture. Sailors usually went barefoot, and when they stepped on the barbs accidentally they could really hurt themselves.

- There were some famous female pirates!

- Some pirates were not outlaws. The king or queen of their country gave them letters of marquee, which meant they could attack the ships of other countries—as long as their own king or queen got a nice share of whatever treasure they captured. These pirates were called privateers, and the most famous one is someone you may have heard of—Sir Francis Drake.

Take a look at the pictures of some of the most famous Chinese pirates on page 84.

And that is just the beginning!

Rubin, Susan Goldman, with Ela Weissberger. *The Cat with the Yellow Star: Coming of Age in Terezin.* Holiday House, 2006. ISBN 0823418316. 40 p. Grades 4–6.

Ela Stein was only eight years old when the Nazis invaded Czechoslovakia, the country where she lived with her parents and her older sister. They didn't stay in their home for long after the invasion, for Ela's father publicly spoke out against Hitler. That night he was arrested, and his family never found out what happened to him. Her mother knew one thing, though: they had to move immediately, or they might be arrested too. They escaped to their Uncle Otto's apartment in Prague, but watched conditions get worse and worse there. By 1940, Jews were being concentrated in small areas of the city, and everyone Jewish had to wear a gold star. Jewish children were not allowed to go to public schools.

Then even more awful things started to happen.

In December 1941, the Nazis began rounding up Jews and transporting them elsewhere. In February, Ela and her family were put on a train to a place called Terezin.

It was a concentration camp, and Ela was there until the war ended.

But there she was involved an extraordinary thing. The inmates of the camp gave many performances of an opera written for children called *Brundibar.* Ela got the part of a black cat!

She survived, and today she lives in America. This is her story.

Show the picture of Ela as the cat on page 23.

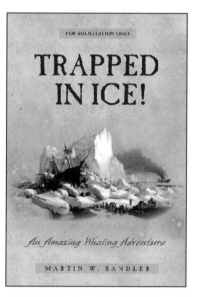

Trapped in Ice! An Amazing Whaling Adventure
by Martin W. Sandler.

Sandler, Martin W. *Trapped in Ice! An Amazing Whaling Adventure.* Scholastic Nonfiction, an imprint of Scholastic, 2006. ISBN 043974363X. 168 p. Grades 4–8.

Going whaling, sailing through the ocean looking for whales, chasing them and harpooning them—wow! It sounded like a glamorous life in the 1800s, and young men and boys signed up to go on whaling voyages, hoping to make a lot of money and see the world.

Very few of them made much, if any, money, and mostly what they saw was the ocean. And chasing and killing the whale (if they were lucky and caught the whale) *was* extremely exciting. But what happened after they caught the whale was backbreaking, smelly, dirty work. Sometimes they even had to work inside the rotting corpse of the dead whale. The ship decks ran with whale blubber and blood.

By 1871 whales were getting harder to find. A lot of the most desirable ones, the bowhead whales, valued for the huge number of their bones, were to be found in the Arctic. So whalers, sometimes including the captain's wife and children, headed north. And, in 1871, they faced a crisis unlike any most of them had ever seen.

Winter came early that year, and it was a hard winter. The Eskimos warned the sailors that the ice was coming fast, but the sailors paid no attention. They knew what they were doing, or so they thought.

The Eskimos were right. The thirty-two ships carrying 1,219 men, women, and children became completely stuck in the ice in below zero temperatures. It was getting colder, and there was no hope at all for getting unstuck. If they didn't get out of their ships and get rescued, they would all die for sure. What was going to happen to them? Who could save them? What could they do?

This is a scary and true story.

Schlitz, Laura Amy. *Good Masters! Sweet Ladies! Voices from a Medieval Village*. Illustrated by Robert Byrd. Candlewick, 2007. ISBN 0763615781. 85 p. Grades 4–8.

Do you like the Middle Ages? Do you like hearing about knights and castles and fine ladies?

Well, unfortunately, most of the people who lived then were not knights and fine ladies, and very few of them lived in castles. Most of them were ordinary people, and a great number of them were terribly poor and did not get enough to eat.

This is a series of plays about kids who live in the village and the farmlands surrounding a small castle in England around the year 1255. Almost all of them tell about one young person who tells us about his or her life and what it is like.

If you read them all, you will learn a great deal about how kids lived so long ago. And you and your class or friends might like to read them in a group, each taking a different part. These plays were written for kids in a school.

You'll hear about a kid who was happy, very happy, to get some dog food to eat, a girl whose job it was to trap eels, a Jewish boy who has almost no legal rights, and more.

This Newbery Medal winner is a fine read.

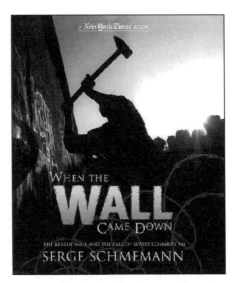

When the Wall Came Down: The Berlin Wall and the Fall of Soviet Communism **by Serge Schmemann.**

Schmemann, Serge. *When the Wall Came Down: The Berlin Wall and the Fall of Soviet Communism*. A New York Times Book. Kingfisher, 2006. ISBN 0753459949. 127 p. Grades 5–up.

It was November 9, 1989, and Serge Schmemann was writing like crazy on his laptop in his hotel room in West Berlin. At about midnight, someone knocked at his door. He was annoyed. He had work to do. When the door opened, it was his assistant from East Berlin, and he tried to get rid of him. Viktor was trying to tell him something, and all of a sudden it him! What was Viktor doing in *West* Berlin? Viktor lived in *East* Berlin and could have been shot for trying to get to the other side of the great wall that had been built between the two parts of the city almost forty years earlier.

Viktor told him what was going on. The wall was down! People were crossing over, climbing over, scrambling over any way they could—and no one was shooting!

A lot of events led up to that exciting night, and this is their story.

After Germany was defeated in World War II, its victors, the United States, the Soviet Union, Great Britain, and France, divided up the country so that it could never start another war. Berlin landed right in the middle of the Soviet area—but the other countries wanted access to Berlin because it was the capital as well as the largest city. The Soviets let them have access for a while, and then closed all the roads and railroad tracks leading into the city. The Allies succeeded in making them change that rule, but the Soviet Union wanted Germany to be communist and did not want their part of Berlin or Germany to be able to see what was going on in the other part. They especially did not want their citizens to escape. Eventually they built a wall between the two parts of the city. People were separated from their families and their friends. Many people died trying to escape from East Berlin. Now all of that was over. What would happen next?

This is an astounding story, and this book is loaded with excellent photographs that show us what was happening.

Shoveller, Herb. *Ryan and Jimmy: And the Well in Africa That Brought Them Together.* Kids Can Press, 2006. ISBN 1553379675. 56 p. Grades 4–6.

Ryan Hreljac (pronounced Hurljack) learned something that really bothered him when he was in first grade. He learned that many people in Africa had no safe drinking water. In fact, it was very hard for them to get water at all. Some of them had to walk twelve miles to get water, and the water they got was often disgustingly dirty and made them sick. The teacher told his class that it only cost $70 to build a well, and Ryan decided he was going to make enough money to send to Africa to build one.

Making $70 isn't the easiest thing to do when you are in first grade. Ryan's parents were pretty sure he might work on it for a little while and then lose interest, but they were wrong. Ryan did it—and found he needed a lot more than $70. In fact, the whole well would cost $2,000. How could he *ever* make that much money?

But he did. People started getting interested and donating money, and before too long passed, he had the money. And then he heard that $25,000 would buy a power drill that could go around digging lots of wells. How could Ryan raise $25,000?

This is the true story of how he did it, how this Canadian boy went to Africa to see the well, and how he met his pen pal there, a Ugandan boy who became his best friend and, eventually, his new brother.

There are lots of great photos here. Show the one of a typical pond of water used for drinking on page 19.

Simon, Seymour. *Knights and Castles* (Seemore Readers: Level 3). Chronicle Books, 2006. ISBN 0811854086. Unpaged. Grades 2–4.

Just about everyone thinks knights are pretty neat. Most of them were really good, trained soldiers, and they worked in the service of a king or a lord, during the time we call the Middle Ages. They wore armor, they rode horses, and they carried shields that had their family emblem, or coat of arms, on them. They did not have guns. They used bows and arrows, swords, and shields.

You'll learn about them, the way they fought and the castles in which they lived in this interesting book.

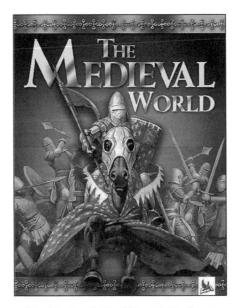

The Medieval World by Philip Steele.

Steele, Philip. *The Medieval World*. Kingfisher, 2006. ISBN 0753460467. 96 p. Grades 4–8.

If you like knights and castles and knowing about what life was like in the Middle Ages, this is a great place to start. It is loaded with pictures and gives us all sorts of great information.

Did you know that:

• At that time, all that held together all of the tiny principalities, kingdoms, and dukedoms in Europe was that they shared a common faith—Christianity. Most modern countries did not exist. Every once in a while they would get organized and attack the people who were not Christians.

• From the 1100s on, knights were expected to follow a code of honor.

• Women could not become knights and had almost no rights at all.

• Very few people could read or write.

And that is just the beginning. Take a look at some of the illustrations—you'll want to know more.

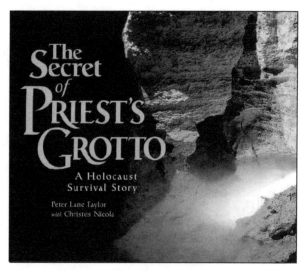

The Secret of Priest's Grotto: A Holocaust Survival Story **by Peter Lane Taylor with Christos Nicola.**

Taylor, Peter Lane, with Christos Nicola. *The Secret of Priest's Grotto: A Holocaust Survival Story*. Kar-Ben, 2007. ISBN 158013260x. 64 p. Grades 4–8.

Only one place on earth has "Gypsum Giant" cave systems. That place is the Ukraine. The caves do not descend deep into the ground, although they are deep enough, but instead are horizontal caves, made of a substance with a crystalline structure. They are dark and treacherous, long and bewildering. To get lost in them, which happens easily in the dark, is terrifying.

But one of those caves saved the life of a group of Jewish families that was hunted by the Nazis during the Holocaust. The Jews in their little town of Korolowka were being executed and deported. They knew their only hope of surviving the horror was to hide—and the best place to hide was in the caves.

They had very little food, almost no tools, and very little wood for heat. The caves were always damp, and people were always wet. Some of them had to leave the caves occasionally to find food and supplies, and they were helped by a few family members and friends on the outside. They had almost no furniture, and not many blankets. Amazingly, some of them stayed underground in the dark for 344 days—more than any other known human has ever stayed underneath the ground.

This book has many photographs of the extraordinary survivors and of the cave itself and the men who explored it. It is an amazing story.

Chapter 4

Animals

What is it with kids and animals? Nonfiction books about animals are a perennial favorite with young readers—they just can't get enough of them. And if there are cute pictures (see *Owen and Mzee* by Isabella and Craig Hatkoff) or gross pictures (see *Slippery, Slimy, Baby Frogs* by Sandra Markle), all the better. Publishers come out with many animal books every year, and the subject matter ranges from dinosaur droppings to modern-day rescue dogs. We've selected the cream of the crop here—these books are both well reviewed and appealing to kids.

Aston, Diana. *An Egg Is Quiet.* Illustrated by Sylvia Long. Chronicle Books, 2006. ISBN 0811844285. Unpaged. Grades K–3.

We've all seen eggs. We see them often. Mostly we see chicken eggs and they all look pretty much alike, but there are lots of other kinds of eggs. Some of them are not white or brown. Some are blue, or green, or speckled. Some are almost round, and some are oval. Some are pointy. Some of them are almost camouflaged to hide in the places where they are laid. They are different sizes. Ostrich eggs can weigh as much as eight pounds! Hummingbird eggs and jellybeans are about the same size. Some are smooth, and some are rough. Some are fossilized dinosaur eggs!

We see a lot of eggs in the book and a lot of animals that hatched out of them at the end. Take a look at the amazing pictures. You'll learn a lot about eggs.

Author Profile: Jacob Berkowitz

After seeing drawers of fossil poop, or coprolites, in a museum, Canadian author Jacob Berkowitz was convinced that he had found the perfect topic for a children's nonfiction book. Since writing Jurassic Poop: What Dinosaurs (and Others) Left Behind, *he's now working on more kids' nonfiction books that explore unusual and fun science topics.*

What made you start to write nonfiction for kids?

Ten years ago I was working at the Canadian Museum of Nature as an educator. The curator of paleontology was giving a tour of the collection. We saw dinosaur skeletons, a saber-toothed tiger skeleton, and then the curator opened a drawer and said, "These are coprolites, fossil poop." I was sure it was a joke, a stunt they pull on all the new educators. Then he opened another drawer and another drawer—all full of coprolites.

One of the photographs in the book is of him holding one of these. I was fascinated by fossil poop—that something so normally ephemeral could fossilize and hold an enormous amount of information about the ancient world. I thought this would be a fantastic kids' book because it combines paleontology, dinosaurs and other neat animals of the past with poop, and the things we can learn from it. For me it just screamed "kids' book."

How did you sell this book?

Initially I sent out query letters to publishers I thought would be a good fit and I got several rejection letters. Then, having been a professional writer for a number of years, I put on my business hat. I began to work the contacts that I knew and finally a colleague put me in touch with Valerie Wyatt, the science editor for Kids Can Press. She saw the title *Jurassic Poop* in the outline and was sold right from the start. From there it was a great journey.

How did you do the research for Jurassic Poop?

There was no comprehensive text on coprolites, so I spent a lot of time doing basic research. I went to all the original scientific sources, and talked to a lot of scientists, which was a hoot because I got information right from the researchers' mouths. I was lucky enough that while I was at the museum I'd arranged a speaking event that involved Karen Chin, the world's dinosaur coprolite expert. So I knew her personally. The founder of research into human coprolites, Eric Callen—now deceased—was from Montreal. I visited his son who generously shared his father's original papers and took me to his former lab at McGill University, which ironically has now been turned into the men's washroom.

How do you put scientific concepts in terms kids will understand?

The biggest challenge is taking the complex scientific vernacular, the technical gobbeldy-gook, and turning it into fun and engaging language for children. Fortunately with *Jurassic Poop* the topic is so full of puns that I loved writing it. I knew I was having a good writing day when I'd sit and laugh because I was having such a good time writing. I always have to remember to play when I'm writing. If I'm working hard, I know the writing's going to be bad. This doesn't mean that the writing isn't full of solid content. On the one hand it's funny, it's fossil poop. But if you go through the book and learn the skills to figure out *"Who dung it?"* you have all of the essential skills to be a paleontologist.

What was the most exciting research moment you have had while researching Jurassic Poop?

One of the most interesting insights was talking to Hendrik Poinar. His father is the "insects in amber" scientist on whom Michael Crichton based his book *Jurassic Park*. Hendrik Poinar worked with his dad for a while then went off to do his own ancient DNA research. He asked his Ph.D. advisor if anyone had tried to get DNA out of Ice Age sloth coprolites, and he was told they'd tried and it was impossible. That's the best thing to tell a striving Ph.D. student. So Hendrik Poinar did it. In the end, it meant dad inspired *Jurassic Park*, and his son inspired *Jurassic Poop*. Hendrik has now shown that fossil poop is the best source of ancient DNA—better than bones or teeth—and he's looking to extract DNA from Neanderthal coprolites. He might provide seminal insight into human evolution all based on getting DNA out of poop.

What would you be doing if you were not writing for young people?

That's a good question. I've been thinking about this. Someone once described writing as a long journey in a small room, and I'd add a long and often lonely journey. It's why I'm now doing kids theatre—the play *The Mysterious Case of Who Dung It?* which is based on the book. I love acting, and its another venue of expression and storytelling that I'm exploring and that is more social than writing.

Learn more about Jacob Berkowitz at www.jacobberkowitz.com

Berkowitz, Jacob. *Jurassic Poop: What Dinosaurs (and Others) Left Behind.* Illustrated by Steve Mack. Kids Can Press, 2006. ISBN 1553378601. 40 p. Grades 3–6.

So what on earth *is* Jurassic poop? Do you have a clue? Read the first two pages in chapter one, and you will have your answer.

An ancient dinosaur poops in a river delta. The poop sinks and is covered up for a long time—until about 75 million years later, when a dinosaur hunter finds it in Alberta, Canada. It is about as big as a loaf of bread, and there is an amazing photograph of it on page 6.

The fact is that poop is all around us. Even the soil in which we grow our food is made up largely of the poop of worms and other small animals, which is a darn good reason to wash the food before we eat it.

In this colorfully illustrated book you will learn more about poop than you ever dreamed you wanted to know! You'll even find a recipe for how to make your own fake coprolite—which is fossilized poop. You will learn how to recognize ancient poop if you stumble across some—although it is not easy. You will learn what preserves poop, and how many kinds of poop are preserved on our planet. You will learn why scientists love to find ancient toilets and outhouses—places where people went to the bathroom.

You will have a blast learning about science by learning all about old poop.

Nic Bishop Spiders by **Nic Bishop.**

Bishop, Nic. *Nic Bishop Spiders*. Scholastic Nonfiction, an imprint of Scholastic, 2007. ISBN 0439877563. 48 p. Grades 3–6.

This book has some of the most incredible photographs you will ever see: close-ups of all different kinds of spiders. Not only will you get to see them, but you will learn some great things about them, such as:

- Spiders have been around for 350 million years, even before *Tyrannosaurus Rex.*

- There are more than 38,000 kinds of spiders, but the biggest one is the Goliath birdeater tarantula from South America.

- Spiders drink all of their food. They turn the animal's insides into soup before they eat it.

- Most spiders have eight eyes, but they do not have very good vision. Some are blind. The hairs on their legs can sense all sorts of things.

- Spiders molt. They squeeze out of their old skin. It is hard, hard work. Look at the photograph on page 18.

- Jumping spiders can jump twenty times their body length! Take a look at the photo on page 28.

- Male spiders often fight with each other when they are looking for mates. Look at the photos on pages 36–37.

You won't be able to put this book down!

Bonner, Hannah. *When Fish Got Feet, Sharks Got Teeth, and Bugs Began to Swarm: A Cartoon Prehistory of Life Long Before Dinosaurs.* National Geographic, 2007. ISBN 1426300786. 45 p. Grades 4–6.

What do you suppose our planet looked like before there were even dinosaurs? It was a long time ago, and if you guessed that it looked completely different, you are absolutely right.

Take a look at the picture of what is now Pennsylvania on pages 8 and 9. Here is what it says about it: "430 million years ago the tallest plants around would have been knee-high to a grasshopper, had there been any grasshoppers. There weren't. Instead there were some small millipedes and other bugs crawling around under equally tiny plants. There were moss relatives a few inches tall, lichens on the rocks, and slimy mats of algae and bacteria in the wetter spots. Mostly though, it was just rocks, rocks, and more rocks, with some gravel, sand and silt thrown in for good measure" (p. 9).

Wow! That's hard to imagine.

Four hundred thirty million years ago, most of North America was underwater—a sea! And although there was a lot of life, there were not many creatures alive that are still around today. We would be astonished at what we would see. The biggest animals around were eurypterids, some of which were six feet long. They looked sort of like scorpions, and that is a scary thing to think about. Look at the picture of one on pages 12–13.

Kathy's Top Ten Animal Booktalking Favorites

- Berkowitz, Jacob. *Jurassic Poop: What Dinosaurs (and Others) Left Behind.* Kids Can Press, 2006.

- Bishop, Nic. *Nic Bishop Spiders.* Scholastic Nonfiction, 2007.

- Chrustowski, Rick. *Turtle Crossing.* Henry Holt, 2006.

- Hatkoff, Isabella, Craig Hatkoff, and Dr. Paula Kahumbu. *Owen & Mzee: The True Story of a Remarkable Friendship.* Scholastic, 2006.

- Hatkoff, Isabella, Craig Hatkoff, and Dr. Paula Kahumbu. *The Language of Friendship (Owen and Mzee).* Scholastic, 2007.

- Jenkins, Steve. *Dogs and Cats.* Houghton Mifflin, 2007.

- Marrin, Albert. *Oh Rats! The Story of Rats and People.* Dutton Children's Books, 2006.

- Markle, Sandra. *Musk Oxen* (Animal Prey). Lerner, 2006.

- Ryder, Joanne. *Toad by the Road: A Year in the Life of These Amazing Amphibians.* Henry Holt, 2007.

- Souza, D. M. *Look What Whiskers Can Do* (Look What Animals Can Do). Lerner, 2007.

From *Gotcha Good! Nonfiction Books to Get Kids Excited About Reading* by Kathleen A. Baxter and Marcia Agness Kochel. Westport, CT: Libraries Unlimited. Copyright © 2008.

There were fish with no jaws. There were no trees. Some of the continents were still stuck together, like what is now North America and northern Europe.

And then things started to change.

You'll be surprised at what you will learn about the earth and its life before the dinosaurs in this fun book.

Bradley, Timothy J. *Paleo Sharks: Survival of the Strangest.* Chronicle Books, 2007. ISBN 0811848787. 47 p. Grades 4–8.

Sharks have been around for hundreds of millions of years. Not many animals have that kind of a history. This book tells us a little bit about their past and the kinds of sharks that existed over time. All the pronunciations for the shark names are in the book.

- Cladoselache, which was six feet long, appeared about 375 million years ago. Though it had sharp teeth, it ate everything tail first! Today many fish do this to avoid barbs and spines and the problems they cause going down.

- Orthacanthus, about 360 million years ago, had a long spike that grew from the back of its skull.

- Perhaps the most bizarre looking shark was Helicoprion, about 250 million years ago. It "had hundreds of teeth tightly packed into a compact spiral that looked like a 10-inch buzz-saw blade!" (p. 26). Look at the picture. It is scary!

- Carcharodon Megalodon, which lived about 25 million years ago, was colossal. It might have weighed about twenty-five times as much as a blue whale. It went around eating anything it felt like. Nothing could stop it.

If you like sharks, you will have a great time reading and looking at the pictures in this book.

Bredeson, Carmen. *African Elephants Up Close* (Zoom in on Animals!). Enslow Elementary, 2006. ISBN 0766024997. 24 p. Grades 1–3.

Did you know that African elephants are bigger than any other animals that live on the land? Or that they can live to be as old as 50?

In this neat book you will learn about their ears, their skin, their eyes, their food, their tusks (sometimes they use them to fight each other), their feet, and their babies.

When those babies are born, they weigh 200 to 300 pounds, and the other elephants hug the new baby with their trunks. You'll enjoy learning about these fun animals.

Show the picture on page 21.

Brown, Charlotte Lewis. *After the Dinosaurs: Mammoths and Fossil Mammals* (I Can Read Book 2). Pictures by Phil Wilson. HarperCollins, 2006. ISBN 0060530537. 32 p. Grades 1–3.

Small mammals lived at the same time as the dinosaurs, but they were very different. Take a look at the pictures on pages 4 and 6.

After the dinosaurs died out, it took millions of years, but those small mammals started to get bigger. This book gives us some great illustrations and interesting information about some of those mammals.

You'll enjoy learning about

- The Glyptodon, which sort of looks like an armadillo—but was a lot bigger. It was the size of a small car.

- The Platybelodon, which kind of looks like an elephant—except that its front teeth were shaped like shovels. It could use them to dig up plants to eat.

- The Macrauchenia—an animal that had a body like a camel, feet like a rhinoceros and a trunk somewhat like that of an elephant, only shorter. It was definitely weird looking.

You'll have fun reading this book!

Brown, Charlotte Lewis. *Beyond the Dinosaurs: Monsters of the Air and Sea* (I Can Read Level 2). Pictures by Phil Wilson. HarperCollins, 2007. ISBN 0060530561. 32 p. Grades 1–3.

Scientists are learning lots of new things about prehistoric times. This book tells us about some of the animals that lived at the same time of the dinosaurs—and there were some really cool ones. Take a look at:

- The Deinosuchus, which looked a lot like a crocodile but was five times bigger! It waited underwater for a dinosaur to come get a drink—and then it pulled the dinosaur underwater and had it for dinner. Look for it on pages 10–11.

- The Mosasaurus had flippers instead of feet and a thin body and head. It was the fastest swimmer in the ocean. See it on pages 16–17.

- "Kronosaurus was a giant that hunted the ocean for food. It was longer than a bus. It had teeth as big as bananas. Its jaws were bigger and stronger than the jaws of Tyrannosaurus rex. It ate fish, ichthyosaurs, and even turtles. Kronosaurus ate everything it wanted!" (pp. 24–25).

If you like dinosaurs, you will want to know about these amazing animals.

Brown, Charlotte Lewis. *The Day the Dinosaurs Died* (I Can Read 2). Illustrated by Phil Wilson. HarperCollins, 2006. ISBN 0060005289. 48 p. Grades 1–3.

Millions of years ago, dinosaurs were everywhere, all over the earth. And, fairly suddenly, they all died. All we have left are fossils to show they once existed. What happened?

Most scientists believe something big happened. One big thing caused a whole lot of other things to happen. Most believe that big thing came from outer space.

It was an asteroid. That asteroid landed in what is now Mexico. You can still see the huge crater it made. It blew up! It killed everything anywhere near it, and then the effects started spreading.

Read this interesting book to find out what really happened.

Chrustowski, Rick. *Turtle Crossing*. Henry Holt, 2006. ISBN 0805074988. Unpaged. Grades K–3.

Rick Chrustowski writes about ordinary animals and makes you want to know more and really appreciate them. Take a look at this colorful book about a painted turtle that comes out of an underground nest in the mud and slowly walks to a pond, a place where she is safe.

She is very small, only as big as a quarter. She has to hide a lot, because there are other animals that would like to eat her. When she gets to be older, her shell will be hard, and then no one wants her for dinner, but now her shell is very soft. One threat is a big snapping turtle.

Why is this book called *Turtle Crossing?* What would a turtle cross? Is it dangerous? You bet. Read it and find out what happens.

Clarke, Ginjer L. *Bug Out! The World's Creepiest, Crawliest Critters* (All Aboard Science Reader). Illustrated by Pete Mueller. Grosset & Dunlap, 2007. ISBN 9780448445434. 48 p. Grades 1–3.

There are a lot of bugs in the world—more than any other kind of animal. All insects are bugs, but not all bugs are insects—spiders aren't. Their bodies are built differently. But spiders are still bugs!

Read this neat book to find some fun things about them. For instance,

- A tarantula hawk wasp may be smaller than a tarantula, but it swoops down and stings one. That sting paralyzes that poor tarantula. The hawk wasp drags the tarantula to a tunnel in the desert and then lays an egg on it. When the baby is born, it eats that tarantula! Yuck.

- Never touch a scorpion. Read about what they can do on page 11.

- Giant water bugs grab small frogs and stab them with their sharp beaks. The frog's insides turn to a liquid mush. Then the bug drinks that mush—the frog's blood and guts—and leaves only the frog's empty skin.

- Learn about crab spiders, which sit inside of flowers and wait for bees. When a bee lands, it hasn't got much longer to live. Find out what happens on page 39.

And that is just the beginning!

Clarke, Ginjer L. *Freak Out! Animals Beyond Your Wildest Imagination* (All Aboard Science Reader Station Stop 2). Illustrated by Pete Mueller. Grosset & Dunlap, 2006. ISBN 0448443082. 48 p. Grades 1–4.

A lot of the animals in this book are probably ones even your parents and maybe teachers have never heard of, and they are indeed really weird. Take a look at the picture of the blue-tongued skink on pages 24 and 25. Its tongue is as big as its head, and its size and color just plain scare other animals away.

Or how about the giant pangolin on pages 40 and 41? It is a lizard, and it can be as big as six feet tall. Scales overlap its body, and it raises them to make itself bigger when it is threatened. If it figures the threat is too great, it rolls itself into a ball—and hardly anything can hurt it then.

You will learn about electric eels and pink dolphins, giant squids and walking sticks, viper fish and kiwi birds, and much much more.

Coren, Stanley. *Why Do Dogs Have Wet Noses?* Kids Can Press, 2006. ISBN 1553376579. 64 p. Grades 2–5.

Anybody who has a pet dog probably has a lot of questions, but so do a lot of other people! This book has some great information for dog lovers.

- Dogs really did start out as wolves, and we can tell this because they can have babies with wolves—and jackals, coyotes, dingoes, and some kinds of foxes. That means they are a family.

- Greyhounds are amazingly fast. They can run at their top speed for as much as seven miles. Cheetahs can run faster, but only for a few seconds. Greyhounds can keep running at speeds of about thirty to thirty-five miles an hour. That's fast!

- The most popular dog breed of all is the same in three countries: Britain, Canada and the United States. Can you guess what it is? Find the answer on page 17. (It is the Labrador Retriever.)

- Dogs have more than 220 million smell-detecting cells. Humans only have five million. No wonder dogs are sniffing all of the time.

- On page 39, you will learn how to get your dog to stop barking.

- Dogs can learn to understand about 120–150 words and hand signals.

- Male dogs raise their legs to pee on trees so they will give other animals the impression that they are actually bigger than they are. The higher up it goes, the bigger the dog must be.

You will love telling your friends about the facts in this book.

Extreme Animals: The Toughest Creatures on Earth **by Nicola Davies.**

Davies, Nicola. *Extreme Animals: The Toughest Creatures on Earth.* Illustrated by Neal Layton. Candlewick Press, 2006. ISBN 0763630675. 61 p. Grades 3–6.

    "We humans are such a bunch of wimps!

We can't stand the cold,

We can't stand the heat, we can't live without food, or water,

And just a few minutes without air is enough to finish us off" (p. 7).

    Well, *we* may be wimpy, but there are a lot of animals out there that can easily survive things that we cannot even dream of enduring.

You will love the interesting facts in this book:

- Bowhead whales, which live in the Arctic Ocean, have a layer of fat underneath their skin that is almost *two feet* deep. No wonder they stay warm!

- Emperor penguins have an amazing coat of feathers. Inside the feathers can be 140 degrees Fahrenheit warmer than outside the feathers.

- Hummingbird temperatures can drop below normal by thirty-five to fifty-five degrees Fahrenheit. If our bodies tried to do that, we would be dead long before we came anywhere close.

- In desert heat of 113 degrees Fahrenheit, humans would have to sweat almost a gallon of water an *hour* to keep cool. You will be surprised how desert animals, like camels, have adapted to survive.

- A bird called a blackpoll warbler migrates from North America to South America in a flight that takes eighty hours—with no stopping. The bird uses its own body as fuel and so usually loses about half its weight on the flight. Yikes!

- Some creatures just love to live in boiling water or in volcanoes. Not us!

And that's just the beginning. This is *really* interesting. Bet you can't guess what the toughest animal on earth is (see page 57).

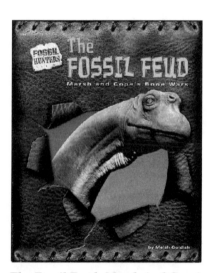

The Fossil Feud: Marsh And Cope's Bone Wars **by Meish Goldish.**

Goldish, Meish. *The Fossil Feud: Marsh and Cope's Bone Wars* (Fossil Hunters). Bearport, 2007. ISBN 1597162566. 32 p. Grades 3–6.

In the late 1800s, a lot of people were dinosaur crazy. Dinosaurs had not really been discovered until the early 1800s, and just about everyone thought they were really cool—just like we do today. A lot of people wanted to find fossils.

Two of the most famous fossil finders were Othniel Charles Marsh and Edward Drinker Cope. Marsh was at Yale University, in charge of the new Peabody Museum of Natural History. Cope worked for the Academy of Natural Sciences in Philadelphia. Both men had studied paleontology, which is the science of ancient plants, animals, and rocks, and early on they became friends.

But they didn't stay friendly for very long. They had worked together in an area in New Jersey where dinosaur bones were found. They found several good fossils, and Marsh supposedly went back to Yale but really snuck back to New Jersey and offered the pit workers money to get them to send him the dinosaur bones they found.

Cope was furious. And the Fossil Feud began! Pretty soon they headed west. Not only did they each want to be the first to find a fossil, they also were even willing to destroy valuable fossils just so the other guy would not get them.

This is an amazing story—and a pretty sad one. Think of the dinosaur fossils that were destroyed. You will have fun reading about those fossil feuders.

Saber-Toothed Cats **by Susan E. Goodman.**

Goodman, Susan E. *Saber-Toothed Cats* (On My Own Science). Illustrated by Kerry Maguire. Millbrook Press, 2005. ISBN 157505759x. 48 p. Grades 1–3.

This is the true story of the *Smilodon,* a saber-toothed cat that lived in what is now California 13,000 years ago. We certainly don't know everything about them, because they all died out by 11,000 years ago, but scientists can make some guesses.

They know from examining its fossils that the smilodon had a powerful, short body, built more like a bear's than a cat's. Cheetahs have light bodies, and they can run up to seventy miles an hour. These saber-tooth cats probably could only run about 30 miles an hour, but their two saber teeth were seven inches long!

Scientists also know that saber-toothed cats could eat fifty pounds of meat at one meal. That is a lot of meat!

This book tells us what scientists think they may have been like, and some of the things they disagree about. It also shows us some of the other saber-toothed cats and some of the other animals that lived at that time. It's an interesting read.

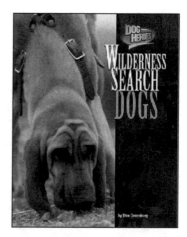

Wilderness Search Dogs by Dan Greenberg.

Greenberg, Dan. *Wilderness Search Dogs* (Dog Heroes). Bearport, 2005. ISBN 1597160199. 32 p. Grades 3–5.

When a human being disappears or a child wanders away, one thing that police often do is call in a wilderness search-and-rescue team that consists of a dog and its handler.

Dogs have found missing people for hundreds of years. They hunt down people who escape from prison. They rescue mountain climbers who are injured. They find small children.

Part of the reason that they do this so well is that dogs have an incredible sense of smell—they can smell things over a thousand times as well as we can. Some dogs are tracking dogs. Their handlers give them a piece of clothing, for instance, that was worn by the missing person, and then the dog tries to match up that smell to the smells in the air. The dogs are well trained, and this book describes exactly how it is done.

Most rescue dogs are pretty large, because they can run further and faster and do not tire out as quickly as smaller dogs do. Their handlers reward them in many ways.

You'll have a lot of fun learning about these amazing animals.

Owen & Mzee: The Language Of Friendship by Isabella Hatkoff, Craig Hatkoff, and Dr. Paula Kahumbu.

Hatkoff, Isabella, Craig Hatkoff, and Dr. Paula Kahumbu. *Owen & Mzee: The Language of Friendship*. With photographs by Peter Greste. Scholastic Press, 2007. ISBN 0439899591. Unpaged. Grades 4–6.

If you have read the book *Owen and Mzee* (see below), you probably loved learning the story of the baby hippo orphaned by the 2004 tsunami that was moved to a wildlife sanctuary and almost immediately became best friends with a 130-year-old turtle. This book tells us more.

Mzee, the turtle, did not much like other animals, and he was grumpy most of the time. When Owen first crouched down by him, Mzee crawled away. But Owen followed him, and by the next morning, they were snuggled up next to each other. Mzee surprised the people in the wildlife sanctuary, too. He started showing Owen what to do—for instance, how to find and eat grass.

Owen takes care of Mzee now, and Mzee takes care of Owen. Mzee bosses Owen around, too! Neither one of them ever hurts the other, and they have even developed their own sounds to communicate with each other.

They were separated once for two weeks when Mzee needed medical care. Owen was lonely at first, but then he made friends with a younger turtle named Toto, and now all three of them hang out together sometimes.

You will love reading about these two extraordinary animals—and you will especially love looking at all of the wonderful pictures of them.

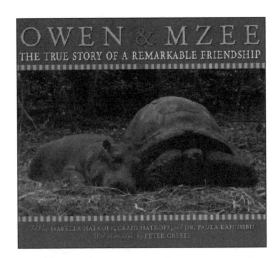

Owen & Mzee: The True Story of a Remarkable Friendship **by Isabella Hatkoff, Craig Hatkoff, and Dr. Paula Kahumbu.**

Hatkoff, Isabella, Craig Hatkoff, and Dr. Paula Kahumbu. *Owen & Mzee: The True Story of a Remarkable Friendship.* With photographs by Peter Greste. Scholastic Press, 2006. ISBN 0439829739. Unpaged. Grades 1–4.

In December 2004, there was a huge tsunami, a gigantic ocean wave that killed thousands of people. Everyone felt terrible about all of the people whose homes and lives were destroyed in the tragedy, but people were not the only ones who died.

This is the true story of Owen, a baby hippopotamus, who was about one year old and weighed about six hundred pounds when the tsunami came. He lived with his mother in a pod of hippos in Kenya, and the whole pod was caught up in the tsunami. Only one hippo survived—Owen. He could not live on his own without his mother, so the people in the village who found him tried to capture him and bring him on to dry land. It was not easy, trying to move an angry, upset six-hundred-pound animal, but they did it. They moved him by pickup truck to an animal sanctuary called Haller Park about fifty miles away.

Owen was not a happy camper. He wanted his mother.

When he got off the pickup, he saw something, something that looked sort of familiar. It was big, like his mother, and about the same color, too. It was a giant tortoise, about 130 years old, and its name was Mzee. And Owen wanted to be with Mzee.

This is the true story of the two of them and their unlikely relationship.

The last full-page photo in the book will make *anyone* want to read it.

The World's Greatest Elephant
by Ralph Helfer.

Helfer, Ralph. *The World's Greatest Elephant.* Illustrated by Ted Lewin. Philomel Books, 2006. ISBN 0399241906. Unpaged. Grades K–4.

In Germany many years ago, a baby and an elephant were born on the same day. The baby boy, Bram, was the son of the elephant trainer for a small circus. Modoc, the elephant, and Bram became best friends and learned to do wonderful tricks together. Bram vowed that they would always stay together.

But they were going to have a lot of difficulty making that happen, for the circus was sold to an American man who fired all of the circus employees and took away the elephants.

Bram refused to be separated. He stowed away on the ship and began a series of almost unbelievable adventures with the creature he loved the most in the world.

This book will make you laugh and make you cry.

Hickman, Pamela. *Animals Hibernating: How Animals Survive Extreme Conditions.* Illustrated by Pat Stephens. Kids Can Press, 2005. ISBN 1553376625. 40 p. Grades 3–5.

What do you think "hibernation" means? Do you know? A lot of people don't. This book tells the difference between true hibernator animals and deep sleepers. The main difference is that true hibernators lower their body temperature and both their breathing and heart rates. Some of their bodies even partially freeze in the cold and thaw out in the spring. "True hibernators shut down their body functions until they are barely alive. This extreme state is called torpor" (p. 6). The deep sleepers drop their breathing and heart rates, but their body temperature lowers only a little.

Hibernators must hibernate because there is not enough food for them to survive a winter. Their bodies, like ours, require a lot of food to keep up their energy level, and so their bodies shut down. Painted turtles stay partially frozen for up to five months!

You'll enjoy reading the book and looking at the illustrations. Some of them show us different animals and how they prepare for hibernation. Look at the one on pages 14–15. A woodchuck would:

- Start gaining a lot of weight late in the summer

- Dig a deep burrow and block itself in it by the end of October

- Roll itself into a ball and tuck its head between its hind legs

- Breathe as little as one breath every five minutes during hibernation

- Lose as much as one third of its body weight during the winter.

This is great information!

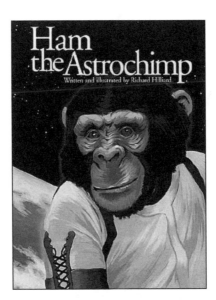

Ham the Astrochimp by **Richard Hilliard.**

Hilliard, Richard. *Ham the Astrochimp*. Boyds Mills Press, 2007. ISBN 1590784596. Unpaged. Grades 3–5.

Chang was a chimpanzee born in Africa, but he had the most extraordinary adventures of any chimpanzee in history!

When he was old enough to leave his mother, he was brought to New Mexico. He had a special job to do. There he was renamed Ham, and he was one of many chimpanzees being trained to go into space. Scientists decided he was the best and the brightest of all of the chimps, so he was chosen.

On January 13, 1961, he was fitted into a little pod, which was called a biopack, which sat in the human-sized seat in the *Mercury* capsule. His job was to follow directions, see clearly, and make decisions quickly. And he did everything exactly the way the scientists wanted it done.

Everyone was excited, because the experts were afraid that being in space might do terrible things to the human body and brain—and chimpanzees' bodies are a lot like ours. And here was Ham, whose body and brain were working just fine!

This is the story of that incredible ride into space, as well as the rest of Ham's life, illustrated with a lot of fine color pictures.

Author Profile: Steve Jenkins

Steve Jenkins, known for the collage illustrations in his innovative science books for young people, has been writing and illustrating nonfiction books since 1994. His publications include more than twenty books that he has both written and illustrated, as well as a dozen books illustrated for other authors. Five of his books are collaborations with his wife, Robin Page, and one of those, What Do You Do with a Tail Like This? *was a Caldecott Honor Book. He intended to become a scientist but went into graphic design instead.*

What was the breakthrough that took you from graphic designer to author/illustrator?

A New York publisher asked our office to design a series of children's books that required illustrations. I'd been doing illustrations for corporate clients and book jacket design, and I talked them into letting me to the illustrations. It was a series called the Photolog books, and it was collage work. After doing those, I realized that perhaps I could try an idea of my own. I did a proposal for two books. One of them sunk without a trace, but the other one is *Biggest, Strongest, Fastest,* and it's still in print. At that time Houghton Mifflin was starting a new imprint, and through a friend of a friend I heard they were looking for submissions. I put the proposals together and took them into the editor, and she liked both of them. So it was kind of a painless way to enter the field compared to what most people seem to go through. *Biggest, Strongest, Fastest* was the first book I did that tapped into the interest I had in natural science.

What drives you to write and illustrate nonfiction books for kids?

Partly it's because I don't think I could write fiction. Maybe someday. With nonfiction, I'm really writing about things I'm interested in. Some are inspired by my kids and things they were interested in, but it comes back to me having a fascination with it. I like the process.

Which comes first for you—the writing or the illustrations?

They sort of parallel in a way. The idea always comes first, so in that sense I guess the word comes first because I usually have some sense of how I'm going to talk about a topic. But then when I'm beginning illustrations, researching and doing sketches, that always changes what my original idea was. If it's a book I'm doing with Robin, a lot of times it's her idea, and she does a lot of the research and sketches. Then it's a little more dynamic because it gets kicked back and forth. So it varies a little bit, but I think it would be safe to say that both of them are being worked on at the same time.

Is one easier than the other?

Yes. Illustrating is much easier. I always know I can solve those problems one way or another. I might have to change perspective or even change subject, but the writing is much harder, I find.

How do you research the topics you write about?

I primarily use books. We have quite a large library now of natural science books. The Internet is also helpful, and to some extent natural history museums and photographs that we take.

Do you enjoy the research aspect?

I do. It's an important part of it. It always informs what ends up in the book. We always find new and unexpected stuff. We start out looking for one thing to illustrate a point and find quite often something that's actually a lot more interesting or a lot more fun or that we realize would make a better illustration. So the research is a pretty critical part of the process.

Of all the books you've written and illustrated, which are you most proud of?

Life on Earth, which is a book about evolution. I just wasn't sure I was going to be able to pull it off, to make a book for a second or third grade audience about evolution, but I feel like I did.

Do you have a nonfiction book that you dream of writing someday?

I'd love to do a young adult nonfiction book along the lines of John McPhee or Bill Bryson. That's an age where it might be kind of a challenge to interest kids. Maybe that's why it's intriguing.

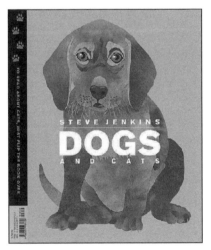

Dogs and Cats by Steve Jenkins.

Jenkins, Steve. *Dogs and Cats.* Houghton Mifflin, 2007. ISBN 0618507671. Unpaged. Grades 3–5.

Steve Jenkins knows quite a bit about dogs and cats. He has one of each in his home, and he made a beautiful book about them. If you open it front to back, the first half is about dogs. If you open it back to front (the other way up), the first half is about cats. Either way you'll find some great information here, such as:

- Today dogs are bred to look a certain way. They used to be bred to do different jobs, like herd sheep. Lots of dogs did work. Most dogs today are mixtures of breeds—mutts—and a lot of dog lovers adore them.

- If the fastest mammals on earth were to race for three miles, the saluki, one of the oldest dog breeds, would win.

- Dogs are easy to housebreak because they instinctively understand that you should not mess up your home.

- There are more than four hundred dog breeds, but only forty cat breeds, probably because most cats were never really trained to work.

- Cats are the only animals that purr. They purr for a whole bunch of reasons.

- There are charts of amazing cat and dog facts that are fun to talk about. You might be surprised what you will learn.

This is a really neat book.

Kaner, Etta. *How Animals Defend Themselves* (Kids Can Read). Illustrated by Pat Stephens. Kids Can Press, 2006. ISBN 1553379047. 32 p. Grades 1–4.

Animals defend themselves from attack in many really cool ways.

Look at the picture of the Blue-ringed octopus on page 4, and then see how it changes colors on page 5 when it senses that danger is near.

Opossums and hognose snakes pretend they are already dead. Some different animals live together because they can protect each other. Some are brightly colored to scare off a predator—would you want to attack a skunk? If it sprays you, not only will you smell disgusting, but it can even make you blind for several hours.

Some animals look like other poisonous animals. Some have amazing hiding places.

You will enjoy learning about these great ways animals defend themselves.

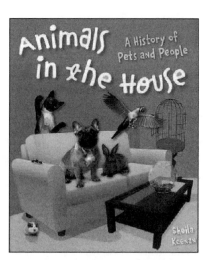

Animals in the House: A History of Pets and People **by Sheila Keenan.**

Keenan, Sheila. *Animals in the House: A History of Pets and People*. Scholastic Nonfiction, 2007. ISBN 0439692865. 112 p. Grades 4–8.

Do you have a pet in your home? The odds are pretty good that you do! There are about 290 million people in the United States and close to 378 million pets. So, if you do have a pet, what kind is it? And what do you think is the most popular kind?

If you guessed fish, you are right. Over half of the pets in the United States are fish! Cats are only half as popular—there are about 90 million of them. There are 74 million dogs, 17 million birds, 17 million small animals like rats, gerbils, hamsters, mice, and 9 million reptiles.

This book is filled with great information about pets. Here are a few facts:

- In Europe in the Middle Ages, usually only royalty had pets. In China, people had pet crickets and pet katydids.

- Two dogs arrived in America on the *Mayflower* in 1620. One was a mastiff and one was an English spaniel.

- The American Society for the Prevention of Cruelty to Animals was founded in 1866. Before that, people could do whatever they wanted to animals. No laws protected them.

- Leonardo da Vinci loved cats and painted and drew many pictures of them.

- There are more varieties of dogs than there are of cats, because dogs work for human beings and are bred to do particular kinds of work. Cats don't usually do much work for us.

- Greyhounds have been around for a long, long time. Even Egyptian royalty had them!

- There is a sign saying "Beware of the Dog" in Latin in Pompeii. That saying has been around at least 2,000 years!

- Whenever a dog is a big hit in the movies, that dog breed becomes popular with pet owners. Think of Lassie, Rin-Tin-Tin, or *101 Dalmatians.*

- Nobody kept rabbits as pets until the 1800s.

And there's a lot more fun stuff in this interesting book. See if your favorite pet is in it.

Kelly, Irene. *It's a Butterfly's Life.* Holiday House, 2007. ISBN 082341860X. Unpaged. Grades 1–3.

This is a really interesting look at one of the most beautiful creatures any-where—the butterfly. There are a lot of different kinds of butterflies, and this gives us some great information about them. Here's a sample:

- Butterflies and moths are a lot a like, but not exactly the same. There are about 17,500 types of butterflies and about 160,000 types of moths in the world.

- A butterfly's taste buds are in its feet—a butterfly can taste something by stand-ing on it!

- You should never touch a butterfly because you might accidentally damage its wings.

- Monarch butterflies migrate the farthest, but they also gain an incredible amount of weight. After Monarch caterpillars hatch, they take two weeks to be-come 2,700 times their original weight!

At the end of the book, take a look at a few of the endangered butterflies in the world. It's pretty scary.

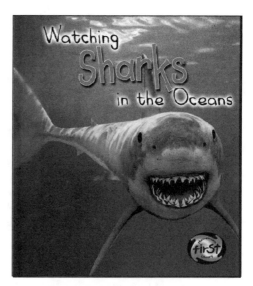

Watching Sharks in the Oceans
by L. Patricia Kite.

Kite, L. Patricia. *Watching Sharks in the Oceans* (Wild World). Heinemann Library, 2006. ISBN 1403472467. 32 p. Grades 3–5.

There are more than four hundred kinds of shark, and just about everyone thinks they are pretty cool animals. The biggest one is the great white shark—the adults may be as long as a pickup truck and weigh more than a large car. That is big! Their backs and sides are gray, and their bellies are white. That means it is hard to see them above the water, because they look like the water. And it is hard to see them from below, because they look like the sky. This makes it easier for them to catch other animals.

Here are a few interesting facts about sharks:

- Their skins are covered with tooth-like prickles. These are called skin teeth or denticles.

- They can only swim forward, never backward.

- They do not chew their food. They just swallow it!

- If their teeth break or wear out, another tooth moves in to take the place of the bad tooth.

- They can smell even one drop of blood in the water.

- Their worst enemies are us: human beings.

And that is just a bit of the interesting information you will find in this book.

First Dive to Shark Dive **by Peter Lourie.**

Lourie, Peter. *First Dive to Shark Dive.* Boyds Mills Press, 2005. ISBN 159078068X. 48 p.
Grades 3–7.

Suzanna, the author's daughter, had a wonderful twelfth birthday present. She got
to learn how to scuba dive. And she not only learned how to dive on the island of
Andros in the Bahamas, but she became a certified diver and even got to dive with
sharks!

This is the story of how it happened.

Peter Lourie, who wrote this book, loves rivers and water and having adventures.
A diver himself, he knows where to go to have a really good experience. He picked
Andros because it is the largest, most unexplored island in the Bahamas and because it
is simply a spectacular place for diving. It has the world's third largest coral reef.

Suzanna was scared—scared she might not pass the written certification test,
scared she might do something stupid underwater, and especially scared of sharks.

Fortunately, she had a great teacher, a man whose nickname is Skeebo, an extremely competent diver who has done more than five thousand dives. He taught
Suzanna what she needed to know, and she learned what kind of equipment you need
and what you have to do to dive safely and avoid injuring yourself.

She had a blast, and the best part of all was the day she swam with seven sharks!

The beautiful photos were taken by Peter Lourie.

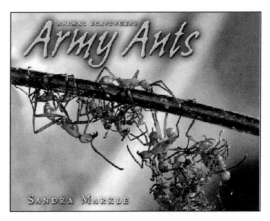

***Army Ants* by Sandra Markle.**

Markle, Sandra. *Army Ants* (Animal Scavengers). Lerner, 2005. ISBN 0822531968. 40 p. Grades 3–5.

　　Army ants are scavengers. Scavengers eat dead animals in order to live themselves. They clean up all of the dead bodies lying around.

　　Army ants live in tropical areas in Africa, South and Central America, and Asia, and they not only eat dead animals, they kill sick, weak, and old animals and eat them, too. What is unique about them is that they all work together in groups so large that they are called army ants—because they look like an army!

　　There are many excellent color photographs in this book. Take a look at the one on page 3—a whole bunch of army ants are attacking what looks like the body of a grasshopper. Or look at the photo of the army ants marching out on page 12—or the one of the army ants making a bridge with its body so that other ants can walk across it on page 15. Or maybe look at the one on page 29, of thousands of ants forming a living curtain surrounding their queen. You will learn exciting information about these unusual creatures.

***Little Lost Bat* by Sandra Markle.**

Markle, Sandra. *Little Lost Bat.* Illustrated by Alan Marks. Charlesbridge, 2006. ISBN 157091656X. Unpaged. Grades K–3.

　　In one area of Bracken Cave near Austin, Texas, mother and baby Mexican free-tailed bats cling to the ceiling. A mother gives birth to her baby, and then that mother takes excellent care of her child until it is old enough to go off and live by itself.

But every night the mother has to leave the baby to go get food. She needs to eat nearly as many insects as she weighs herself to stay alive, and it is hard work. Finding her baby when she returns is hard work, too! There are so many babies and so many mothers. How do you find the right one?

And what happens to the baby if one night its mother does not return? How will it live? Who will take care of it?

Show any of the pictures in this lovely book.

A Mother's Journey by Sandra Markle.

Markle, Sandra. *A Mother's Journey.* Illustrated by Alan Marks. Charlesbridge, 2005. ISBN 1590916217. Unpaged. Grades K–3.

Did you ever see the movie *March of the Penguins*? It shows us how penguin chicks hatch and are protected and cared for by their parents.

This book tells us about and shows us the emperor penguin mothers. After they lay their eggs, they give the egg to their mate. Then they leave.

They march about fifty miles, sometimes walking, sometimes flopping on their bellies, until they get to the open ocean. Penguins cannot move very quickly. And there, diving carefully into the ice-cold water, they can eat. At the same time they must avoid the leopard seals that like to eat them.

This book has beautiful pictures that show us this amazing animal. You'll find out what happens next when you read it.

Musk Oxen **by Sandra Markle.**

Markle, Sandra. *Musk Oxen* (Animal Prey). Lerner, 2006. ISBN 082256064X. 40 p. Grades 3–6.

Musk oxen live in the furthest northern area of the world: the Arctic.

The musk ox looks a lot like a short, shaggy buffalo, but it is not as big. It is about five feet high at the shoulder. It eats a grass-like substance called a sedge, and it must *always* watch out for other animals that want to eat it.

The animals that really eat a lot of musk oxen are arctic wolves. These white wolves attack them, especially any young musk ox that might have gotten separated from the group. If you look at the picture on page 7, you will see wolves attacking a group of musk oxen. They are not always successful. Big musk oxen can be really tough and hard to fight! But the wolves keep at it, and if you read this book, you will find out exactly how they go about catching something they like to eat.

You'll learn a lot about musk oxen in the process—and they are an extraordinarily interesting, unusual animal.

Octopuses **by Sandra Markle.**

Markle, Sandra. *Octopuses* (Animal Prey). Lerner, 2007. ISBN 0822560631. 40 p. Grades 3–5.

Octopuses are unusual creatures. Unlike most animals, they do not have a bony skeleton, and this enables them to hide and squeeze into all sorts of tight and unusual spaces. They eat other animals, so that makes them animal predators. But other animals eat *them,* too, and that makes them animal prey. And octopuses as animal prey is what this book is about.

Take a look at the incredible photographs of these amazing animals. Octopuses are often able to hide in plain sight. Take a look at the octopus on page 17. She looks like just another part of the sea floor. Or look at the giant Pacific octopus on page 19. The way she hides six tentacles down a hole and spreads out the other two makes her look like a poisonous snake. Some of them bury themselves—look at the southern keeled octopus on page 21.

Octopuses also have other ways to defend themselves. Some can change their coloring or camouflage themselves. Some squirt out ink that manages to hide them from predators. Some can even snap off their tentacles and grow new ones.

You will be amazed at the way octopuses protect their eggs!

Anyone who loves animals and surprising information will have fun reading this book.

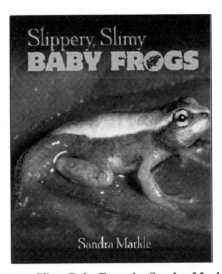

Slippery, Slimy Baby Frogs **by Sandra Markle.**

Markle, Sandra. *Slippery, Slimy Baby Frogs*. Walker & Company, 2006. ISBN 0802780628. 32 p. Grades 3–5.

If the really amazing photographs in this book don't gross you out, you will probably be absolutely fascinated by them. Sandra Markle, the author, is fascinated, and she shows us several baby frogs, including eggs, as well as how they grow up. Take a look at the frog with her babies on the title page.

Markle tells us that frogs are amphibians, and the word "amphibian" means "leading two lives" (p. 4). Baby frogs can live only in the water, but adult frogs live outside of the water much of the time. They need the oxygen they get in the air.

Baby frogs are shaped like fish because they need to be good swimmers. They all start lives as eggs, and you will be amazed at the different ways that the parents take care of their eggs. The Foam Nest Frogs create a nest that looks like stiff egg whites. They wrap their babies in this, and it becomes hard, protecting the babies but making it hard for predators to eat.

Pygmy marsupial frogs have lumps on their backs when they are carrying their eggs. The lumps on their backs *are* their eggs! Take a look at the photo on page 11.

Darwin's frogs finish growing up in their father's mouth! Look at the picture of them coming out on page 23.

You will enjoy learning a lot about many different types of frogs.

Oh Rats! The Story of Rats and People
by Albert Marrin.

Marrin, Albert. *Oh Rats! The Story of Rats and People.* Illustrated by C. B. Mordan. Dutton Children's Books, 2006. ISBN 0525477624. 48 p. Grades 4–7.

Rats give most of us the creeps. And there are good reasons for that. When you read this book, you'll learn more bad things than you ever even guessed, but you will be surprised that you will learn some really good things about them, too.

First, of all mammals in the world, rodents are the largest group. About 4,000 species of mammals (that includes us) live today, and rats make up about 1,500 of those. They have been around longer than humans—they probably began appearing around the time of the end of the age of the dinosaurs.

Marrin tells us that a rat can:

• "Squeeze through a pipe the width of a quarter

• Scale a brick wall, straight up

• Fall off a five-story building and land safely on its feet

• Rear up on its hind legs and box with its front paws

• Get flushed down a toilet and live

• Climb up a drainpipe into a toilet bowl" (page 10)

And this is just the beginning. Rats eat almost everything. They can eat one-tenth of their body weight every day. Brown rats first arrived in New York City in 1776. Before then America did not have rats. (Darn!)

They only live a few months. A rat is old at age nine months. But a rat couple can have as many as 381 babies a *year*. And the babies have babies, and those babies have babies, and—you get the picture.

This is mind boggling stuff. You'll love finding out about these unsettling creatures.

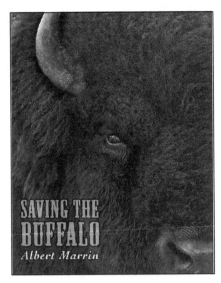

Saving The Buffalo by Albert Marrin.

Marrin, Albert. *Saving the Buffalo*. Scholastic Nonfiction, 2006. ISBN 0439718546. 128 p. Grades 5–up.

The way that the settlers dealt with the millions of buffalos in the American West is a true horror story. And this book, loaded with great illustrations and photographs, tells it unforgettably.

The homeland of the buffalo was the Great Plains, west of the Mississippi, which is bigger than all of Western Europe combined. These animals were essential to the health of the plains, for their hooves stirred up the soil, and their grazing made the grass short enough for other plains animals to live in. They fertilized the soil in many ways.

The buffalo is the largest animal on the North American continent. An adult bull is twelve feet long, stands seven feet high at the shoulder, and can weight up to 2,500 pounds. They have thick layers of both fat and hair so that they can stand cold weather very well. They can also run up to thirty-five miles an hour, for up to five miles, which is pretty amazing. And the natives of the country respected and depended on the buffalo for their food, clothing, and shelter—almost everything. After the Spanish conquerors brought the horse to North America, many natives became hunters on horses, and their skills at riding a horse and doing other things simultaneously were astounding. A talented band of hunters could easily kill up to three hundred buffalo in a buffalo running that lasted only about ten minutes.

But the natives only killed about 450,000 buffalo a year. It was when the prairies started being settled by pioneers that everything changed.

The buffalo was in the way, a pest, dangerous, and the settlers wanted no more of them. People organized trips to the West just to kill as many buffalo as possible.

And that was the beginning of the end of the buffalo.

This is a wonderful read.

Quest for the Tree Kangaroo: An Expedition to the Cloud Forest of New Guinea by Sy Montgomery.

Montgomery, Sy. *Quest for the Tree Kangaroo: An Expedition to the Cloud Forest of New Guinea* (Scientists in the Field Series). Photographs by Nic Bishop. Houghton Mifflin, 2006. ISBN 0618496416. 80 p. Grades 5–8.

Kangaroos that live in trees! Have you ever heard of such a thing?

A lot of people have not. They are very rare and extremely good at hiding, so they are hard to find.

Matschie's tree kangaroo lives in the cloud forests in Papua New Guinea. Cloud forests look like the forests that were around when the dinosaurs existed. They are beautiful, strange, wet, and often cold places, with tall trees. (Show the photograph on page 36.)

Sy Montgomery, who wrote this book, loves animals and adventures. She and the photographer, Nic Bishop, joined a scientific expedition to try to capture some of the tree kangaroos, study their bodies, attach a radio collar to them, and then release them back into the wild. They had the incredible help of local natives, who were their friends—and who used to hunt and eat the tree kangaroos themselves.

Just getting to the site where the expedition was going to camp was an adventure. It was a long hike in high altitudes where breathing is difficult. And when they arrived, living conditions were pretty primitive.

These tree kangaroos are so cute and cuddly that everyone wants to hold them and hug them and protect them. Finding them took huge amounts of patience and ingenuity.

Take a look at the photographs of the kangaroos (the frontispiece is fantastic) and you'll want to know more.

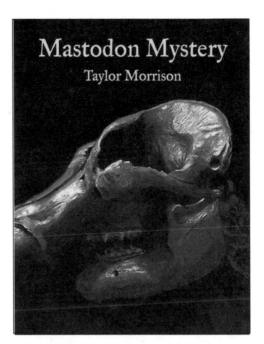

Mastodon Mystery **by Taylor Morrison.**

Morrison, Taylor. *Mastodon Mystery*. Houghton Mifflin/Walter Lorraine Books, 2001, 2006. ISBN 0618771301. 32 p. Grades 3–6.

Mastodons lived in New York State during the Ice Age, and there many of them got stuck in peat bogs and died. They were huge creatures, looking quite a bit like today's elephants, and they became extinct about 10,000 years ago.

In 1799, a group of farmers were digging out peat bogs, and they discovered a bigger bone than any of them had ever seen before. They kept on digging and found more and more bones, but the pit flooded with cold water and stopped them from finding any more.

Two years later a man who had created America's number one natural history museum in Philadelphia read about the discovery. Charles Willson Peale wanted to see those bones and, hopefully find a complete skeleton for his museum. And he was prepared to travel and pay!

He did not get exactly what he wanted, but he did eventually put a couple of skeletons together and get most of a complete one—and his customers at the museum were only too happy to pay to see this amazing discovery.

If you like prehistoric animals, this is a fine book for you.

Polar Bears in Danger **by Helen Orme.**

Orme, Helen. *Polar Bears in Danger* (Wildlife Survival). Bearport, 2007. ISBN 1597162647. 32 p. Grades 3–6.

Polar bears live in the Arctic. In the Arctic Circle, a large part of the sea is frozen all year long. It is called the ice cap. And the fact that the ice cap is melting, which many people believe is due to global warming, is causing a big problem for the polar bears.

Polar bears eat seals. And the way they catch those seals means that they need the sea to be frozen.

They look for holes in the ice and wait until a seal comes up from underwater to breathe. Then they grab the seal and eat it.

If there is no frozen water, there are no holes in it, and polar bears starve.

This interesting book has beautiful, informative pictures of the polar bear and its cubs and tells us what scientists are trying to do to help the polar bear, which is perfectly adapted to live in cold areas. You'll enjoy finding out about these animals.

Ryder, Joanne. *A Pair of Polar Cubs: Twin Cubs Find a Home at the San Diego Zoo*. Photos by the World-Famous San Diego Zoo. Simon and Schuster Books for Young Readers, 2006. ISBN 068985871X. Unpaged. Grades K–3.

Two little orphaned polar bears were found in northern Alaska. Unless someone helped right away, there was not much hope for them to live. Polar babies need their mothers!

Fortunately, the San Diego Zoo agreed to take them for its polar bear exhibit.

But first they had to stay in the zoo hospital and eat and grow. One weighed twelve pounds and one weighed seventeen pounds when they arrived, but pretty soon they were gaining fourteen pounds every week. They got big fast.

There are great photographs here of the two bears growing and changing and finally, curiously, learning to live in the Polar Bear Plunge exhibit. If you like animals, you will love this book.

Face to Face with Grizzlies **by Joel Sartore.**

Sartore, Joel. *Face to Face with Grizzlies* (Face to Face). National Geographic, 2007. ISBN 1426300506. 32 p. Grades 2–5.

If you like bears and beautiful photographs, you'll love this book.

Joel Sartore is a wildlife photographer, and he has spent two years studying and photographing grizzly bears in the wild. A lot of his time was spent in Alaska.

The first thing we need to know is that brown bears and grizzly bears are really the same. Brown bears tend to be a little bigger because they live near the coast and have better eating. Inland the bears are generally smaller and have light-tipped fur, which people call grizzly. But the bears here are all North American brown bears that eat almost anything, although they do not like to eat human beings.

They hibernate, which means that they have to eat a lot to prepare for winter. In fact, when they are not hibernating, they are almost constantly trying to find food. Finding food gets harder all of the time, for human beings are building homes and living in areas that used to be great hunting grounds. And that has become a real problem.

Scientists are catching bears and tagging their ears or collaring them so that they can learn where they go, and they are finding out a great deal.

This book has great photographs and wonderful information. Give it a try.

Ballet of the Elephants by Leda Schubert.

Schubert, Leda. *Ballet of the Elephants*. Illustrated by Robert Andrew Parker. Roaring Brook Press, 2006. ISBN 1596430753. Unpaged. Grades 1–3.

Probably one of the most astounding dances of all time took place in 1942 in New York City.

John Ringling North, who managed a very famous circus, had an idea. He thought audiences would love to see elephants dancing a ballet. With ballerinas! He called the best choreographer in the world, George Balanchine. George Balanchine called a good friend of his—one of the most famous composers in the world, a man named Igor Stravinsky. They decided they were *in*.

And they did it!

What, we all wonder today, would it be like to see fifty elephants dancing in tutus?

This is a true story. You will enjoy the illustrations and love seeing the actual photographs of the elephants dancing at the end of the book.

Singer, Marilyn. *Cats to the Rescue: True Tales of Heroic Felines*. With illustrations by Jean Cassels. Henry Holt, 2006. ISBN 0805074333. 154 p. Grades 4–8.

You always are hearing about heroic dogs that save people's lives and do all sorts of noble things, but do you know that there are heroic cats, too? This tells the story of some of them. You'll love reading about:

- The 14,000 cats that were dropped by parachute into Borneo on a rescue mission. Their job was to kill the rats that were causing diseases and eating the people's rice crops.

- Towser, who lived in Scotland and worked at a distillery that made whiskey from barley. Towser's job was to keep mice away from the grain, and boy was she good at it. She caught 28,899 mice in her lifetime and left them for people to find. When she died, they put up a statue of her.

- Taco was an old, blind dog that wandered away from his backyard. The family cat, Big Boy, saw him heading toward a cliff. Big Boy got very excited and blocked his path to the cliff, gently turning him around and leading him back to safety.

• Sugar, an Oklahoma cat that traveled with her owners to California. She hated the trip so much that they decided to leave her there with some neighbors in a new home. She stayed there for fifteen days—and then she left. Fourteen months later she walked into the home of her original owners. And no one knows how she did it!

You'll love reading about these amazing cats.

Sklansky, Amy E. *Where Do Chicks Come From?* (Let's-Read-and-Find-Out Science 1). Illustrated by Pam Paparone. HarperCollins, 2005. ISBN 0060288930. 33 p. Grades K–2.

Have you ever looked at the inside of an egg? Have you ever wondered what the parts of an egg are *for?* Why is there a yellow egg yolk? Why is there egg white? What are those stringy things in the egg white? Why are they all there?

Well, this book tells you those answers.

Chickens have many tiny eggs inside them. For one to become a chick, a rooster must mate with the hen. Then the egg changes and grows and the hen lays the egg. This not only shows what happens outside that freshly laid egg, which the hen is usually sitting on, but also what is happening inside that egg shell—and how the chick gets out.

You'll enjoy looking at the neat pictures.

Look What Mouths Can Do by D. M. Souza.

Souza, D. M. *Look What Mouths Can Do* (Look What Animals Can Do). Lerner, 2006. ISBN 0761394621. 48 p. Grades 2–5.

Look at the frontispiece photo of an anteater eating away. He can eat far away, for his tongue can reach about two feet! He wins the prize for the longest tongue in the animal kingdom.

You will not believe the things animals can do with their mouths. Look at the picture of the archerfish on page 12. It sees an insect to eat on a branch above it. It spits at the insect, hits it, and the insect falls into the water—where the archerfish eats it!

Learn about how hippopotamuses fight (look at the picture on page 14—that guy's two big teeth are as long as your arm!), how paper wasps make their papery nests, and how leeches suck blood. If you thought that doctors using leeches were a thing of the past, you will be surprised to find out that they are still doing that today. Look at the picture of a leech sucking on a human being on page 28. There is a great photo of rattlesnake fangs on page 36, and you will love the color photo of a mother alligator carrying her baby.

The pictures make you want to know more—and the text tells you what it is you were wanting to know.

Look What Whiskers Can Do **by D. M. Souza.**

Souza, D. M. *Look What Whiskers Can Do* (Look What Animals Can Do). Lerner, 2007. ISBN 0761394591. 48 p. Grades 3–5.

A lot of animals have whiskers. "Scientists call whiskers *vibrissae*. The word once meant to shake or vibrate. Whiskers let many animals called mammals feel movements or vibrations in both air and water" (p. 8).

Here are a few of the interesting things whiskers can do:

- In the dark, rats cannot see well, so they use their whiskers like we use our hands—to feel their way around and to try to collect information about objects they find—such as food.

- Blind cats can catch prey—such as mice—by using their whiskers to sense vibrations in the air. (Show the picture of a cat that just caught a mouse on page 16.)

- Manatees have about six hundred short whiskers that act like fingers.

- The walrus uses its hairs, which look something like a mustache, to find food on the sea floor. (Show the picture on page 27.)

There are lots of color photographs. You will be amazed at what whiskers can do.

Packed with Poison! Deadly Animal Defenses
by D. M. Souza.

Souza, D. M. *Packed with Poison! Deadly Animal Defenses* (On My Own Science). Illustrated by Jack Harris. Millbrook Press, 2006. ISBN 1575058774. 48 p. Grades 1–3.

What would happen if you were bitten by a rattlesnake? What about a black widow spider? Or an Australian funnel-web spider? What happens if you get stung by a stingray? Or a bee? Or a scorpion?

What kind of poison do these animals have, and what does it do to you?

This isn't a hard book to read, and it is fun to look through. It has some great information you will enjoy sharing with your friends. For instance, do you know about a food called fugu? It is prepared in Japan, and it is cooked puffer fish. Puffer fish have poison in many parts of their bodies. Fugu is a very special food. It costs as much as four hundred dollars a serving.

But here is the problem: if the puffer fish is not cleaned and cleaned and cleaned, there may be specks of poison left. If there is any poison left, it can kill the person eating it. About one hundred to two hundred people die from eating cooked puffer fish every year. Would you want to try some?

You'll enjoy learning about poisonous animals.

Bengal Tiger by Louise Spilsbury and
Richard Spilsbury.

Spilsbury, Louise, and Richard Spilsbury. *Bengal Tiger* (Save Our Animals!). Heinemann
Library, 2006. ISBN 1403478031. 32 p. Grades 2–5.

Where do tigers live? Do you even know which continent they live on?

Most people would probably say tigers live in Africa, but Bengal tigers live in
Asia. They are beautiful animals. Each one has a different pattern of stripes, so no two
look exactly alike.

Sadly, they are in big trouble. Unless serious efforts are made to try and save
them, they are in danger of becoming extinct in the wild. About 300 are in zoos around
the world, but that is not the same as living in the places where they have always lived.

Like all tigers, Bengal tigers eat meat—usually antelopes, buffalo, pigs, and deer.
They need quite a bit of that meat, and it is getting harder and harder to find. People are
moving into areas where the tigers used to roam, and there is less space and less food
for them.

This book is full of good information about what these beautiful animals are like.
They have three or four cubs at a time—look at the picture on page 12. Cubs face a lot
of danger. They are small, and other animals can kill them. If a tiger does grow up, it is
safe from other animals—none that live near them would dare attack a healthy tiger.
But it could starve to death.

It is against the law to kill the tigers, but people called poachers do it because they
can make a lot of money selling the skins.

You'll enjoy learning about these tigers. What could you do to help save them?

Starosta, Paul. *The Bee: Friend of the Flowers*. Text and photos by Paul Starosta. French
series editor, Valerie Tracqui. Charlesbridge, 2005. ISBN 1570916292. 28 p. Grades
3–6.

The photographs in this book are great. Take a look at the beautiful pictures of the
bees at work. On page 4, you can see what a field of flowers looks like to a bee, whose
vision is completely different from ours, and then there is a picture of the way it looks
to us.

All of the worker bees are female. They have a sac called a honey stomach, and they need to fill it up with nectar. They have to get nectar from about one hundred flowers to fill it up. They also gather pollen, which they store in pollen baskets—these are hollows on their rear legs (see the photo on page 7).

You'll learn about the bee's dance, why honey comes in different colors, how bees build nests, and what happens to male bees, called drones, which have no other job except to mate with the queen bee. You won't believe all the interesting things you'll learn!

Saving Manatees **by Stephen R. Swinburne.**

Swinburne, Stephen R. *Saving Manatees*. Boyds Mills Press, 2006. ISBN 1590783190. 40 p. Grades 4–6.

They are mammals. They are really big. They live in the waters off of Florida, and there are only about 3,000 of them. They are an endangered species. In 2005, 396 of them died. Eighty of those died because a boat ran into them. Boat collisions happen a lot. Motorboats tend to go fast, and manatees move slowly. When they come out of the water, it happens too often. A boat collides, and even if the manatee survives, it may be horribly wounded.

Stephen Swinburne loves manatees and believes that people should respect them and watch for them.

One species of manatee is already extinct: Stellar's sea cow became extinct in 1768. Shipwrecked Russian explorers saw that they were slow and easy to kill. They first saw them in 1741, and it only took twenty-seven years to destroy them forever. Now there are four species of manatees left. The ones off the Florida coast are the West Indian manatee.

This has great information about manatees:

• The closest land animal that manatees resemble is the elephant.

• An adult manatee eats about two hundred pounds of greens a day—it weighs more than a ton.

• Manatees need to surface to breathe every three to five minutes, on the average.

• Manatees need lots of warm water just to survive.

• Manatees' whiskers can work almost like fingers.

Show the picture of the different kinds of manatees on page 15.

Tatham, Betty. *Baby Sea Otter.* Illustrated by Joan Paley. Henry Holt, 2005. ISBN 0805075046. Unpaged. Grades K–3.

Doesn't just about everybody think that sea otters are really neat animals? Isn't it cool the way they lay in the water, belly up, happily eating their food? And if the adults are really fun to look at, imagine how cute the babies must be!

This book is loaded with great illustrations that show us how a baby sea otter grows up and some of the scary things that can happen to it.

• Sea otter mothers bring up food and a stone from the water. They use the stone to crack open their food—often things like crabs.

• Sea otter pups can be attacked by eagles and carried away, eaten by sharks, or even kidnapped by a male sea otter—who sets a ransom. He wants the food the mother has before he lets the pup go.

• Sea otters have the thickest fur of any animal on earth.

You'll enjoy learning about these adorable animals.

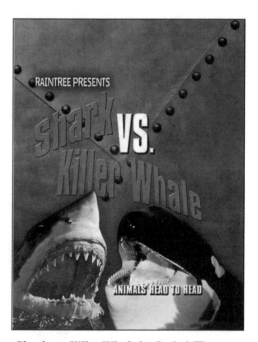

Shark vs. Killer Whale **by Isabel Thomas.**

Thomas, Isabel. *Shark vs. Killer Whale* (Animals Head to Head). Raintree, 2006. ISBN 1410923924. 32 p. Grades 3–6.

Let's have a contest. Which is the fiercest, strongest, top-dog animal in the ocean? The author compares two really scary ones: the orca, also known as the killer whale, and the great white shark. She scores them on a bunch of points, including speed, size, deadly weapons, hunting skills, and stamina. She includes a bunch of awesome information, such as that once a shark was caught that had two entire sea lions in its stomach. Yikes!

Here are a few cool facts:

- Sharks have to swim all the time. Their gills work only if water is flowing over them.

- Killer whales usually stay near the surface of the ocean because they need to breathe air. They are also good at holding their breath—for up to fifteen minutes. This lets them dive way down.

- Humans do not taste good to great white sharks—but if they accidentally bite one, the bite can kill.

- "Shark skin would feel smooth if you stroked it from head to tail. But stroking it back to front would make you bleed" (p. 21).

Who do you think will win the fight?

Thomson, Sarah L. *Amazing Dolphins!* (I Can Read Book 2). Photographs provided by the Wildlife Conservation Society. HarperCollins, 2006. ISBN 0060544538. 32 p. Grades 1–3.

Almost everybody loves dolphins, and scientists are learning a lot more about them all of the time. One thing they know is that dolphins are always making noises that sound like clicks or claps. What they are doing is telling other dolphins that they are around: "I'm here!"

Dolphins are really a kind of whale, which means they are mammals, and mammals must have air to breathe. They breathe through the blowholes on top of their head—the same part of their body that makes sounds.

This is full of really interesting information and excellent photographs. You'll enjoy finding out about these amazing animals.

Tokuda, Yukihisa. *I'm a Pill Bug.* Illustrated by Kiyoshi Takahashi. Kane/Miller, 2006. ISBN 1929132956. Unpaged. Grades 1–3.

A pill bug can look like a ball with an eye, but not all the time: only when it is frightened or disturbed. It has a hard shell, which combined with the ball position can protect it.

Pill bugs live near people, because they like things that people have around—dead plants and bugs, leftover food, pet food, newspapers, cardboard, and concrete.

They are interesting animals. When they shed their old shells, they shed half one day and half the next, and they eat them because they are delicious!

They really are not insects. They are related to crabs and shrimp—and they hibernate in the winter.

This neat book has a lot of interesting pictures. Have you ever seen a pill bug? You'll enjoy finding out about them.

Author Profile: Sally Walker

Sally Walker has written children's nonfiction for seventeen years and has published more than fifteen nonfiction titles. In 2006 she received the Robert F. Sibert Medal for Secrets of a Civil War Submarine: Solving the Mysteries of the H.L. Hunley. *Her passion for research, archaeology, and history has since led her to write* Written in Bone, *about excavations at Jamestown, and* The Search for Antarctic Dinosaurs.

What drives you to write nonfiction for kids?

I love doing research. I really enjoy digging up facts and looking for snippets of information. It's like going on an adventure, and when I was a kid I loved to do adventuresome sorts of things. I did anything that let me poke into places that people don't ordinarily go. Nonfiction is a way that you can explore, and you have this valid reason for doing it so people are always willing to let you explore more.

What is the most exciting research moment that you've had when researching a book?

It was definitely with *Written in Bone*. I was able to go on an archeological dig with the archeologists and anthropologists from the Smithsonian. While I was on that dig, we excavated the remains of twelve colonial settlers, and I personally excavated the remains of a six-month-old baby. As a mother, it was a very moving moment.

How do you feel about series nonfiction?

I think it serves an important function for kids. When a series has a certain look to it, kids feel comfortable with it. It's kind of like going out with a friend. They expect it to work for them or help them through the project. Series nonfiction today is so different than it was thirty years ago. It's bright, it's colorful, and most of the series I have seen are written by reputable authors who know what they're talking about.

With all your success, are you continuing to do series books or focusing on your own projects?

If the series topic is something that interests me, I still do it. That said, there is something more satisfying for an author, especially when you've been doing it as long as I have, to have the flexibility to do stand-alone projects.

Of all the books that you've written, which are you most proud of?

Secrets of a Civil War Submarine, but *Written in Bone* may replace it as the one I'm most proud of because it was so hard to write.

How has winning the Sibert changed your life or your writing?

I think it has made me a little more confident in myself. It's really satisfying to receive that kind of recognition for your work. On a day-to-day basis, I don't know that it does change your life, but many people all of the sudden know your name. That's kind of a cool thing.

Other than being a writer, what jobs have you done?

I have been a chemical lab technician, a booktalker, a children's book buyer for an independent bookstore, and a stay-at-home mom for many years. In high school, my guidance counselor told me I shouldn't become a writer. I told her specifically that I wanted to write children's books, and she told me no, it wasn't something people could do for a living. That's when I went into science and I stopped writing for many years.

What would you be doing if you were not writing for young people?

My dream profession would probably be to be an archaeologist. My college degree was in archaeology and geology. I like to play in the dirt.

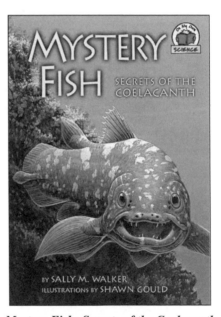

Mystery Fish: Secrets of the Coelacanth
by Sally M. Walker.

Walker, Sally M. *Mystery Fish: Secrets of the Coelacanth* (On My Own Science). Illustrated by Shawn Gould. Millbrook Press, 2006. ISBN 1575056380. 48 p. Grades 1–3.

A lot of the animals that once lived on Earth became extinct thousands of years ago, maybe even millions of years ago. They were like dinosaurs. We have fossils of them, but no more exist.

Except once in a while we get a surprise! In 1938 a scientist in South Africa saw a strange-looking fish. She had never seen anything like it. No one had room in their refrigerator for this big dead body, so she had it stuffed. Then she drew a picture of it and sent it to a fish expert.

He was completely surprised. It looked like a coelacanth, which scientists believed was an extinct fish. How could this be? There were fossils of coelacanth, but could they still be alive?

It took fourteen years before someone found another one. Scientists were astounded. And that was just the beginning.

This is an almost unbelievable true story.

Winter, Jeanette. *The Tale of Pale Male: A True Story*. Harcourt, 2007. ISBN 9780152059729. Unpaged. Grades K–3.

Redtail hawks like to put their nests way up high where they can see everything. And they like to stay in that nest, period. It is their nest.

This is the true story of a redtail hawk and his mate who happened to build their nest near the top of a fancy apartment building in New York City. People really liked to watch them and were excited when their baby chicks started peeking out of the nest.

But some people did not like it at all. They hated the mess that the hawks made that fell down on their balconies and around their building. They wanted those hawks out.

And this is the story of what happened.

Chapter 5

Science

What do junk food, Typhoid Mary, and the atomic bomb have in common? They're all high-interest topics that happen to have a lot to do with science. From seemingly mundane topics such as salt and glass to the more ostensibly exciting topic of the first moon landing, these books prove that science can be fun. In the hands of talented authors, these and many other surprising science topics come to life and make for engrossing reading for kids.

Bradley, Kimberly Brubaker. *Forces Make Things Move* (Let's-Read-and-Find-Out Science 2). Illustrated by Paul Meisel. HarperCollins, 2005. ISBN 0060289074. 33 p. Grades 2–4.

Have you ever thought about what happens when you move? Or when you make something else move? Or stop? "Forces get things moving. Forces also make things stop" (p. 5).

Anything that moves at all is started by a force. A car starts when someone turns a key and presses a foot on a gas pedal, causing all sorts of other things to happen. Big people need to use more force than smaller people because they weigh more. If you are running, for instance, only force can stop you. Your feet will push on the ground to make you stop. And it takes more force to stop in a hurry than it does to stop slowly.

You will think about force in a completely new way after you read this book.

Author Profile: Loree Griffin Burns

Loree Griffin Burns, author of Tracking Trash: Flotsam, Jetsam, and the Science of Ocean Motion *came across the idea for the book in 2003. With her science background (she has a Ph.D. in biochemistry), she saw the exciting story behind thousands of floating ducks and tennis shoes and wrote her first nonfiction book for children.*

What made you start to write nonfiction for kids?

I worked as a research scientist until I had my children and decided to stay home with them. I've spent a lot of time in the lab doing science. It's what I'm passionate about. It just made sense for me to write about other scientists and their work. It excites me. It thrills me. In the spring of 2003 I read an article in the local paper about some rubber ducks that had fallen into the Pacific Ocean twelve years ago and were now supposed to wash ashore on the Atlantic Coast near where I live and I was really intrigued.

How did you sell the book?

My first instinct was to try and write a picture book, but I was discouraged to discover that Eve Bunting had already written a book called Ducky. She published it right around the time of the spill. Although it's a fabulous picture book and it's great for young kids, I began to realize that the part that most interested me was the science. So I started to envision a book for older readers who could really sink their teeth into the science behind these rubber ducks traveling around the ocean. I was already a fan of Scientists in the Field books. I modeled my proposal after those books and I pitched the book to Houghton Mifflin as a new title in that series. My editor pulled it out of the slush pile and bought the book. It was all very surprising to me.

What was the most exciting part of researching Tracking Trash?

For me, hands down, the most fun was meeting with the scientists. I was able to go to Seattle and meet with Curt Ebbesmeyer and spend a day with him looking through his collection of beachcombed debris. I also spent a day with him at a beachcomber fair, with hundreds of beachcombers coming up and sharing their stories and dragging in boxes of things they found on the beach for him to analyze. That was really fun for me.

You've been getting great reviews and feedback. How has the success of Tracking Trash changed what you're writing now?

It took me awhile to figure out that nonfiction was where I should be focusing my writing. It took the writing of *Tracking Trash* for me to realize that. It opened the floodgates for me. There are so many scientists and areas of science I want to explore in books. I have more projects than I have time to actually carry out. It brought together two parts of my life that used to be very separate—my writing and my passion for science. It seems so obvious to me now that that's what I should be writing about but I didn't realize it for a long time.

What are your favorite nonfiction books/authors for children or teens?

I have lots of them. Jim Murphy is amazing. He does such a good job of attending to story at the same time he's delving into whatever his subject happens to be. I love Peter Sis's books also, especially his nonfiction biographies. Don Brown is another author of picture book biographies that I really enjoy. As far as science goes, I have learned a lot by reading Sy Montgomery who also writes Scientists in the Field books.

What would you be doing if you were not writing for young people?

I'd be back in the lab doing science. The thing about science that was always hard for me is how scientists become very focused on one topic. I knew a lot about the small world that I studied, but there was no time for me to explore the really neat science everyone else was doing. What appeals to me as a writer is that I get to go out and learn a little bit about everyone else's science and everyone else's projects.

Tracking Trash: Flotsam, Jetsam, and the Science of Ocean Motion **by Loree Griffin Burns.**

Burns, Loree Griffin. *Tracking Trash: Flotsam, Jetsam, and the Science of Ocean Motion* (Scientists in the Field). Houghton Mifflin, 2007. ISBN 0618581316. 58 p. Grades 5–up.

This is a scary book.

It starts by telling us about currents in the ocean. Sailors have known about them for centuries. They seem like rivers in the middle of the ocean. If a ship got on the current, it could get to its destination more quickly. Fighting the current could slow it down. Ben Franklin, of all people, studied one of those currents called the Gulf Stream and made the first map of it.

Scientists have identified many of these currents and know where they are. They also know that weather patterns can alter currents somewhat. And one man, Curt Ebbesmeyer, has become a leader in the field of studying currents and how they carry things in the ocean. Scientists have learned a great deal from his studies.

How do you think he studies currents? He uses trash! Curt's mother got him interested in tracking trash in the ocean. Hundreds of Nike shoes were washing up on beaches near Seattle. She thought he should find out where they came from. Curt listened to his mom and found out. Five cargo containers full of Nikes had been tossed into the Pacific Ocean during a storm. Thousands of Nikes went floating. And where and when they landed told Curt and other scientists a great deal about ocean currents—and where ocean trash was going.

You might think that most of the plastic and trash in the ocean comes from ships or from people who live nearby. This is not true. Most of it comes from storm sewers and rivers that flow into the ocean. This means that all of us need to be careful what we use and how we dispose of it. And the number one thing we need to be careful about is plastic.

You will be horrified when you find out what happens to plastic when it gets in the ocean and how it hurts animals and birds.

If you care about the environment, read this book and tell your friends all about it.

Junk Food **by Vicki Cobb.**

Cobb, Vicki. *Junk Food* (Where's the Science Here?). Photographs by Michael Gold. Millbrook Press, 2005. ISBN 0761327738. 48 p. Grades 4–6.

There's a reason that almost everyone loves to eat junk food. It tastes really good. Absolutely delicious. And there is a scientific reason for that.

This book is full of fascinating facts like these.

- An explosion makes popcorn what it is. The water inside the kernel turns to steam when it is heated and eventually bursts out of the hull. And there are two shapes of popcorn—butterfly and mushroom. Find out the difference on page 11.

- Chocolate came from Mexico, but the first chocolate was pretty bitter for European tastes. Somebody came up with the idea of mixing it with sugar and, wow, it has been a hit ever since!

- You can make your own rock candy, and on pages 29–30 you'll find out how.

And much, much more.

The Quest to Digest by Mary K. Corcoran.

Corcoran, Mary K. *The Quest to Digest.* Illustrated by Jef Czekaj. Charlesbridge, 2006. ISBN 1570916640. 32 p. Grades 2–5.

So, are you hungry? Feel like eating something? What would you like to eat? This book is not about food before you eat it. It's about what happens *after* you eat it.

It all starts, of course, in the mouth. If you eat an apple, your canines rip up the food, and your molars grind it up. You better chew it a lot. Always chew it a lot before you swallow.

Then your food gets mixed with your saliva, and that slimy, slippery stuff helps it go right down the throat. Think of saliva. Think of your favorite food right now. What does your favorite food look like? How does it taste? How does it smell? Is that saliva really flowing in your mouth right now, getting you ready to eat?

This tells what happens to any food as it makes its journey into your body. But remember that some of it comes out, too! It's a fun way of beginning to learn about what happens inside the body when food comes in.

David, Laurie, and Cambria Gordon. *The Down-to-Earth Guide to Global Warming.* Orchard Books, 2007. ISBN 0439024943. 112 p. Grades 4–8.

It is a fact. Our beautiful planet is heating up. It has gotten hotter before, but never before has it gotten this much warmer this quickly. This book tells us exactly what is going on and what we can do about it.

The number one problem can be stated very simply. We are producing way too much carbon dioxide. What can we do to absorb all the carbon dioxide? For starters, we can plant a lot more trees because trees absorb huge amounts of that deadly gas. We have been cutting them down and using them up like crazy.

"If the Earth's average temperature increases even a few degrees, gigantic changes can happen:

• Glaciers will melt.

• Oceans will get too warm, causing fiercer hurricanes.

- Animals and plants might die because they can't adapt to the change in temperature.

- And humans can suffer too" (p. 5).

What are some of the bad things that are going on?

Well, the Arctic permafrost is melting. Permafrost means we thought it would be frozen forever. We were wrong.

Some of the coral reefs are turning white. They become weaker and break apart more easily.

There are a lot more floods. And the oceans are getting more water in them because the icebergs are melting. When that happens, beaches flood. Take a look at the abandoned beach house on page 44. It is in Cape Hatteras in North Carolina, which has been losing about twelve *feet* of beach every year.

And that is just the beginning. Read what you can do to help. Kids have done a lot already!

DiSpezio, Michael A. *How Bright Is Your Brain? Amazing Games to Play with Your Mind.* Illustrations by Catherine Leary. Sterling, 2004. ISBN 14027065160. 80 p. Grades 4–8.

Your brain is probably the most interesting thing about you, and you are going to learn a great deal about it—and have a lot of fun at the same time—if you start taking a look at this book. It is loaded with information and activities you can do to test some of the information you will discover.

Do you know how to make a quick model of your brain? Make your hands into fists and put them together, with the heels of your palms facing and touching each other. It looks like the brain in both shape and size! The brain has two halves, or hemispheres, and so does another thing it represents: a walnut!

There are tests to show whether you are more left brained than right brained, a test to show why your hair helps protect your brain, and all sorts of games and activities to play. You will have a blast!

Editors of YES Magazine. *Science Detectives: How Scientists Solved Six Real-Life Mysteries.* Illustrated by Rose Cowles. Kids Can Press, 2006. ISBN 1553379942. 48 p. Grades 4–7.

Scientists, this book tells us, are like detectives. When they don't understand why something is happening or why it is the way it is, they start looking for clues. And the answers to their clues can be amazing!

The first case involves a mystery in New York City early in the twentieth century. People started getting sick. Lots of people. In one beautiful home owned by a wealthy man, two of his daughters, his wife, the gardener, and two maids got very sick indeed. They had, it was determined, a disease called typhoid fever. It was usually caused by contaminated food or water. Experts called in said the water wasn't contaminated. It turned out the food *was,* and the reason for this was that the family cook was a typhoid fever carrier. She never got it herself, but seven of the eight families she had cooked for had gotten it. Her name was Mary Mallon, and she did not believe she ever made anyone sick. Hey, she herself was very healthy! She ran away from the doctors and the detectives, but they eventually caught up with her, tested her and found she was a typhoid breeding place. Then the trouble really started! You may have even heard of her: they called her Typhoid Mary.

Other mysteries in this book concern the huge numbers of vultures that died in India in the 1990s; the mysterious corpse of a 5,300-year-old man found in the Alps in 1991; the Diamond detective, a man who knows exactly what to look for if you are trying to find diamonds (and he found a lot of them in British Columbia!); the deciphering of the DNA code that allowed us to learn all sorts of things about ourselves; and the case of Swissair Flight 101, which crashed into the water near Peggy's Cove, Nova Scotia, killing everybody on board. What happened?

This is an excellent read with a lot of other interesting information in it as well.

Forsyth, Adrian. *How Monkeys Make Chocolate: Unlocking the Mysteries of the Rain Forest.* Maple Tree Press, 2006. ISBN 1897066783. 48 p. Grades 4–6.

I bet it never even occurred to you that monkeys help us get chocolate. It does seem like a wild idea, but it is true.

Adrian Forsyth, who wrote this book, has spent most of his life working in rain forests around the world. A lot of people know that rain forests are being cut down, causing a problem for our air. What he tells us is that the disappearing rain forests can affect our food and our medicine as well—and he shows us how this happens.

In the rain forests, the people who have lived there for generations know exactly what plants and

Kathy's Top Ten Science Booktalking Favorites

- DiSpezio, Michael A. *How Bright Is Your Brain? Amazing Games to Play with Your Mind.* Sterling, 2004.

- Burns, Loree Griffin. *Tracking Trash: Flotsam, Jetsam, and the Science of Ocean Motion* (Scientists in the Field). Houghton Mifflin, 2007.

- David, Laurie, and Cambria Gordon. *The Down-to-Earth Guide to Global Warming.* Orchard Books, 2007.

- Gore, Al. *An Inconvenient Truth: The Crisis of Global Warming.* Viking, 2007.

- Editors of YES Magazine. *Science Detectives: How Scientists Solved Six Real-Life Mysteries.* Illustrated by Rose Cowles. Kids Can Press, 2006.

- Romanek, Trudee. *Squirt!: The Most Interesting Book You'll Ever Read About Blood* (Mysterious You). Illustrated by Rose Cowles. Kids Can Press, 2006.

- Slavin, Bill, with Jim Slavin. *Transformed: How Everyday Things Are Made.* Kids Can Press, 2005.

- Morrison, Taylor. *Tsunami Warning.* Houghton Mifflin, 2007.

- Mallory, Kenneth. *Diving to a Deep-Sea Volcano.* Houghton Mifflin, 2006.

- Thimmesh, Catherine. *Team Moon: How 400,000 People Landed Apollo 11 on the Moon.* Houghton Mifflin Company, 2006.

From *Gotcha Good! Nonfiction Books to Get Kids Excited About Reading* by Kathleen A. Baxter and Marcia Agness Kochel. Westport, CT: Libraries Unlimited. Copyright © 2008.

animals do—which ones are good to eat, which are not, and how they work with each other. Mr. Forsyth is afraid that as the people are driven out of the forests, all of us will lose the incredible knowledge that they have. Many plants are used for medicine, and even in modern countries, many plants discovered by natives of the rain forests are used for medicine. One very famous one is aspirin!

The way monkeys make chocolate is just one of the many amazing stories that he tells. In the rain forests in Peru, on the Mau River, Capuchin monkeys and spider monkeys travel in large troops. That way, more of them will be aware if a predator that wants to eat them is nearby.

The monkeys that look for fruit are really looking hard for one particular tree, and when they find it they get it all excited. They pull the pods off that tree and smash them open in a two-handed smash. Inside the broken pods are rows of seeds covered with a white coating. The coating tastes wonderful, even to humans. But the seeds are bitter. The monkeys eat the coating and spit out the seeds—and the seeds grow into more cacao trees. And we make chocolate from those pods.

This is great to read, and has lots of excellent color photographs. Take a good look!

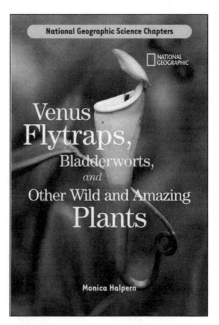

Venus Flytraps, Bladderworts, and Other Wild and Amazing Plants by **Monica Halpern.**

Halpern, Monica. *Venus Flytraps, Bladderworts, and Other Wild and Amazing Plants* (National Geographic Science Chapters). National Geographic, 2006. ISBN 0792259572. 48 p. Grades 3–6.

Plants can be killers—in different ways. "Many plants have developed interesting ways to find food and to protect themselves. Some produce poisons to keep animals from eating them. Others have sharp thorns that scratch animals that get too close. Still others catch and eat animals!" (page 9).

Only about four hundred plants eat meat, and most of those eat insects. A few are big enough to eat frogs, mice, and small birds. All of them offer a small treat (like a sugary substance) to attract the animals, catch them in the trap, and then dissolve them into a kind of soup, which they then digest. The most famous of these is the Venus flytrap. You'll enjoy looking at the pictures of it catching a fly.

Bladderworts suck tiny insects up. Pitcher plants drown their victims. Sundew plants trap insects in their sticky leaves. Poisonous plants taste bitter, so most things will not eat them—but some of them can even kill human beings.

This is full of fascinating information and great photos.

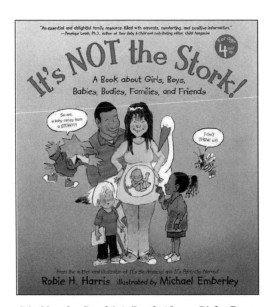

It's Not the Stork! A Book About Girls, Boys,
Babies, Bodies, Families, and Friends
by Robie H. Harris.

Harris, Robie H. *It's Not the Stork! A Book About Girls, Boys, Babies, Bodies, Families, and Friends.* Illustrated by Michael Emberley. Candlewick, 2006. ISBN 0763600474. 64 p. Grades K–4.

In the latest of Harris and Emberley's excellent series on our bodies, a bird and a bee explain exactly how babies are made. The illustrations show it like it is, and the text tells it like it is—and you are either comfortable or uncomfortable with this. I'm a mature adult and I even learned a couple of things! This is wonderful information.

Harrison, David L. *Cave Detectives: Unraveling the Mystery of an Ice Age Cave.* Illustrated by Ashley Mims. Cave photographs by Edward Biamonte. Chronicle Books, 2007. ISBN 0811850064. 48 p. Grades 4–8.

The cave has been there for at least hundreds of thousands of years, maybe millions, but ages ago, as the Ice Age ended, its entrance was blocked, and nothing could enter it anymore. It was completely hidden in the ground.

In September 2001, a road crew was using explosives to blow off part of a hill that was in the way of the construction. They waited for the debris to crash outward. It didn't. Instead, the debris fell back into the earth. When the men rushed to see what had happened, they saw a cave.

Soon a local geologist was notified, and he decided that the cave needed to be explored. He called a paleontologist, Matt Forir, and Matt's team member, Lisa McCann. They would be looking for signs of ancient life—and did they ever find it!

This book is loaded with photographs that show what they found in that cave—some of it almost unbelievable. Take a look at the claw marks of a gigantic bear in the cave wall on page 27. Look at the tracks of hoof prints on page 29. They were made by peccaries, distant relatives of the modern pig, and they look fresh. But they are thousands of years old! They found a peccary foot that had been bitten off by a bear—see the illustration of that about to happen on page 31.

When they started dating their samples, they learned that they had found one of the oldest Ice Age caves ever—and that all sorts of wonderful new information could be learned from it.

This is an exciting book to read.

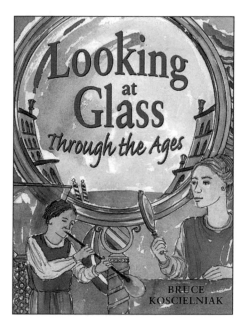

Looking at Glass Through the Ages
by Bruce Koscielnak.

Koscielnak, Bruce. *Looking at Glass Through the Ages.* Houghton Mifflin, 2006. ISBN 0618507507. Unpaged. Grades 3–5.

Is there anyone who doesn't use glass at least several times a day? Do you drink water out of a glass? Do you look in a mirror? That's glass. Windows are glass. There are glass vases, glass dishes, maybe you wear glasses, made of—what else—glass.

But do you know how glass is made or who made it first? This book tells us.

Scientists have discovered that Egyptians made glass about 4,500 years ago, and no one has discovered any glass that is older than that so far. There are diagrams showing us how they made some beautiful glass objects. Then, about 2,500 years later, people in what is now Syria figured out that hot, molten glass could be blown into a bubble. That was called handblown glass, and some artists still make it that way today. Constantinople in present-day Turkey became a famous center of glass production, and Venice, Italy, became famous for its glass. It still is today. Glassmakers in Venice were the first to figure out how to make glass that was almost clear. Clear glass led to many developments, such as eyeglasses and magnifying glass—and clear windows.

Artists over the centuries have made glass into beautiful objects, such as stained-glass windows.

You'll be fascinated by all of the interesting things you learn about glass.

The Story of Salt **by Mark Kurlansky.**

Kurlansky, Mark. *The Story of Salt*. Illustrated by S. D. Schindler. G. P. Putnam's Sons, 2006. ISBN 0399239987. 48 p. Grades 3–6.

Human beings and other mammals eat only one rock. But we *have* to eat that rock. We have to have it because without it we would die. That rock is salt, or sodium chloride.

"Sodium chloride is needed for breathing and for digestion, and without salt, the body could not transport nourishment, oxygen, or nerve impulses, which means that the body would not function at all" (page 7).

So how do we get it? How is it made? How much does it cost? Why is something that is readily available for free in so many places and sometimes very expensive to buy? Why have people fought wars over salt?

All of the answers are in this book.

Did you know that:

- historians and scientists believe that farmers offered salt to wild animals, and that is how those animals became tame?

- salt preserves food, and when people started preserving food, that meant they could travel away from home because they would still have food that was not spoiled and safe to eat?

- there would be no mummies without salt?

- the Roman word for salt was *sal?* And that Roman soldiers were often paid in salt, and that word became our word *salary*? That is also where we get the expressions "worth his salt" and "to earn his salt."

And there is a lot, lot more. You would never dream that salt has such an incredible history.

***Hurricanes, Tsunamis, and Other Natural
Disasters* by Andrew Langley.**

Langley, Andrew. *Hurricanes, Tsunamis, and Other Natural Disasters* (Kingfisher Knowledge). Kingfisher, 2006. ISBN 0753459752. 64 p. Grades 4–8.

Take a look at the first picture in this book. It shows one of the most famous places and buildings in the world: Saint Mark's church and square in Venice, Italy. There are tables and chairs set up for a restaurant in the front part of the picture. But there is something really unusual going on—a few feet of water have flooded the entire square. It is still neat and tidy, but there is a *lot* of water there.

In this book, you will learn about some of the disasters that have happened on our planet. Earthquakes are particularly prevalent around the Pacific Rim, the edges of the Pacific Ocean. Take a look at what happened to a building in San Francisco in 1989 on page 11. Then look at the great photo of lava flowing out of a volcano on page 21. You would not want to be anywhere near *that*—unless, perhaps, you were wearing a full thermal suit as the scientist is on page 29.

Weather creates all sorts of disasters too—from tornadoes to hurricanes to rogue, or freak, waves in the ocean to floods and avalanches. You'll be interested in reading about how diseases are spread, how droughts happen, and how fires break out.

This book is just loaded with photos and interesting information.

Latta, Sara L. *What Happens in Summer?* (I Like the Seasons!). Enslow Elementary, 2006. ISBN 0766024164. 24 p. Grades K–2.

If you live in the northern part of the United States or in Canada, do you ever wonder why it is sometimes hot and sometimes cold and sometimes snowy, and sometimes cool with leaves falling or lots of new things growing? This book tells you how that happens and why it happens, and especially all the neat things that happen during the warmest part of the year, the summer. You'll learn some of the things that people and animals and plants do during the summer.

Show the picture of the boy on page 19.

Diving to a Deep-Sea Volcano **by Kenneth Mallory.**

Mallory, Kenneth. *Diving to a Deep-Sea Volcano.* Houghton Mifflin, 2006. ISBN 0618332057. 60 p. Grades 5–8.

Since the beginning of history, no human being really knew what was growing and what lived (if anything) at the bottom of the ocean. People had no way of checking it out. Human beings die if they dive that deep.

It was not until the 1960s that small submersibles were built that were strong enough to be able to go miles down in the ocean with human beings safely protected inside them to see what was there.

And, boy, did the scientists who went get a surprise!

All sorts of astonishing things were growing and living in the darkest, most remote areas of our oceans. Furthermore, there were volcanoes down there spewing out hot water—sometimes as hot as 752 degrees Fahrenheit! And creatures were living in that hot, hot water.

Those creatures were unusual looking. Many were pale or white. One was a protozoan—a single-celled animal, which ordinarily you can see only through a microscope, but this one was the size of a volleyball.

There were tubeworms, and clams, and mollusks, which were much bigger than the ones you can catch in the ocean. There were all sorts of strange and exotic creatures, and most of them had never been seen by human beings before.

The scientists who study these creatures are excited by all they are seeing—and all they have yet to see. "Scientists have explored a lot more of outer space than the deep ocean. Although they have mapped nearly 100 percent of the surface of Venus, they've charted only .001 to 1 percent of the ocean floor. Scientists discover new species on nearly every dive, and more than 95 percent of the life forms they find there are new to science" (p. 49).

You will enjoy looking at the incredible illustrations and photographs and reading about the unimaginable creatures that live at the bottom of the ocean.

Miller, Mara. *Hurricane Katrina Strikes the Gulf Coast: Disaster & Survival* (Deadly Disasters). Enslow Publishers, 2006. ISBN 0766028038. 48 p. Grades 4–6.

On August 26, 2005, Hurricane Katrina whipped through the whole Miami, Florida, area, with speeds of 87 miles an hour. Not many people had expected that bad of a storm. Over one million people were left without power, and eleven died. The damage done totaled more than 600 million dollars.

But that was just the beginning. The hurricane kept going, straight into the Gulf of Mexico, where the water was warm and gave the hurricane even more power and energy. It was on its way to New Orleans. It was coming from the south. A hurricane expert had said in 2002 that if any hurricane was so strong that it would wash over the levees there, it could fill up New Orleans, which is surrounded by water on every side, like a bathtub.

And that is exactly what happened.

This is the story of what went on when it happened and how people coped. They did not cope well, because they got very little, mostly inept help. Forced to evacuate into the Superdome and the Convention Center, they found there was very little food and water, and bathrooms quickly overflowed. People just had to go to the bathroom on the floor. Many homes were flooded.

It was a terrible catastrophe, and this is the true story of how it happened.

Show your audience the picture on page 18 and the fantastic photograph on the front cover.

Tsunami Warning **by Taylor Morrison.**

Morrison, Taylor. *Tsunami Warning*. Houghton Mifflin, 2007. ISBN 9780618734634. 32 p. Grades 2–5.

Some people might not have even known what a tsunami is, but in December 2004, they found out. More than 230,000 people died in the Indian Ocean tsunami. Scientists decided they needed to better prepare to give people advance warning of the next one.

This is the true story of how scientists began working together in 1925 to learn more about the earth. Some believed that undersea earthquakes were in some way related to tsunamis, but no one really understood how.

They were horrified when on April 1, 1946, an earthquake happened in the Aleutian Islands off of Alaska. Giant waves built, and, almost five hours later, they landed in Hawaii.

Hawaiian workers that day had been surprised to find that Hilo Bay was dried up, and stranded fish were flopping around. Men ran into the bay to grab them, and heard a roaring noise. It was a tsunami.

Though there had been some warnings, not big ones, but small ones, no one believed them because it was April Fools' Day. Now people's homes, cars, and workplaces were being swept away by the huge wall of water.

This is the story of that tsunami and of what researchers started to do and are continuing to do to improve upon ways to predict tsunamis and prepare people who are going to be struck by them in the future.

Show the pictures on page 14 and 15.

Wildfire **by Taylor Morrison.**

Morrison, Taylor. *Wildfire.* Houghton Mifflin, 2006. ISBN 0618509003. 48 p. Grades 4–8.

Almost everyone is afraid of forest fires and thinks they are a bad thing. This book tells us the truth about what goes on in a forest fire. Have you ever heard that they might actually be a *good* thing that forests need?

"The people who work with wildfire are like lion tamers, attempting to control an extremely powerful and unpredictable force of nature. And as lion tamers do, they need to learn as much as they can about what they are trying to restrain" (p. 6).

Ponderosa pine forests give scientists *and* firefighters clues. What researchers have learned and observed is that the forests need fire to keep the healthy trees alive and growing and to get rid of the dead trees and the debris on the forest floors. Really healthy trees have ways of resisting fires and surviving them. The author of this interesting book compares the work of a forest fire as similar to getting rid of the trash in your house. If the forest is not kept clean, much worse fires can happen.

You will learn about the firefighters who try to tame the fires—and also set fires to help keep the forests healthy and try to keep fires from going out of control. Their job is extremely dangerous. You will also learn about the solitary forest rangers whose job is to see if they can spot fires anywhere around them—and how their information is used.

You will learn many surprising things about wildfires when you read this colorful, interesting book.

Rockwell, Anne. *Why Are the Ice Caps Melting? The Dangers of Global Warming* (Let's-Read-and-Find-Out Science 2). Illustrated by Paul Meisel. Collins, 2006. ISBN 0060546697. 40 p. Grades 2–4.

Have you heard of global warming? Do you know what it is? A lot of people think it is happening right now, although not everyone is sure what causes it. This book explains what many scientists think is happening.

What does it mean when the earth gets too hot? For starters, ice starts to melt. When ice melts in the colder areas of the earth, the water level in the ocean goes up. More floods occur as the sea covers the land. Birds like robins may not need to migrate to warmer places. It is warm enough where they are all year round. Rivers dry up, and there are many hot, dry places on the planet where there is not enough water. More deserts develop.

Most scientists believe that people like us are causing global warming. First of all, we are creating too much carbon dioxide, in all sorts of ways. Using fossil fuels, such as coal and oil and gasoline for automobiles, creates more carbon dioxide.

And that's just the beginning. This is an interesting look at what is happening —and what we can do to help.

Romanek, Trudee. *Squirt! The Most Interesting Book You'll Ever Read About Blood* (Mysterious You). Illustrated by Rose Cowles. Kids Can Press, 2006. ISBN 1553377761. 40 p. Grades 4–7.

We have all seen blood squirt out—think, for instance, of what happens when you squash a wood tick or a mosquito! This book gives us a great deal of interesting information about blood. Here are a few things you might want to know more about.

- The average person has a little over one ounce of blood for every pound he or she weighs. An eighty-pound kid has about eighty-eight ounces of blood flowing in his or her body. That's more than you'd find in a giant soda bottle!

- "A bruise is … red blood cells that have leaked out of a broken blood vessel under your skin. When they die, they turn black. Bruises disappear as fresh blood carries off the dead cells" (p. 8).

- Vampire bats have no choice—they have to eat blood. If they do not get any for two days in a row, they will die.

- Do you know why your eyes sometimes look red when you have your picture taken with a flash camera? It's because light bounces off the tiny blood-filled vessels in the back of your eyeballs.

And that's just the beginning. This book is loaded with great stuff!

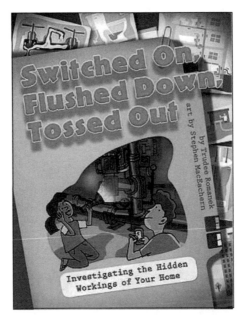

Switched On, Flushed Down, Tossed Out:
Investigating the Hidden Workings of Your
Home by Trudee Romanek.

Romanek, Trudee. *Switched On, Flushed Down, Tossed Out: Investigating the Hidden Workings of Your Home.* Art by Stephen MacEachern. Annick Press, 2005. ISBN 155037902x. 48 p. Grades 3–7.

All sorts of things happen sort of automatically around your house. Maybe you never wondered how or why they happen, but maybe you *did* wonder such things as:

- Where does the water in the faucets come from? How come it sometimes smells funny?

- How does water get hot?

- What happens to the stuff that goes down your drains and toilets?

- How does electrical power get to the lights? The TV? The computer? How does that work?

- How does air-conditioning cool down a house?

There are a lot of pictures in this interesting book. I bet a lot of the things in it will surprise you!

Romanek, Trudee. *Wow! The Most Interesting Book You'll Ever Read About the Five Senses* (Mysterious You). Illustrated by Rose Cowles. Kids Can Press, 2004. ISBN 1553376293. 40 p. Grades 4–8.

This book is just loaded with great information about the senses. Here are just a few of the fun facts.

- On the average, women have better senses of smell, but men are better at seeing small movements. That is why prehistoric men hunted, and women found plants that were safe to eat.

- "Cats and some other animals have a thin extra eyelid that covers the eye and protects it from sand or bright light. Humans used to have them, too. All that's left are those bits of white tissue in the corners of your eyes" (p. 6).

- We need two eyes so we can see depth. Seeing depth with just one eye does not work well. Try threading a needle with one eye closed and see what happens.

- If you want to hear what your voice sounds like to other people, plug your ears while you are talking. It sounds weird! But it is the real thing. Read the explanation on page 15.

- With the sense of touch, usually your brain does not pay any attention to things that stay the same—like the way clothes feel on your body. What it does pay attention to are things that change—like the feel of an insect walking around on you.

And that is just the beginning!

Sneeze by Alexandra Siy and Dennis Kunkel.

Siy, Alexandra, and Dennis Kunkel. *Sneeze*. Charlesbridge, 2007. ISBN 1570916535. 45 p. Grades 3–6.

What makes you sneeze? And what happens when you do sneeze? What's going on here?

You'll be surprised at what you find out in this book. The author and the photographer have included many photographs that are called electron micrographs. They are taken with electron microscopes and can magnify the object up to 500,000 times. The micrographs are always black-and-white images, but they are colored here so we can see them better. You will be amazed at what you see.

Look at the micrographs of pollen on page 9, of a piece of ground pepper on page 11, of a dust mite (yuck!) on page 13, of house dust on page 17, and of a tissue on page 39. No wonder some of these things make you sneeze.

Learn some of the fascinating facts about sneezing—like why we say "God Bless You" or "Gesundheit" when someone sneezes, and why we do not sneeze when we are asleep. Did you know that sometimes pinching your nose can stop you from sneezing?

Did you know that the first copyrighted motion picture ever was of a sneeze? See pictures from it on page 41.

Slavin, Bill, with Jim Slavin. *Transformed: How Everyday Things Are Made.* Illustrated by Bill Slavin. Kids Can Press, 2005. ISBN 1553371798. 160 p. Grades 4–8.

Do you know what is the most *famous* drink in the world? Do you know what is the most *popular* drink in the world? (Let your audience guess. The answers are Coca-Cola and tea.) Now, how do you suppose these drinks are made? Do you know what ingredients are in Coca-Cola? The Coca-Cola Company isn't telling. How about tea? Where is that from?

This is a book just packed with interesting information about where things come from and how they are made. Who thought up the idea of chewing gum? How come baseballs have so much yarn in them? Who makes marbles, and who got the idea for them, anyway? How is licorice made? How about jelly beans? How does a ship get in a bottle? Who invented kitty litter, and what is it made of? Do you know that when erasers were invented, parents and teachers got worried? They thought it would be too easy for kids to erase their mistakes! Do you know you can make your own tooth-paste? This book has a recipe for it.

All of these questions and many, many more are answered in this fascinating book. Show the picture of the baseball being made on pages 12–13.

Strauss, Rochelle. *One Well: The Story of Water on Earth.* Illustrated by Rosemary Woods. Kids Can Press, 2007. ISBN 1553379543. 32 p. Grades 3–5.

The earth has so much water that when astronauts look at it from space, it looks blue! It's a good thing, too, because every animal and every plant and every human be-ing needs water. Without water, we are all dead.

But there is a problem, even with all the water on Earth. We never can get more water than we already have. And Earth has had the exact same amount of water for bil-lions of years. Most of it, over 97 percent, is in the oceans. But oceans have saltwater, and we need freshwater for drinking and most of our needs.

We keep using the same water over and over and over. The process is called the water cycle. So any water we are drinking today might have been drunk by a dinosaur millions of years ago! And we human beings have a lot of water in our bodies—they are made of about 70 percent water.

We are using more water today than we have ever used in all of history. In North America, about three-quarters of all of our water is used in the bathroom—for bathing and for flushing. It takes water to manufacture things and to grow things.

In North America, at least in most places, we have plenty of water, but there are people all over the world who do not have readily available water. What would it be like to walk at least fifteen minutes to get a pail of water? And then what would it be like to carry that pail, now weighing twenty-two pounds, home?

This is a scary book. Read it and see what you think about the water situation in the world right now.

Wired by Anastasia Suen.

Suen, Anastasia. *Wired*. Illustrated by Paul Carrick. Charlesbridge, 2007. ISBN 1570915997. 32 p. Grades 1–4.

It's dark in the room. When you walk in the door, you flip on the switch, and suddenly the lights go on. Throughout most of the history of the world, people would have thought you were doing something magical, but we just take it for granted.

What really happens when you turn on the light? Or plug in an appliance? How does electricity work? Where does it come from, and how does it get to our homes?

This book tells us the answer to that question and makes it simple and interesting, with lots of colorful illustrations. There is even a list of basic safety rules at the end of the book. You'll enjoy beginning to understand electricity.

Sullivan, Edward T. *The Ultimate Weapon: The Race to Develop the Atomic Bomb*. Holiday House, 2007. ISBN 0823418553. 182 p. Grades 5–up.

By 1945, the American people—and much of the rest of the world—were totally sick of World War II. Young men were dying at a horrifying rate, and the lives of civilians in war-torn countries was chaotic. When Germany surrendered in the spring, everyone heaved a sigh of relief. Now Japan was the only country left fighting the Allied forces, and the United States was leading those forces in the Pacific.

Many Americans hated Japan. Their attack on Pearl Harbor in 1941 brought the United States into the war. They always fought to the death, and they were tough and savage enemies who were willing to kill themselves to win the war for their homeland.

Even before the war started in Europe, Germany was developing new weapons. A rumor spread that German scientists were splitting the atom. They might be able to develop a nuclear weapon.

In 1939 Albert Einstein wrote a letter to President Franklin Roosevelt urging him to begin nuclear research in the United States. By 1940 the government began giving money to fund the project that became the Manhattan Project, the design and construction of an atomic bomb in the United States.

There were three places where the work took place. The most famous is Los Alamos in New Mexico, but two others contributed materials: Black Oak Ridge, now known as Oak Ridge, in Tennessee, and Hanford, Washington, on the Columbia River. Thousands of people were employed in these almost obsessively secure sites. The government was terrified that enemy agents might find out what was happening.

This is the story of what happened, how the bomb was designed, tested, and built, and what it was first used for in the summer of 1945.

It is an incredible true story.

Author Profile: Catherine Thimmesh

Catherine Thimmesh, a former art gallery owner, began writing full time in 1997. Her visually stunning nonfiction book Team Moon *won the Sibert Medal in 2007, and she continues to write creative and visually appealing books for young readers.*

What made you start to write nonfiction for kids?

It was sort of accidental. I have always loved writing but never dreamed that I wanted to be an author. It just didn't occur to me. I owned a contemporary art gallery, and while I was doing that, I decided to take a class in writing. The only class they had available was writing for kids, and so I took it and loved it. I always loved kids and always loved writing, but it never occurred to me to put the two together.

Tell me about your first nonfiction book.

When I wrote *Girls Think of Everything,* it actually started out as a fiction book. I just set out to write a story, but this particular book was a fiction story that had nonfiction content in the middle. It was kind of a book within a book. The editor that read it said it was convoluted, but she loved the nonfiction part of it. She asked if I had thought about writing it as a nonfiction book. My initial reaction was no, because I thought that kids didn't read nonfiction. Her response was that they'll read nonfiction if it's good. When I got to thinking about it, I asked if I could do it my way—with fun sidebars and a more colloquial writing style and lots of illustrations. When the answer was yes, it sounded like fun. So that's how that got started.

What was the design process for Team Moon like? Did you have any input?

I had quite a bit of input actually. In my initial proposal to the publisher, I outlined how I envisioned the overall design of the book. I knew I wanted it to be an oversized book.

I knew I wanted these great swaths of black behind the photos. I knew I wanted photos and images on every page. I knew the design before the whole book was even written. Part of what was nice about me working as the photo illustrator in this case was that I got to do it my way. Clearly, of course, we worked with a design team at the publisher, but my editor was on board from the very beginning. There was a little give and take with the designer, but we all worked together to make it happen, and eventually we got what we wanted.

How do you choose the books you want to write?

I pick topics that are absolutely fascinating for me, first and foremost. Then I ask myself, would this be as interesting to kids? I tend to hope they are and think they will be, but you never know. First it has to be something I'm just intensely curious and intensely fascinated with before I'll devote the time and the research and all that's involved to a project.

How do you research the topics you write about?

I'm kind of haphazard in my process. I'm actually fairly disorganized. In general I start with library material—books and articles and Internet searches. But I'm always looking for as much primary material as I can, so I try to seek out people for interviews. That has its problems as well. I found that especially with *Team Moon*. You think by getting the information straight from the horse's mouth it will be correct, but memories are faulty, and people don't always remember things accurately. People have a tendency to cast an event in a particular light based on where they sit. First-person accounts need to be corroborated, and that can be difficult. I cast out a wide net in terms of trying to soak up as much information and talk to as many different people as possible.

Have you had any amazing research moments?

The interviews for *Team Moon* were fun. You're talking to the guys who put the guys on the moon. That's pretty cool. Hearing their stories firsthand is always exciting. There was one gentleman that I spoke with who was in hospice care. He was the chief engineer for NASA. When I called I spoke to his daughter, and I hadn't known he was ill. I apologized and said I wouldn't have called if I had known that. She said *Apollo* was his life, and he ended up wanting to talk to me. He had a nurse nearby helping him with breathing and helping if I couldn't understand what he said. It was a touching time to talk to this gentleman who cared so much about this that he wanted to share his information with kids. That was really memorable.

***Team Moon: How 400,000 People
Landed Apollo 11 on the Moon*
by Catherine Thimmesh.**

Thimmesh, Catherine. *Team Moon: How 400,000 People Landed* Apollo 11 *on the Moon.* Houghton Mifflin, 2006. ISBN 0618507574. 80 p. Grades 4–8.

Most people in America weren't even alive when it happened, but it was truly mind-boggling.

It was July 20, 1969. Everyone who could get anywhere near a television set was watching one. Something so big that it was almost unbelievable was about to happen. Two men—men from Earth—were going to land on the moon!

The Moon! We had all stared at it throughout our lives. It was so far away, so beautiful, so mysterious. It was unimaginable that we would ever be able to go there, like something out of a science fiction story.

But this was no story. Two Americans, Neil Armstrong and Buzz Aldrin, were actually about to land on the moon. Two men, alone, over 200,000 miles away.

But they were not really alone. More than 400,000 people were on Earth making absolutely sure that nothing went wrong. They wanted the two soon-to-be-moonwalkers back on Earth alive and well, and they wanted them to bring samples of the moon with them, too.

This is the true story of how they did that: how the United States decided to try to land a man on the moon by the end of the 1960s and of all the different teams of designers, engineers, artists, and other workers who planned, created, and executed everything that was needed for an almost perfect expedition to the moon and back.

It is also the story of what went wrong—and what might have gone wrong. What if, for instance, there were deadly germs on the moon and the astronauts brought them back with them? Would everyone on Earth die? What if there was a computer failure of some sort? The author tells us that the computers of 1969 had less power than the average electronic calculator does today.

Look at the photographs of the people gathered together to watch one of the most famous historic events of all time. Look at the photograph of the LM, the lunar module that carried the men from the spaceship directly to the moon itself. It's on page 16 and it looks like an insect. Check the photograph of a footprint on the moon on page 38. You'll have a grand time reading this Sibert Medal–winning book.

Chapter 6

Playing with Words

Poems and wordplay can spice up any booktalk. You can booktalk several poetry books at once, or throw in poems and poetry books as they relate to other nonfiction topics you are booktalking. Kids will enjoy hearing poems read aloud, and they just may catch your enthusiasm for the written word and check out a poetry book on their own.

Shout! Little Poems that Roar **by Brod Bagert.**

Bagert, Brod. *Shout! Little Poems that Roar.* Illustrated by Sachiko Yoshikawa. Dial Books for Young Readers, 2007. ISBN 0803729723. Unpaged. Grades 1–4.

Lead your entire booktalk or storytime audience in "The Library Cheer" for some fun audience participation. Or try "Shout" when introducing a poetry unit, "I Can't Wait" near the end of the school year, or "Alphabet Boogie" for a fun new approach to learning the alphabet. These poems are great fun.

Bernier-Grand, Carmen T. *Cesar: Si, Se Puede! Yes, We Can.* Illustrated by David Diaz. Marshall Cavendish, 2004. ISBN 0761451722. 48 p. Grades 4–up.

    If you are booktalking a biography of Cesar Chavez, this lovely collection makes a superb companion. Read one of these excellent poems about the life of Cesar Chavez, illustrated by David Diaz's gorgeous paintings.

    Try "Who Could Tell" on page 4, "Happy Moments" on pages 10–11, or "I am a Clown" on page 20.

Flamingos on the Roof by Calef Brown.

Brown, Calef. *Flamingos on the Roof.* Poems and Paintings by Calef Brown. Houghton Mifflin, 2006. ISBN 0618562982. Unpaged. Grades 3–5.

    The colorful pictures and fun poems in this collection will enliven your day or any booktalk program. Try reading "Bob," about a burly biker, or "Sally," the silly sister of Medusa (she only has one snake instead of hair).

Hey There, Stink Bug! by Leslie Bulion.

Bulion, Leslie. *Hey There, Stink Bug!* Illustrated by Leslie Evans. Charlesbridge, 2006. ISBN 158089304x. 45 p. Grades 4–8.

    Do you like bugs?

    Do you like knowing all sorts of little weird, fascinating things?

    Do you like to laugh?

If you say yes to all those questions, this may be just the book for you. There are poems about many different kinds of bugs, and amazing facts about each of them.

Read aloud "Making Scents" on page 17, or "The Hot Shot" on page 13, or "Thanklessness" on page 32, and then read the facts that follow the poem. They are guaranteed crowd pleasers. If you are doing a booktalk on gross things, this is just the ticket for a poetry filler. Of course, it also works well with booktalks on animals and insects.

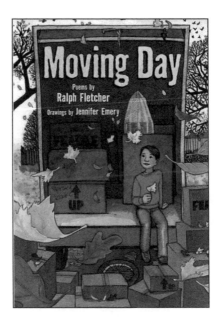

Moving Day **by Ralph Fletcher.**

Fletcher, Ralph. *Moving Day.* Drawings by Jennifer Emery. Wordsong, 2006. ISBN 1590783395. 40 p. Grades 2–5.

A twelve-year-old kid named Fletch is devastated by the news his father tells the family at dinner: they are moving to Ohio. Fletch has no plans to move, and thinks about the things he loves about his home and his neighborhood (and once in a while, the things he doesn't).

Ralph Fletcher, who wrote these poems, had to move to Ohio when he was twelve, and he remembers exactly what it was like. Try reading "New Home" on page 34 or "Defrosting the Freezer" on page 23 to add zip to a booktalk.

A Writing Kind of Day: Poems for Young Poets **by Ralph Fletcher.**

Fletcher, Ralph. *A Writing Kind of Day: Poems for Young Poets.* Illustrations by April Ward. Wordsong/Boyds Mills Press, 2005. ISBN 1590782763. 32 p. Grades 3–6.

You really can write poems about everyday things—like your evil little brother. Ralph Fletcher writes poems about all sorts of things, such as a squished squirrel in the road. Read some of these and see if you don't get some great ideas for your next writing assignment.

Read aloud one of these poems: "My Little Brother" on page 12, "Squished Squirrel Poem" on page 23, or "Bill of Sale" (this works especially well with a unit on the Civil War or African-American history) on page 16.

Florian, Douglas. *Autumnblings.* Poems and Paintings by Douglas Florian. Greenwillow Books, an imprint of HarperCollins, 2003. ISBN 0060092785. 48 p. Grades 2–5.

Florian's poems about autumn are a great way to kick off the school year. Read "What I Love about Autumn" on page 10 or "Falling" on page 37 to add a bit of spice to a fall booktalk.

Florian, Douglas. *Comets, Stars, the Moon, and Mars: Space Poems and Paintings.* Harcourt, 2007. ISBN 0152053727. 48 p. Grades 1–5.

The delightful Douglas Florian takes on the universe in this poetry collection, and it will make a fine and funny addition to any books you are booktalking about space. Some particularly good read-alouds are "A Galaxy" on page 10, "Venus" on page 18, "The Earth" on page 21, "Mars" on page 25, "The Black Hole" on page 42, and, above all, "Pluto," on page 37—right up to the minute on this one!

Florian, Douglas. *Handsprings.* Poems and Paintings by Douglas Florian. Greenwillow Books, an imprint of HarperCollins, 2006. ISBN 0060092815. 48 p. Grades 2–5.

Douglas Florian is always a delightful poet and artist, and these poems and paintings about spring are up to his usual standard. We recommend "What I Hate about Spring" on page 21, "Ten Things to Do When it Rains" on page 32, and "Spring Training" on page 28.

George, Kristine O'Connell. *Fold Me a Poem.* Illustrated by Lauren Stringer. Harcourt, 2005. ISBN 0152025014. Unpaged. Grades K–5.

These absolutely charming poems and delightful illustrations will add a lot of spice to a booktalk, especially one on art. Read "Camel," "Rabbit Complains," "White Paper," "Hungry," or "Windstorm."

Sea Stars: Saltwater Poems by Avis Harley.

Harley, Avis. *Sea Stars: Saltwater Poems.* Photographs by Margaret Butschler. Wordsong/Boyds Mills Press, 2006. ISBN 1590782497. 35 p. Grades 2–5.

Aren't the creatures that live in the ocean amazing? Some of them are beautiful and some are ugly, but all of them are at least interesting! Take a look at the great photographs and read the poems to go along with them. Are those the poems you would have written to go with those photos?

Try "Fast Talk" on page 8, "Otter Chatter" on page 12, or "Sips of Sea" on page 17. Use these poems to spice up a booktalk about sea creatures.

Havill, Juanita. *I Heard It from Alice Zucchini: Poems About the Garden.* Illustrated by Christine Davenier. Chronicle Books, 2006. ISBN 0811839621. 29 p. Grades 2–5.

These poems about gardens and their produce include some fine ones to brighten up a booktalk or any school day. Good poems to share include "When I Grow Up" on page 7, "The Monster" on page 10, and "What I Like about July" on page 20.

Behind the Museum Door: Poems to Celebrate the Wonders of Museums **by Lee Bennet Hopkins.**

Hopkins, Lee Bennett. *Behind the Museum Door: Poems to Celebrate the Wonders of Museums.* Illustrated by Stacey Dressen-McQueen. Abrams Books for Young Readers, 2007. ISBN 081091204X. Unpaged. Grades 3–6.

    If you are booktalking to a class that is about to take a field trip to a museum, this is a great choice. Think of booktalking books about objects of the sort they will see, then throw in one of these delightful poems. Some of the best are "Journey of the Woolly Mammoth," "The Mocassins," and "Mummy," but any of these delightful poems will work well.

Hopkins, Lee Bennett. *Days to Celebrate: A Full Year of Poetry, People, Holidays, History, Fascinating Facts and More.* Illustrated by Stephen Alcorn. Greenwillow Books, an imprint of HarperCollins, 2005. ISBN 0060007664. 112 p. All ages.

    If you, as a booktalker or teacher, are looking for a visual feast of poetry, facts, and glorious pictures, this is the book to pick. There are interesting facts for every day of the year, as well poems to celebrate many of them. Try "Groundhog" on page 19, "Spring" on page 31, "Two Lives Are Yours" on pages 98–99, "Treasure Words" on page 88, and "The Year" on page 109 for starters.

Hopkins, Lee Bennett (selected by). *Got Geography!* Pictures by Philip Stanton. Greenwillow Books, an imprint of HarperCollins, 2006. ISBN 0060556021. 32 p. Grades 1–5.

    Geography teachers and poetry lovers will enjoy reading these poems about our Earth and about geography itself.

    Try "Awesome Forces" on page 13 in conjunction with booktalks on volcanoes, "Learning the World" on page 25, or "Lines Written for Gene Kelly to Dance To" on page 30.

Today and Today **by Kobayashi Issa.**

Issa, Kobayashi. *Today and Today*. Pictures by G. Brian Karas. Scholastic Press, 2007.
ISBN 9780439590785. Unpaged. Grades 2–6.

    If you are doing a unit on haiku or if you just want to share a beautiful book with
your audience, try this book by one of the greatest haiku poets who ever lived, Issa. G.
Brian Karas illustrates sixteen of his poems and makes them into a story of a year in
the life of a small and happy family.

    If you just want to read one or two, try the first one, "Once snows have melted …"
or the eighth, "So many breezes …"

Janeczko, Paul B. (selected by). *Hey, You! Poems to Skyscrapers, Mosquitoes, and Other
Fun Things*. Illustrated by Robert Rayevsky. HarperCollins, 2007. ISBN
0060523476. 40 p. Grades 3–6.

    There is a potpourri of fun and moving poems here on topics ranging from a mag-
got in an apple to an octopus, seahorse, hat hair, and a fork. Try one as a booktalk
filler. These are the kinds of poems that help kids understand that poetry can be wonderful. Three favorites are "Lovely Mosquito" on page 10, "To a Maggot in an Apple"
on page 17, and "Soft-boiled" (OK, I admit I've loved that one for decades!) on page
20.

Katz, Bobbi. *Once Around the Sun*. Illustrated by LeUyen Pham. Harcourt, 2006. ISBN
0152163972. Unpaged. Grades K–4.

    This is a fun collection of poetry about the months. Read the one for the month
you are in now, or "January," "June," and "November" are excellent choices.

Pocket Poems by Bobbi Katz.

Katz, Bobbi (selected by). *Pocket Poems*. Illustrated by Marylin Hafner. Dutton Children's
Books, 2004. ISBN 0525471723. 28 p. Grades K–4.

This delightful collection of short poems can provide booktalk fillers. Many are
easy to memorize, and a lot are very funny. Try "Toothpaste" on page 4, "The Drum"
on page 7, "English Is a Pain! (Pane?)" on page 10, or "Raising Frogs for Profit" on
page 20.

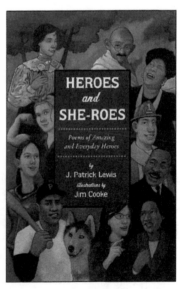

**Heroes and She-Roes: Poems of Amazing and
Everyday Heroes by J. Patrick Lewis.**

Lewis, J. Patrick. *Heroes and She-Roes: Poems of Amazing and Everyday Heroes*. Illustrations by Jim Cooke. Dial Books for Young Readers, 2005. ISBN 0803729251.
Unpaged. Grades 1–5.

Use these poems when you are booktalking biographies and history. There is a
good variety here, each on a two-page spread with a color illustration. Check out the
poems on Helen Keller, Roberto Clemente, Joan of Arc, Togo the Wonder Dog

(Iditarod Race), Cesar Chavez, and more. The last poem is a great inspirational one about people who do what needs to be done.

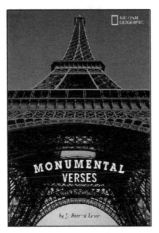

Monumental Verses **by J. Patrick Lewis.**

Lewis, J. Patrick. *Monumental Verses.* National Geographic, 2005. ISBN 0792271351. 32 p. Grades 3–up.

This is a fine companion to George Sullivan's *Built to Last.* The famous monuments in this book are not all American monuments, but they were definitely built to last—and people love them and consider them beautiful.

Read the poem "Statue of Liberty" on page 20, or "Machu Picchu" on page 23, and take a look at the suggestions in the epilogue on page 30. Lewis suggests that if your favorite architectural achievement is missing, you should write a poem about it!

Be sure to show your audience some of the beautiful photographs.

Once Upon a Tomb: Gravely Humorous
Verses **by J. Patrick Lewis.**

Lewis, J. Patrick. *Once Upon a Tomb: Gravely Humorous Verses.* Illustrated by Simon Bartram. Candlewick Press, 2006. ISBN 0763618373. Unpaged. Grades 2–5.

If you are booktalking gross, horrifying, or scary books, add one of these twenty-two poems, each of which deals with an untimely demise, including a school principal, a beautician, a bully, and a cafeteria lady. My favorite is the one about the schoolteacher. Read it aloud while showing the picture.

MacLachlan, Patricia, and Emily MacLachlan Charest. *Once I Ate a Pie*. Illustrated by Katy Schneider. Joanna Cotler Books, an Imprint of HarperCollins, 2006. ISBN 0060735317. Unpaged. Grades 1–4.

    If you are booktalking books about dogs, this will add some spice. Told in the first person by thirteen dogs, these are poems about their lives, ranging from that of a tiny Chihuahua to a sheep dog that insists on herding all of his people. Try reading "Mr. Beefy," from which the title is taken, "Gus," or "Abby." The colorful illustrations are just right!

Snapshots: The Wonders of Monterey Bay **by Celeste Davidson Mannis.**

Mannis, Celeste Davidson. *Snapshots: The Wonders of Monterey Bay*. Words and Pictures by Celeste Davidson Mannis. Viking, 2006. ISBN 0670060623. Unpaged. Grades K–5.

    Have you ever gone to a beach by the ocean? What do you see there that is unusual and interesting and exciting?

    This is a story and poem about one of the most beautiful beaches in the world, Monterey Bay, and the animals that live there and the environment in which they live. There are more than 2,000 sea otters, animals that are both cute *and* clever. They use rocks to crack open the shellfish they eat—which means that they use tools, and not many animals can do that.

    Look at the pinnipeds! Do you know what that means? They are marine animals with flippers, such as sea lions, fur seals, northern elephant seals, and others. "Pinniped" means "feather-footed" in Latin. Look at the pictures and see if you don't think their feet look like feathers.

    Just looking through this beautiful book will make you want to look more carefully at everything you see the next time you go to a beach.

    Show the picture of the sea lion floating or the pinniped riot.

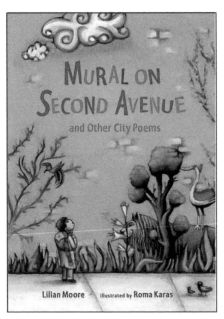

*Mural on Second Avenue and Other
City Poems* **by Lilian Moore.**

Moore, Lilian. *Mural on Second Avenue and Other City Poems.* Illustrated by Roma Karas. Candlewick Press, 2005. ISBN 0763619876. 32 p. Grades K–4.

Living in a big city is definitely not the same as living in a smaller or more rural area, and Lilian Moore spots some of those differences in this lovely collection of short poems. Try "Snowy Morning" (this would work well with booktalks on snow and blizzards) or "Pigeons."

Mozelle, Shirley. *The Kitchen Talks.* Illustrated by Petra Mathers. Henry Holt, 2006. ISBN 0805071431. 40 p. Grades 1–4.

Anytime you need a day brightener, a laugh, or just an example that a poet can write a poem about almost anything, try this book. Some good ones are "Toaster," "Favorite Cup" (how true, how true!), "Rolling Pin," and "Cookie Jar."

Myers, Walter Dean. *Jazz.* Illustrated by Christopher Myers. Holiday House, 2006. ISBN 0823415457. Unpaged. All ages.

This father-son collaboration is a powerful addition to a unit on jazz. It's an example of how poetry can sound like music. In some of it, you can hardly keep from moving to the beat. Christopher Myers's inspired illustrations accompany the delightful poetry. Read "Stride" or "Good-bye to Old Bob Johnson," or "Twenty-Finger Jack" as an addition to a booktalk.

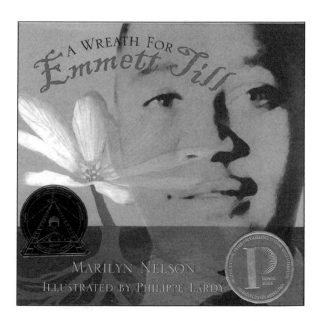

A Wreath for Emmett Till **by Marilyn Nelson.**

Nelson, Marilyn. *A Wreath for Emmett Till.* Illustrated by Philippe Lardy. Houghton
  Mifflin, 2005. ISBN 0618397523. Unpaged. Grades 5–up.

  Emmett Till was fourteen years old when he was lynched: tortured and murdered
by angry white men in Mississippi in 1955. His body was thrown in a river. When it
was found, his mother was horrified to see it and shared her horror with the world by
putting it in an open casket and letting thousands of people view it.

  Marilyn Nelson has written "a crown of sonnets" or "a wreath of sonnets" about
Emmett Till and his murder. It is stunning and beautiful.

  Use this book with Christopher Crowe's *Getting Away with Murder* and read one
of the poems aloud, perhaps "Emmett Till's Name Still Catches in My Throat."

Nye, Naomi Shihab. *A Maze Me: Poems for Girls.* Pictures by Terre Maher. Greenwillow
  Books, an imprint of HarperCollins, 2005. ISBN 0060581905. 118 p. Grades 5–up.

  Naomi Shihab Nye remembers very well what it is like to be twelve, to be a teenager, to be on that uncertain ground between child and adult—and these poems describe her feelings during that time. They're dead on.

  Read aloud "Sometimes I Pretend" on page 61.

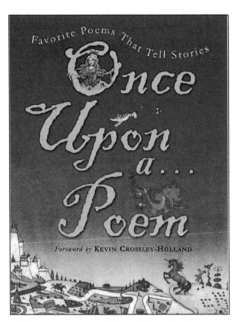

*Once upon a... Poem: Favorite Poems
that tell Stories.*

Once upon a ... Poem: Favorite Poems That Tell Stories. Foreword by Kevin
Crossley-Holland. Illustrated by Peter Bailey, Sian Bailey, Carol Lawson, and Chris
McEwarn. The Chicken House, 2004. ISBN 0439651085. 124 p. Grades 4–up.

  If you like poems that tell stories—and have lots of great pictures to look at while
you read them—this is the book for you. Try reading "The Grateful Dragon" or
"Brave Boy Rap" (the story of Theseus and the Minotaur) to get started, and I bet you
will want to read them all!

Peters, Lisa Westberg. *Earthshake: Poems from the Ground Up.* Pictures by Cathie
Felstead. Greenwillow Books, an imprint of HarperCollins, 2005. ISBN 0060292652.
32 p. Grades 2–5.

  Use this colorful book in conjunction with science units or units on Earth—or on
Earth Day. Our favorites include "Plain Old Rock" on page 7, "Living with Lava" on
page 12, and "Obituary for a Clam" on page 21.

Prelutsky, Jack. *Good Sports: Rhymes about Running, Jumping, Throwing, and More.* Illustrations by Chris Raschka. Alfred A. Knopf, 2007. ISBN 0375837000. Unpaged.
Grades 2–5.

  Jack Prelutsky's poems, as always, make wonderful booktalk fillers, and if you
sing them, the kids will be clamoring for more—and trying to figure out songs that
work for other poems as well.

  Try the rhyme that starts with "Though I like to swim ..." with either "The Daring
Young Man on the Flying Trapeze" or "On Top of Old Smokey." "The Battle Hymn
of the Republic" works well on the rhyme that starts with "I'm going to dunk this basketball ...." Or let the kids see if they can find songs that fit the words. They'll love it!

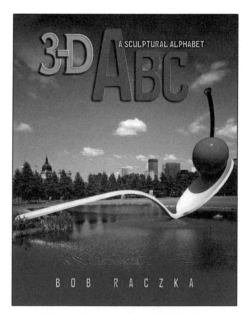

3-D ABC: A Sculptural Alphabet
by Bob Raczka.

Raczka, Bob. *3-D ABC: A Sculptural Alphabet.* Millbrook Press, 2006. ISBN 0761394567. 32 p. Grades 2–6.

    Starting with the fun cover, this is an introduction to twentieth-century sculpture. There is not a lot of text here, but show the audience two or three of the pictures (G, N, and R are great starting places), and they'll get interested.

Rex, Adam. *Frankenstein Makes a Sandwich and Other Stories You're Sure to Like, Because They're All About Monsters, and Some of Them Are Also about Food. You Like Food, "Don't You?" Well, All Right Then.* Harcourt, 2006. ISBN 0152057668. 40 p. Grades 2–5.

    Do *you* like monsters? Adam Rex, who wrote this book, thinks everyone does, so he has written a bunch of poems about monsters like the Creature from the Black Lagoon, The Phantom of the Opera, the Mummy, Godzilla, Bigfoot, Wolfman, and many, many more. Did I tell you these are very funny poems? Read "Count Dracula" on page 17, and you will know what I mean.

Ruddell, Deborah. *Today at the Bluebird Café: A Branchful of Birds.* Illustrated by Joan Rankin. McElderry Books, 2007. ISBN 0689871538. Unpaged. Grades 1–4.

    Twenty-two fun and hilariously illustrated poems about birds fit in well with any booktalk that includes about penguins, eagles, cardinals, loons, or any other kind of bird. Try "Hummingbird Search," "The Loon's Laugh," or "The Cardinal" for starters —and be sure to show the pictures.

Ryder, Joanne. *Toad by the Road: A Year in the Life of These Amazing Amphibians.* Illustrations by Maggie Kneen. Henry Holt, 2007. ISBN 080507354X. 37 p. Grades 1–4.

    What are toads like? Have you ever seen one outside?

    This book tells us, in short poems, the story of a year in the life of toads. It starts out when the toads are all making noises in the spring, and it ends one year later. In the meantime, toads have to escape from other animals (like snakes, who eat them) and also from the cars that will squash them flat if they cross the road at the wrong time.

We learn what toads eat and how they drink (not always through their mouths!). Read the poem on page 23. You'll also learn how they hibernate.

This has some fun poems and some great information about toads. You'll want to take a close look at the next one you see.

Read aloud a poem—three good ones are "Yummy Bugs" on page 19, "Old Toad's Warning" on page 12, or "Just Fooling" on page 29.

Shields, Carol Diggory. *American History Fresh Squeezed! 41 Thirst-for-Knowledge Quenching Poems* (BrainJuice). Illustrations by Richard Thompson. Handprint Books, 2002. ISBN 1929766629. 80 p. Grades 3–5.

Fans of painless learning mixed with frequent humor will enjoy these amusing looks at American history. You can almost certainly find one to mesh with a unit being studied or to introduce a subject. Try "The First" on page 5, the depressingly true "Job Available" on page 18, or "Poor You" on pages 44–45.

Sidman, Joyce. *Butterfly Eyes and Other Secrets of the Meadow.* Illustrated by Beth Krommes. Houghton Mifflin, 2006. ISBN 061856313X.

Do you know what a meadow really is or what kind of creatures live in one? You will by the time you finish reading this beautiful book that includes both poetry and information. Start by reading the first poem, "In the Almost-Light." Each one is also a riddle. What does the poem describe? Guess! Or maybe you know! There are clues in the illustrations.

Then turn the page, and the answers are on the next two pages.

That is the way the whole book is set up, and you will have fun with this guessing game.

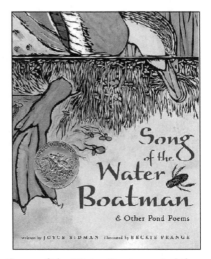

Song of the Water Boatman & Other Pond Poems **by Joyce Sidman.**

Sidman, Joyce. *Song of the Water Boatman & Other Pond Poems.* Illustrated by Beckie Prange. Houghton Mifflin, 2005. ISBN 0618135472. Unpaged. Grades 2–5.

If you like nature, bugs, and small animals, you will enjoy reading about some of the unusual animals that live in ponds. There is a poem and a beautiful picture of each one, and then there is some factual information. You will be surprised at what you do not know. Try reading "Diving Beetle's Food-Sharing Rules," "Travel Time," or "Into the Mud."

***This is Just to Say: Poems of Apology and Forgiveness* by Joyce Sidman.**

Sidman, Joyce. *This Is Just to Say: Poems of Apology and Forgiveness.* Illustrated by Pamela Zagarehski. Houghton Mifflin, 2007. ISBN 0618616802. 48 p. Grades 4–6.

Mrs. Merz asks her sixth-grade class to write poems of apology—real ones, to really apologize. And then the kids, who end up really enjoying the assignment, decide to get the people to whom they apologized to write poems back. This is both funny and moving. As a booktalk filler (and maybe a great way to get your audience to read the book), try reading "This Is Just to Say" on page 8 or "Fashion Sense" on page 12, or pairing "It Was Quiet" on page 20 with "Losing Einstein" on page 38.

Sierra, Judy (selected by). *Schoolyard Rhymes: Kids' Own Rhymes for Rope Skipping, Hand Clapping, Ball Bouncing, and Just Plain Fun.* Illustrated By Melissa Sweet. Alfred A. Knopf, 2005. ISBN 0375825169. Unpaged. Grades K–4.

How many schoolyard rhymes do *you* know? Probably more than you think. This book is loaded with some of the funniest ones.

Read aloud "Tarzan, Tarzan, Through the Air" on page 10, or "Burp" and "Nobody Likes Me" on page 15.

Singer, Marilyn. *Central Heating: Poems About Fire and Warmth.* Illustrated by Meilo So. Knopf Books for Young Readers, 2005. ISBN 0375829121. 48 p. Grades 3–5.

These poems about fire and warmth are real winners. Try reading "Fire Fighters" on page 14, "Dragon" on page 16, or "Toasting Marshmallows" on page 35 to enliven a booktalk or a school day.

Singer, Marilyn. *Monday on the Mississippi*. Illustrated by Frane Lessac. Henry Holt, 2005. ISBN 080507208x. Unpaged. Grades K–4.

With two poems for each day, we follow the Mississippi River from its origin in Lake Itasca down all the way to New Orleans. On the way we see Tom Sawyer's fence, the Gateway Arch in St. Louis, Mud Island in Memphis, and many other wonderful sights. Great for geography units!

Truss, Lynne. *Eats, Shoots & Leaves: Why, Commas Really DO Make a Difference!* Illustrated by Bonnie Timmons. G. P. Putnam's Sons, 2005. ISBN 0399244913. Unpaged. Grades 2–5.

If you think punctuation is really boring, take a look at this book. You'll be laughing out loud at these examples of how commas really are important.

Show the students any one of the examples in the two-page spreads.

Truss, Lynne. *The Girl's Like Spaghetti: Why You Can't Manage Without Apostrophes!* Illustrated by Bonnie Timmons. G. P. Putnam's Sons, 2007. ISBN 9780399247064. Unpaged. Grades 2–5.

This follow-up to *Eats, Shoots & Leaves* deals with the apostrophe, otherwise known as the "Good Punctuation Fairy." It's full of cartoons showing how the meaning of a sentence can completely change with just one apostrophe.

Kids will enjoy the cartoons and teachers will appreciate the fun way to teach grammar. Show the page illustrating "Those smelly things are my brothers."

Whitehead, Jenny. *Holiday Stew: A Kid's Portion of Holiday and Seasonal Poems*. Henry Holt, 2007. ISBN 0805077154. 64 p. Grades 2–5.

This is a fun book of poems celebrating holidays of all sorts throughout the year: Labor Day, Ramadan, Chinese New Year, Birthdays, Martin Luther King Day, Daylight Savings Time, Cinco de Mayo, and so on.

Take a look at "Spring Fever" and "Worm Talk" on page 6 and "Teacher Appreciation Day" on pages 18–19 to brighten a booktalk.

Wolf, Allan. *Immersed in Verse: An Informative, Slightly Irreverent & Totally Tremendous Guide to Living the Poet's Life*. Illustrated by Tuesday Mourning. Lark Books, 2006. ISBN 9781579906283. 112 p. Grades 6–up.

Allan Wolf says, "There are three essential elements of a poet's life: a bloom, a boom, and a secret room" (p. 9). What does he mean? Well, it's not as confusing as it sounds. Young people who want to write poetry need to look for something eye-catching (the bloom), then transform it into something extraordinary (the boom). And what is the "secret room"? It's the heart of the poet that lives deep inside and is able to find meaning in everyday things.

Wolf tells lots of practical information for poets, including how to make your own journals, how to read and perform your poetry, and, of course, how to write good poems. There's lots of humor here and also many ideas and models for poets. If you have any interest in poetry, you will want to own this book. It just might change your life.

Booktalkers can show the Stereotype Poets' Hall of Fame on pages 12 and 13. Are you a Gothic Poet? An Angry Poet? A Hip-Hop Poet? Or some other kind of poet? Young writers and their language arts teachers will love this book.

Chapter 7

Monsters, Mysteries, Mummies, and Other Quirky Books

Werewolves, underwear, the Bermuda Triangle, ice cream, roller coasters, and mummy kids. How do you categorize these books? They're the offbeat titles that certain kids (usually the most reluctant readers) love the most. Don't overlook them—they don't necessarily fit neatly into the school curriculum, but they will get kids reading and that's what matters.

Alillaud, Cindy Lou. *Recess at 20 Below.* Alaska Northwest Books, 2005. ISBN 0882406094. Unpaged. Grades K–3.

How cold does it get where you live? When does your mom, or your teacher, tell you that it is too cold to go outside? When do *you* think that it is too cold to go outside?

Have you ever been outside when it was 20 degrees below zero Fahrenheit? If you have, what did it feel like? Have you ever *played* outside, or gone outside for recess when it was 20 below?

This is a book about kids who do. They live along the Alaska Highway in the coldest state in the United States, and the winter there lasts a long, long time. There's snow on the ground, usually, from September until April.

Getting dressed to go outside when it is 20 below takes a while. You have to wear lots of layers of clothes and you always have to wear a hat. Some kids wear masks. Their clothes can make them look like sumo wrestlers, they are so thick!

But there are great photos and fun facts about what it is like to play outside when it is 20 below. Find out—and decide whether you would ever want to do it!

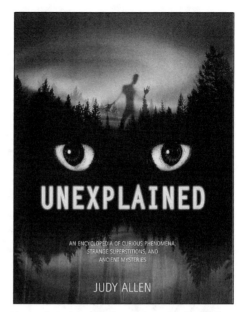

*Unexplained: An Encyclopedia of Curious
Phenomena, Strange Superstitions, and
Ancient Mysteries* **by Judy Allen.**

Allen, Judy. *Unexplained: An Encyclopedia of Curious Phenomena, Strange Superstitions, and Ancient Mysteries*. Kingfisher, 2006. ISBN 0753459507. 144 p. Grades 4–up.

Everybody loves a mystery. And our world is full of them, all sorts of mysteries. Mysteries from history, mysteries from science, people and objects that disappear, strange creatures, possible ghosts, and other interesting things are all fun to read about.

Take a look at this colorful book, loaded with pictures, and see:

- an actual photograph of a ghost on pages 10–11. Or is it a fake? What do you think?

- a man almost completely covered with bees on page 115. They rarely, says the photo caption, sting him. Bee stings hurt like crazy, but they can also help relieve the pain of arthritis.

- information about real lost treasure, which people have been seeking, in some cases, for hundreds of years (pages 110–111).

- information about people that have gone missing—people like Amelia Earhart and D. B. Cooper—do you know who he was?

This is a fun read! You will want to find out more about many of the things in this book.

Baynes, Pauline. *Questionable Creatures: A Bestiary*. William B. Eerdmans, 2006. ISBN 080285284X. 48 p. Grades 5–up.

In the Middle Ages, one type of book people really enjoyed looking at was called a bestiary. Bestiaries, like most books, were created by monks in monasteries. They drew pictures of creatures they had read about or heard about and then added information about the creatures.

They got a *lot* of the facts wrong. But it really didn't matter—people believed whatever they wrote. It was in a book! It must be true! But some of the creatures were taken from ancient books, and others were only described by travelers (who weren't always a reliable source). Some part of their information may have even been correct once in a while, but not very often.

Now if you are interested in gross information, this may be something you might like to read. And if you are interested in beautiful art, it is definitely something you might want to read. And if you just want to find out how mixed-up people really were a few hundred years ago, you will have great fun reading this book.

Show the picture of the camel on page 10 and then read about the creatures that surround it.

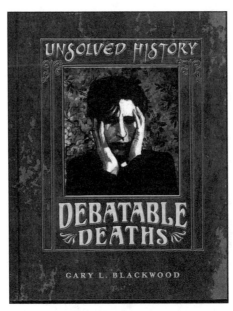

Debatable Deaths **by Gary L. Blackwood.**

Blackwood, Gary L. *Debatable Deaths* (Unsolved History). Marshall Cavendish Benchmark, 2006. ISBN 0761418881. 72 p. Grades 4–up.

Someone is dead. We know the person is dead. But how did he or she die? Was it from a natural cause like a disease? Or did someone murder this person? A debatable death, according to this book, usually involves murder.

Recent murders are not always hard to solve, especially when we still have the body of the victim. But throughout history people have died in ways that made other people think they were murdered. Today it is hard to find the real reasons because we may not even know the location of the of the dead person's body.

This book discusses a few of the most famous debatable deaths, including King Tutankhamen, those of Princes Richard and Edward in the Tower of London (this is a tough one—we are not even sure they really died there), and that of Christopher Marlowe who was killed in a tavern fight (or was he? Did he really die in that fight or did he live and change his name to William Shakespeare?). How about Mozart, maybe the most famous composer of all time? He was only thirty-seven when he died, and we don't even know where he was buried. We know he knew someone who *wished* he were dead. Then there is Meriwether Lewis of the Lewis and Clark expedition. Did he kill himself or did someone else do it? Was Napoleon poisoned? How about Amelia Earhart and her navigator, Fred Noonan? Most people believe they ran out of fuel on their plane flight and fell into the Atlantic Ocean. What if, instead, they landed on a Japanese-held area and were executed?

Fascinating stories and theories abound in this intriguing book.

Enigmatic Events by Gary L. Blackwood.

Blackwood, Gary L. *Enigmatic Events* (Unsolved History). Marshall Cavendish Benchmark, 2006. ISBN 076141889X. 72 p. Grades 4–up.

Do you like mysteries? Doesn't everyone? How about *real* mysteries?

This book deals with mysteries that happened in the past that have never been solved. No one can figure out or get enough information to find out what really happened, who did it, or why it happened.

This book takes six of the most bewildering historical mysteries and describes them to us. First is the death of the dinosaurs. What caused the dinosaurs to become extinct? What really went on? Even the greatest scientists and historians disagree. Some of them are sure that their solution to the mystery is the right one, but others think they are completely wrong. Read this information and figure out what *you* think.

The others include the Roanoke Colony where 115 people just disappeared; the *Mary Celeste,* a ship that lost its entire crew and no one knows where they went; the *Maine,* a ship that blew up and sank off the coast of Cuba (and we don't know whether it was an accident or a real attack or what, but it started a war); the Tunguska event, in which a huge area in Siberia was devastated and no one is sure why or how; and finally, the Hindenburg, an airship that caught fire and was destroyed while trying to land in New Jersey.

These are fantastic mysteries that have kept people wondering for years. Read all about them.

Show the picture of the Hindenburg exploding on page 52.

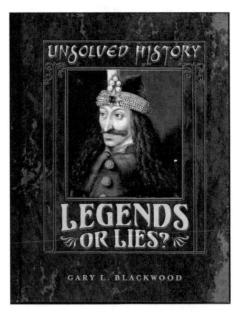

Legends or Lies? **by Gary L. Blackwood.**

Blackwood, Gary L. *Legends or Lies?* (Unsolved History). Benchmark Books, 2006. ISBN 0761418911. 72 p. Grades 4–up.

What is a legend? Could you make a guess as to what that word really means? Can you think of any legends? This book tells us one thing about them, in a great quote: "at the heart of any legend there is usually a kernel of truth. It can be difficult to find and identify, but it's worth the effort because, as scholar Richard Deacon points out, very often 'legends … provide the only clues to what transpired before documentation began' " (p. vii).

You have probably heard of most of the legends in this book. Atlantis—was there ever such a city, now under the ocean? And if there was, where was it? Amazons—women who went into battle just like men. Were they real? Did they exist? King Arthur—everybody who knows it loves the story of King Arthur and Merlin and Guinevere and Lancelot and the knights of the Round Table. Were they real? Did they ever really live? What about Pope Joan? A woman pope? Is it true? Could it have been? And Robin Hood? He has such a great story, but is it fact, or is it fiction?

If you love mysteries, and you like finding out what is real, what might be real, and what is false, this may be just the book you are looking for. The author quotes Peter Stanford, who wrote about the female pope, "People believe in her and go on believing in her because they want her to have happened" (p. 39).

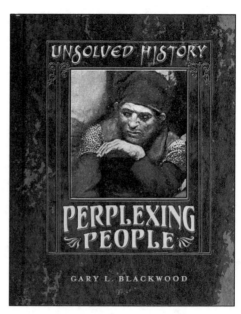

Perplexing People by Gary L. Blackwood.

Blackwood, Gary L. *Perplexing People* (Unsolved History). Marshall Cavendish Benchmark, 2006. ISBN 0761418903. 72 p. Grades 4–up.

This is a book about pretenders. Pretenders are people who claim to be someone else, usually someone famous or royal or wealthy. Some of them may actually be that person. Others are imposters who are perfectly aware that they are lying. But how can we tell which one is which?

DNA testing helps if DNA is available. If people have been dead for hundreds of years, it may not be. And DNA testing still does not have all the answers.

There are lots of photographs here and many intriguing stories of some of the most famous pretenders in history. Read about:

- The women who said they were really Joan of Arc—that Joan was not burned at the stake but someone else was, in her place. Who knows for sure?

- The prisoner in eighteenth-century France who always wore a mask so no one could see his face. Did he look a lot like someone else? Who was he? He became popularly known as the "Man in the Iron Mask," and people are still wondering.

- Brushy Bill Roberts who said he was really Billy the Kid. He was an old man, and he said Sheriff Pat Garrett never killed him. A lot of people believe his story.

You'll want to read more about all of these famous pretenders plus many others.

Borgenicht, David, and Robin Epstein. *The Worst-Case Scenario Survival Handbook: Junior Edition*. Illustrated by Chuck Gonzales. Chronicle Books, 2007. ISBN 9780811860659. 128 p. Grades 4–7.

Have you ever stepped in dog poo? Been stuck at a school dance? Split your pants? Been called to the principal's office? Been forced to eat food you hate? This book is full of advice on how to survive at home, at school, in your social life, and in the outdoors. You'll learn how to survive falling on your face in the school cafeteria (laugh and take a big bow), how to soothe an angry parent (say the never-fail magic words: I'm sorry), and how to survive farting in public (try saying, "Hey, did somebody step on a duck?"). You will not be able to stop reading this addictive book, which also includes some useful lists at the end, such as schoolyard comebacks, excuses for not turning in homework, and contracts for dealing with annoying younger siblings. You will have fun with this book, and you might also get yourself out of some serious trouble.

Buckley, James Jr. *A Batboy's Day* (DK Readers 2). DK, 2005. ISBN 0756612071. 32 p. Grades 1–3.

Do you think it would be fun to be a batboy? Wouldn't it be cool and glamorous? You would get to hang around with all of the great baseball players and carry their bats and talk to them and it would be a blast! Or would it?

This book tells us what a batboy *really* does.

Michael Martinez is a batboy for the Los Angeles Angels, and you will be surprised to learn what he does besides hanging out with baseball players. Did you know that batboys have to do laundry for the team? He has to prepare and then clean up the bull pen. He even has to wash dishes!

You will be surprised at what a batboy does, and if you still want to be one, this book tells you how you can apply for a job to become one.

Kathy's Top Ten Mysterious Booktalking Favorites

- Blackwood, Gary L. *Debatable Deaths* (Unsolved History). Marshall Cavendish Benchmark, 2006.

- Blackwood, Gary L. *Enigmatic Events* (Unsolved History). Marshall Cavendish Benchmark, 2006.

- Blackwood, Gary L. *Legends or Lies?* (Unsolved History). Marshall Cavendish Benchmark, 2006.

- Blackwood, Gary L. *Perplexing People* (Unsolved History). Marshall Cavendish Benchmark, 2006.

- Gee, Joshua. *Encyclopedia Horrifica: The Terrifying TRUTH! About Vampires, Ghosts, Monsters, and More.* Scholastic, 2007.

- Townsend, John. *Mysterious Urban Myths* (Out There). Raintree, 2004.

- Halls, Kelly Milner, Rick Spears, Roxyanne Young. *Tales of the Cryptids: Mysterious Creatures That May or May Not Exist.* Darby Creek, 2006.

- Halls, Kelly Milner. *Mysteries of the Mummy Kids.* Darby Creek, 2007.

- Allen, Judy. *Unexplained: An Encyclopedia of Curious Phenomena, Strange Superstitions, and Ancient Mysteries.* Kingfisher, 2006.

- Townsend, John. *Mysterious Signs* (Out There). Raintree, 2004.

From *Gotcha Good! Nonfiction Books to Get Kids Excited About Reading* by Kathleen A. Baxter and Marcia Agness Kochel. Westport, CT: Libraries Unlimited. Copyright © 2008.

Curlee, Lynn. *Skyscraper.* Atheneum Books for Young Readers, 2007. ISBN 0689844891. 44 p. Grades 4–8.

Skyscrapers! When you are in a big city, you can usually see a lot of them, and they are stupendously intriguing buildings! Above all, they are tall, and most of them are tall and thin, not tall and wide.

They are a relatively new invention in the history of human beings. Skyscrapers would not work without a few inventions. (Think of this: the tallest building for centuries was the Great Pyramid in Egypt!) First of all, there needed to be metal frame construction—steel—strong enough to hold the building together and up. Before steel, massive stone walls were the only way to go. Then there needed to be a way for people to get up and down the many floors: elevators. Then people had to have enough light to work by: electrical lights were needed! Finally, there had to be adequate plumbing and heating and a good way to communicate.

By the late 1800s, at least early versions of all of these were available, and people in America (at first) started constructing buildings so tall it seemed like they would almost touch the sky.

In 1885, the tallest structure in the world was the Washington Monument. Four years later it was the Eiffel tower in Paris. By 1930, the Chrysler Building in New York, today still considered probably the best-loved skyscraper in the world, was around, and a year later it lost its status as the world's highest to the Empire State Building, which lost *its* status a few decades later. Today the Empire State Building may be the most famous skyscraper in the United States, but many Asian skyscrapers are taller.

There are a lot of wonderful illustrations in this colorful book, and you will enjoy reading about these fantastic buildings.

Encyclopedia Horrifica: The Terrifying TRUTH! About Vampires, Ghosts, Monsters, and More **by Joshua Gee.**

Gee, Joshua. *Encyclopedia Horrifica: The Terrifying TRUTH! About Vampires, Ghosts, Monsters, and More.* Scholastic, 2007. ISBN 0439922550. 136 p. Grades 5–up.

Joshua Gee begins this book with a lot of questions. He'd like to find the answers, and so will you, but sometimes *no one* can be certain.

It sure is fun reading, though. There are lots of color photographs and illustrations here, and they show us some of the most interesting things around—including vampires, sea monsters, werewolves, aliens, ghosts and ghost hunters (there is an eyewitness account of what real ghost busters do on pages 53 to 58), superstitions, zombies, mummies, pixies, extrasensory perception, and death itself. There are stories about very strange people and things that actually existed—check out the photos of the giant squid, which may have been what people thought was a kraken, on pages 12 and 13. It is colossal!

Look at the picture of a ghost on page 58. A lot of people think it is not a fake, and the men who took it swore that they did not doctor the photo in any way. You can read the account by the photographer on page 59.

Test your own ESP—there is an actual test you can take on pages 88 and 89.

Here are just a few intriguing things you might want to explore:

- Look at the microscopic photo of the eyelash mite on page 117—yeah, you guessed it, it lives on your eyelash—yuck.

- Take a look at the state-of-the-art ghost-busting equipment on page 48. Does it sound like a good job?

- Look at the picture on page 33 of Petrus Gonsalvus, who had a rare medical condition called Hypertrichosis universalis, which means "hair everywhere." You guessed it—he looks like a werewolf, and you would not want to have that disease!

Kids will have a lot of fun with this book.

Gibbons, Gail. *Ice Cream: The Full Scoop.* Holiday House, 2006. ISBN 0823420000. 32 p. Grades K–3.

Do you like ice cream? Or maybe the question should be this—do you know anybody who *doesn't* like ice cream?

This colorful book tells us how it is made, where it came from, and some of the many ways we enjoy eating it today.

We think the beginnings of ice cream may have been about three thousand years ago in China, but about three hundred years ago the British brought ice cream recipes to their colonies in North America, and people here started making it (but only rich people). It was too hard to get ice.

A lot more people started making ice cream when ice was easier to acquire, and in 1841 a New Jersey woman named Nancy Johnson invented an ice cream maker, very similar to the ones we use to make homemade ice cream even today. Ice cream became very popular.

How many kinds of ways can you think of to eat ice cream? Where do you think the ice cream cone was invented? Why is ice cream with a topping or toppings on it called a sundae? You'll find the answers in this neat book.

Gee Whiz! It's All About Pee
by Susan E. Goodman.

Goodman, Susan E. *Gee Whiz! It's All About Pee*. Illustrated by Elwood H. Smith. Viking, 2006. ISBN 067006064X. 40 p. Grades 3–5.

We all do it several times a day. Human beings have to urinate or they will die. If you are ten years old, you have about 150 gallons of blood passing through your kidneys every day, and the kidneys pull out waste products, salt, and water every day. Kids' bladders can store at least an ounce for every year of their age. Adult bladders hold about two and a half cups, but they feel an urge to pee after about one cup.

You will not believe what you will learn about pee in this book. Here is a start:

- In ancient China, noblemen wearing fancy clothes peed into hollow canes so they would not stain their clothing.

- "Until 200 years ago, European women also peed standing up because of their clothes. They wore long dresses and no underpants. When necessary, they could stand and pee—hopefully outside—without anyone else noticing" (page 11).

- People went to the bathroom anywhere convenient, including the floor and the steps of homes and palaces.

- The White House has thirty-five bathrooms, but when it was built it had only one outhouse.

- Alan Shepard, the first American in space, had to sit and wait for hours for his delayed takeoff. He ended up being the first one to wet his spacesuit.

- Pee in space freezes and looks like stars!

- The mother of newborn bear cubs licks their bottoms after they nurse. Then they pee, and she drinks that pee!

- We do not know how much whales pee a day because it is difficult to measure in the ocean.

- In ancient Rome, spies used pee as invisible ink between the lines of official documents. This is where we get the phrase "Read between the lines."

- In the Civil War, the Confederate army made gunpowder out of pee. Southern ladies saved their pee and gave it to the army.

- Pee is used in medicines, even today. It is also used for cleaning!

- When babies are born, most of the liquid in the sac in which they develop is their own pee.

And that's just the beginning!

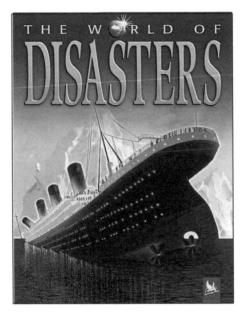

The World of Disasters **by Ned Halley.**

Halley, Ned. *The World of Disasters.* Kingfisher, 2005. ISBN 0753458357. 64 p. Grades 4–8.

The world has survived a lot of disasters, and there are certainly many more to come. In fact, the last third of the book predicts the kinds of disasters that may happen to Earth and its people.

Some of these disasters, like the sinking of the *Titanic,* the eruption of Mount Vesuvius, the Exxon Valdez oil spill, and the nuclear disaster at Chernobyl are famous. Others, in many cases much worse ones, are relatively unknown.

The volcanic explosion of Indonesia's Krakatau Island in 1883 killed more than 36,000 people. No one lived on that island, but people on the surrounding islands were killed. Even 3,000 miles away people could hear the noise of the eruption!

Ice storms, which many of us have seen ourselves, can cause terrible disasters. The one in Canada in January of 1998 caused a national emergency. Tornadoes damage many things in their paths, and bushfires cause problem in dry areas of the world.

Locusts swarming and eating all the food in sight have been around for thousands of years. You may recall hearing about them in the Bible in the story of Moses, and in *On the Banks of Plum Creek* by Laura Ingalls Wilder.

If you are interested in exciting events that really happened, this book is for you.

Show your audience the locusts on page 22.

Author Profile: Kelly Milner Halls

For seventeen years, Kelly Milner Halls has been writing the nonfiction books she wishes she could have read when she was a child. After studying journalism, she turned to writing for kids and has published twenty-one books. Her most recent books, Tales of the Cryptids *and* Mysteries of the Mummy Kids, *fascinate young readers but are full of research and primary source material.*

What made you start to write nonfiction for kids?

I studied journalism in college thinking that I wanted to be an investigative reporter of some kind. When I got out into the adult world, it didn't hold my interest. It wasn't fun and I really wanted a job that would be fun. So I stopped writing for a while and started working for YMCA children's programs. Then when my own kids got old enough to read I had that V-8 moment when I realized that if I write for kids, it will always be fun, it will always be interesting, and I will never have to worry again about whether the assignments are intriguing to me because essentially I'm about a ten year old in my head. So that was when I made the connection that nonfiction was applicable for children as well as adults.

How did you sell your first book?

I went to the newsstand and bought a bunch of children's magazines. I studied them and I started submitting without any understanding of the market. It took me two years to understand that certain editors needed certain articles. My first article was something called "Pistol Packing Paleontologist" about a dinosaur scientist with a law enforcement degree who battled fossil theft. It was a great article, but it took me two years to find the right magazine because I just didn't understand that you had to find the right audience for your material. Once I got the understanding that I had to study the market to know who published what, then the doors started opening.

How do you research your books?

I'm almost fifty years old, so when I first started seventeen or eighteen years ago, the Internet was not an option. I used periodical guides, and libraries were my best friend. Now I find my experts online, then I make direct contact. I know a lot of writers depend on secondary sources, but I really like to go directly to the source and interview the experts because that way I get original material rather than rehashing text that's already out there. My hallmark is expert interviews. I'll go right to the sources and get as many as possible. I think the kids deserve nothing less.

Why do you lean toward unusual subject matter?

When I was a kid, I was a reluctant reader. I was a good reader, but all those years ago, they didn't have quirky material. I only read books about Abraham Lincoln and vampires. Those were my two favorites. I was a strange little girl, kind of quirky. So I thought, I'm gonna write for that kid I was. When I do school visits, I find that there are lots of kids like me. The modern-day equivalents are sitting there waiting just as hopefully as I was for the books that I write. I have two reactions that make me know I want to write about a subject. If it makes me go "What the heck?" or it makes me say "Oh that's gross," then I'm pretty sure those are the topics I should focus in on.

Which of your books are you most proud of?

The six I've done for Darby Creek Publishing are especially meaningful to me because Darby Creek had the vision and the courage to let me use a magazine format in nonfiction for kids. There's a key line of nonfiction material, and sidebars support that information rather than a continuous text. My idea was that if the text was broken into these small segments, even reluctant readers would have a sense of success. Darby Creek let me do that.

Is there a book that you dream of writing someday?

I wish I had the skills to write young adult fiction and I hope someday I'll develop them, but I don't have that power just yet. As far as nonfiction goes, I'm working on one right now about the rescue of the animals at the Baghdad Zoo, and that one has been extremely rewarding to research. I found a captain in the U.S. Army who was the first person to go in and see the animals in such terrible shape, and he coordinated all the rescue missions. It's a dream book, and I feel extremely lucky to be writing it.

Mysteries of the Mummy Kids by Kelly Milner Halls.

Halls, Kelly Milner. *Mysteries of the Mummy Kids.* Darby Creek, 2007. ISBN 158196059X. 72 p. Grades 5–8.

There are mummies all over the world, including some in the United States. Some of them were purposely made into mummies. People prepared the bodies in such a way that they would be preserved, or parts of them would be preserved. But many are accidental mummies. The bodies just happened to be in a place that preserved them.

Here's something most people don't think about—some of all of the different kinds of mummies are kids.

Mummies were real people once, people who had feelings and thoughts. Now we look at them and wonder who they were. Sometimes we know their names or some things about them. Take a look at the El Plomo boy on page 9. He was an Inca child, sacrificed to the gods, given a fermented corn drink, and left to freeze to death on a mountain. His skin has been wonderfully preserved, and we can see his hair and his clothing very clearly. An even more perfectly preserved mummy is pictured on page 49. Rosalia Lombardo is in a chapel in Sicily, and she looks almost alive. No one is sure exactly how she was preserved in about 1920, but the end result is amazing.

You will learn about bog mummies—look at the pictures on pages 44 and 45 of the poor handicapped girl who was probably sacrificed more than two thousand years ago, perhaps because she was handicapped, and at the baby mummy from Greenland on the cover and on page 58 (he's *still* really cute), and at the face of a little girl Egyptian mummy on page 40. You will learn all sorts of great information.

If you like mummies—and who doesn't—you'll enjoy reading this book.

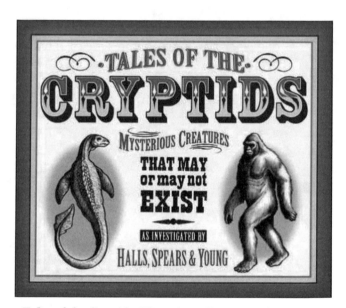

Tales of the Cryptids: Mysterious Creatures That May or May Not Exist **by Kelly Milner Halls, Rick Spears, and Roxyanne Young.**

Halls, Kelly Milner, Rick Spears, and Roxyanne Young. *Tales of the Cryptids: Mysterious Creatures That May or May Not Exist.* Darby Creek, 2006. ISBN 1581960492. 72 p. Grades 4–8.

Do you know what a cryptid is? Have you ever heard of the word "cryptic"? It means mysterious and hard to understand, and a cryptid is a legendary (and mysterious!) animal. Cryptozoology is the study of and the search for legendary animals.

So what is a legendary animal? You've probably heard of some of them: the Abominable Snowman or Bigfoot, the Mermaid, the Loch Ness Monster, the Giant Squid, and the Thunderbird are somewhat famous. But are they *real*?

This book tells the stories of some of the most famous legendary animals throughout world history. There is information on each of them, including maps of the places where people claim to have seen them. Then, at the end of the book, the authors tell us about the different animals and what is believed about them. Five circles mean that they are real, they have been proved to exist, four circles means leaning toward real, three circles means we don't know, two circles means leaning toward a hoax, and one circle means a hoax—an animal that has been proved not to exist.

Here you can see real (or are they fake?) photographs of Bigfoot and the Loch Ness Monster, a mermaid, and many other animals, and learn some great information about them. If you like mysteries and you like animals, you will have a great time reading this fun book.

Harper, Charise Mericle. *Flush: The Scoop on Poop Throughout the Ages*. Little, Brown and Company, 2007. ISBN 0316010642. 25 p. Grades 2–6.

This fits absolutely perfectly into a booktalk on gross stuff. These are humorous poems pertaining to poop and pee, and the audience will love hearing a poem, a few facts, and looking at the fun pictures.

Start with page 3. What did people use before toilet paper? The answers are on page 4, and will blow your audience's mind. A rock in the hand? Lace? A wooden scraper? And that's just the beginning. On pages 6–7, the poem about the Ancient Romans has a particularly disgusting fact at the end.

On pages 11–12, you will learn that a great way for enemies to attack a castle was to crawl up through the garderobe—a little space that sticks out of the castle where people went to the bathroom. It was usually open all the way to the moat, and a good enemy soldier could climb up through it. Yuck. Even worse, he could shoot you in the behind with his arrow!

Show also the picture on page 22 of toilets around the world. What do you think of these? Great fun!

Hocking, Justin. *Taking Action: How to Get Your City to Build a Public Skatepark* (The Skateboarder's Guide to Skate Parks, Half-Pipes, Bowls, and Obstacles). Rosen, 2005. ISBN 1404203419. 48 p. Grades 5–up.

Are you a skateboarder? If you are, where do you skate? Is it a safe place? Is it a legal place?

Maybe you are one of the lucky ones who skates in a skateboard park. Does your city even have a skateboard park? If it doesn't, think how cool it would be to have one in your community.

This book tells you step by step how to go about making that happen. It's not easy. It takes a lot of time and energy, but the end result could be a dream come true.

Take a look at this book, and maybe the other titles in this series: *Awesome Obstacles: How to Build Your Own Skateboard Ramps and Ledges; Dream Builders: The World's Best Skate Park Creators; Off the Wall: A Skateboarder's Guide to Riding Bows and Pools; Rippin' Ramps: A Skateboarder's Guide to Riding Half-Pipes*, and *Technical Terrain: A Skateboarder's Guide to Riding Skate Park Street Courses.*

Katz, Alan, and David Catrow. *Are You Quite Polite? Silly Dilly Manners Songs*. Margaret K. McElderry Books, 2006. ISBN 0689869703. Unpaged. All ages.

This is the fourth in a series of incredibly silly songbooks. If you have the guts, sing them yourself; if not, get the best singer and exhibitionist in the room to do it for you. *Everyone* will want the book! Some sure winners are *Drinkin' at the Fountain, Jimmy Picks Boogers, Don't Talk with Beans in Your Mouth,* and the title song.

Krensky, Stephen. *Creatures from the Deep* (Monster Chronicles). Lerner, 2008. ISBN 9780822567615. 48 p. Grades 4–8.

There are many tales of ancient sea monsters, and they generally came in three varieties—giant serpents, seagoing dinosaurs, and giant squids. It's amazing how people have reported sightings of sea creatures throughout human history. People still see unexplained sea creatures. You've probably heard of Nessie (the Loch Ness Monster), but have you heard of Chessie or Champ? Page 23 has a photo of Nessie that turned out to be a hoax. Page 29 has a photo of the enormous coelacanth, a six-foot long fish that was thought to be extinct until 1938 when one was found near Africa.

The horrifying illustrations in this book will capture the attention of hard-to-please boy readers. Other similar books in the Monster Chronicles series include *Zombies* (ISBN 978082256759) and *The Bogeyman* (ISBN 9780822567608).

***Werewolves* by Stephen Krensky.**

Krensky, Stephen. *Werewolves* (Monster Chronicles). Millbrook Press, 2006. ISBN 0822559226. 48 p. Grades 4–8.

"It's not easy being a werewolf. Werewolves have a lot to deal with. For starters, there are the usual issues—hairy palms, endless howling, and shedding too much fur on the carpet" (p. 6).

Well, there you have it. No one pays nearly as much attention to werewolves as they do to vampires and ghosts. The author tells us that there just plain are not any famous werewolves, and that is part of the problem. Nobody much likes wolves, either, so that doesn't help.

But werewolves are not wolves. A werewolf is a person to begin with, and then that person gets transformed into a werewolf. In most of the old legends, werewolves look just the same as wolves, even though they are really human. But in the movies, werewolves are usually half-human and half-wolf. See the picture of Jack Nicholson as a werewolf on page 17.

Historically, we are not at all certain werewolves ever existed. But some historical people were killed because they were werewolves, and who knows what the truth of *that* is?

In this book, loaded with pictures, you will learn a lot about the legends of werewolves. It's a lot of fun.

Landstrom, Lee Ann, and Karen Shragg. *Nature's Yucky! 2 The Desert Southwest* (Nature's Yucky). Illustrated by Rachel Rogge. Mountain Press, 2007. ISBN 0878425292. 48 p. Grades 2–5.

This book is just filled with extremely interesting gross information. Did you know that:

- Regal horned lizards squirt blood out of their eyes to defend themselves?
- Pack rats use their own urine to glue their nests together?
- The birds called loggerhead shrikes impale the animals they kill on thorns? Think what that means and what that would look like!
- Common ravens eat the eyes of a dead animal first?
- Tarantula hawk wasps lay an egg on a tarantula and paralyze it. Then they bury it alive after they lay an egg in it. The poor tarantula stays alive until the baby is born and eats it up. Yuck!

And that is just the beginning. At the back of the book you will find more information about each animal, an excellent recipe for Raven-gut Upside Down Cake and even a song called Nature's Yucky Blues.

You will have a lot of fun with this book.

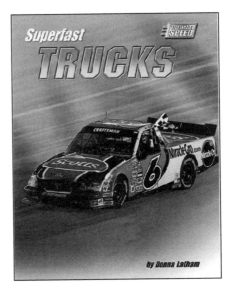

Superfast Trucks **by Donna Latham.**

Latham, Donna. *Superfast Trucks* (Ultimate Speed). Bearport, 2006. ISBN 1597162531. 32 p. Grades 2–6.

As racing goes, truck racing is really new. In 1993 a team of racers built the first racing pickup trucks. They introduced them at a 1994 car-racing event, and the audiences just loved it. Truck racing was in!

Truck races are much shorter than auto races—usually around 150 to 250 miles long (compared with 500 to 600 miles for cars). The trucks go really fast, and such big vehicles are dangerous. "To stay safe, racers are strapped into seats connected to roll cages. A roll cage is a frame made of heavy steel tubes. It helps stop the truck's hard metal body from crushing the driver during a crash" (p. 12). Show the picture on page 15 of the roll cage that saved Geoffrey Bodine from death in his truck's wreck in 2000.

The trucks that are used in racing look pretty much like ordinary pickup trucks, except that they have tractor tires. These tires can get loose when they are driven at such fast speeds.

If you like trucks and racing, you'll love reading this book.

Lauber, Patricia. *What You Never Knew About Beds, Bedrooms, & Pajamas* (Around the House History). Illustrated by John Manders. Simon and Schuster Books for Young Readers, 2006. ISBN 9780689852114. Unpaged. Grades 2–5.

People like to sleep lying down. But they have done that a lot of different ways over the centuries.

We don't really know how the cave people slept. The earliest beds we know about belonged to Egyptians about seven thousand years ago. Their beds were not flat. The head was higher than the foot. They did not use pillows but instead used headrests carved from wood. To us, these headrests look miserably uncomfortable. We are not sure why they did it!

Ancient Romans liked to lie down. They even liked to eat lying down. Nobody had clothes especially for sleeping. They just slept in their underwear.

In the early Middle Ages, people all slept together most of the time. Manor houses had a big room called a hall, and, there "each person was given a sack and some straw to make a bed—that is where our term 'make a bed' comes from. Having made their beds, the important people laid them on the benches, tables and chests. Everyone else slept on the floor." In inns, people usually had to sleep together in one big bed.

By the 1100s some wealthy people began to have separate bedrooms. But it took another five hundred years or so before most sleepers divided themselves into family and nonfamily. And it was not until the 1700s until the bedroom became recognizable as the kind of a bedroom that we have today.

This book is just loaded with interesting facts about sleeping. Here are a few:

- Around 1500 people started wearing different clothes at night from the ones they had worn all day.

- Pajamas became fashionable in the 1890s.

- Bugs were a big problem in most beds. Mattresses were made of straw and other materials that bugs liked. That particular problem was not solved until the coil-spring mattress was invented about 150 years ago.

You will have great fun reading this book.

***Rescues!* by Sandra Markle.**

Markle, Sandra. *Rescues!* Millbrook Press, 2006. ISBN 0822534134. 88 p. Grades 4–7.

Have you ever been in an accident? A really bad one? Have you ever been in a disaster?

This book tells the true story of real people who have been involved in disasters. Many of them were heroes. Some of them were just doing their own thing when nature started doing terrible things to them. Read about:

- The skier who was completely covered up by an avalanche.

- The thirteen-month-old toddler who wandered out of a warm house and into the snow, where parts of her body were covered with ice when rescuers found her.

- The nine miners trapped in a flooded mine. How could they keep from drowning until their rescuers (they hoped!) found them?

- The sailor, all alone in icy-cold Antarctic waters, whose boat was tipped over by an eighty-one-foot tall wave!

- The man sleeping in his bed when an earthquake hit and his building fell over sideways. His head was in a hole in the rubble, but would rescuers find him in time to save his life?

- The baby left all alone in a burning house.

- The tsunami that hit New Orleans, and a young man who needed electricity to keep his heart going.

And more! These are fine and exciting stories with great photos. Show the one on the cover and the one of the firefighter all suited up on page 52.

Masoff, Joy. *Oh, Yikes! History's Grossest Moments*. Illustrated by Terry Sirrell. Workman, 2006. ISBN 0761136843. 308 p. Grades 5–up.

If you want to learn some gross, disgusting, or just plain fascinating information, this is a fun place to start looking. Pick it up and start browsing—it will probably be like eating candy. You won't be able to put it down!

While you are looking, pick up some great facts:

- On page 124, you'll get some fine ideas for April Fools' Day jokes that have been tried—and worked. For example, in Sitka, Alaska, in 1978, people woke up to see black smoke coming out of a nearby volcano. Was it about to blow? No, some local prankster had put old tires into it and set them on fire.

- On page 10, you will learn about the history of diapers. Would you believe that leaves, sealskin, and moss were used in various parts of the world? Or that the pioneers almost never washed diapers? They just air-dried them and put them back on the poor baby.

- Do you know that the very first thing knights had to do before putting on their armor was go to the bathroom? It was really hard to go in armor.

- On page 149, you will learn that Lewis and Clark took a lot of "thunderclappers" with them. Thunderclappers were laxatives, and they needed a lot of them with their weird diet. However, the thunderclappers were full of mercury, which could kill you, but it worked so fast, it went right through the body. Here's the really interesting part: because of the mercury, we are able to tell where the members of the Lewis and Clark expedition camped and where they went to the bathroom, because the mercury is still there!

- On page 152, you will learn where the term "private eye" comes from. The famous Allen Pinkerton founded a detective agency in the mid-1800s, and he had a big banner in front of his building that said "We Never Sleep." Above it was a huge black-and-white eye. That's why detectives are called private eyes!

And lots, lots more.

But this book has a problem. Not everything in it is factually correct. Check the information on the assassin who tried to kill Andrew Jackson (page 205) or on King Charles VIII of England (page 244) for starters. Can you see what might be wrong with those stories? It all goes to prove you can't believe everything you read or hear, even if it is in a book.

But it is a fun read!

Roller Coaster! **by Paul Mason.**

Mason, Paul. *Roller Coaster!* (Raintree Fusion: Physical Science). Raintree, 2007. ISBN 1410925870. 32 p. Grades 3–7.

Have you ever ridden on a roller coaster? Did you like it? Was it fast? Was it steep? Did it ever go upside down? Did you feel sick or did you want to get on it again the minute the ride was over?

This book asks you what you would want if you were to design a roller coaster, and it gives us a great deal of information about them. Here are some intriguing facts.

- They do not have motors or engines. Instead, all of their speed comes from the first hill, which is called the lift hill. Tracks bring them up that hill, and the speed comes when they head down that first hill. The fastest roller coaster so far is in Jackson, New Jersey, and it travels at 128 miles an hour.

- There is a reason that your insides feel like they are rising up inside you over the top of each hill. It is because of the changing of direction. Our insides keep going straight up, just for the moment, even though our bodies are going down—fast.

- Part of the excitement of the roller coaster is the constant changing of direction—up, down, around, and around.

- The first roller coaster that had a loop was in Paris in 1846.

- Some roller coasters have seats that spin around. Talk about confusing our bodies!

You'll have fun with this book and learning what really happens when you get on a roller coaster.

Aliens And UFOs **by Marc Tyler Nobleman.**

Nobleman, Marc Tyler. *Aliens and UFOs* (Atomic). Raintree, 2007. ISBN 1410925145. 32 p. Grades 4–8.

Do you think it would be fun to see a UFO or an alien? Or do you think it would be pretty scary? Do they exist? Are they real?

That's what Marc Tyler Nobleman discusses in this interesting book.

We know for sure that there is one place in the universe where life exists—our Earth. We know that no other life has ever existed in our solar system, but the universe is humongous. Are other life forms out there? Or are we all alone in the universe? That seems pretty unlikely. A lot of scientists think there are bound to be other planets that have life or some kind of beings—in other words, aliens.

So what is the evidence?

Some people believe that they have seen UFOs, which means "unidentified flying objects." Some people say they have actually seen aliens, or even been kidnapped by them. Are they lying or is it the truth? An astronomer called J. Allen Hynek described UFO sightings as close encounters—the witness has to be no more than five hundred feet away. They different kinds of close encounters are:

- seeing a UFO is a close encounter of the first kind,

- finding evidence of a UFO on Earth, such as footprints or burn marks, is a close encounter of the second kind, and

- actually seeing an alien is a close encounter of the third kind.

You will have to make up your own mind. What do *you* think?

The Mystery of the Bermuda Triangle
by Chris Oxlade.

Oxlade, Chris. *The Mystery of the Bermuda Triangle* (Can Science Solve?). Heinemann Library, 2006. ISBN 1403483450. 32 p. Grades 4–7.

Everybody loves a good mystery, and it's even more intriguing if it is a real one—something that has really happened that has no solution.

The mystery of the Bermuda Triangle is something that has intrigued people for many years. The Bermuda Triangle is an area in the Atlantic Ocean. Its three points are the about 150 small islands that make up Bermuda, the city of Miami, Florida, and Puerto Rico. Why is it so mysterious?

Ships and planes have disappeared there, completely vanished. In addition, strange things have happened to people who were flying and sailing there. And people wonder what causes these things to happen.

Could it be strange magnetic forces? Could it be aliens? Could it be weapons set in motion thousands of years ago by the lost city of Atlantis, which some people believe is there?

Or could it be just a really good story, with really logical explanations and no mystery at all?

Read this book and figure out what *you* think!

***Formula One Race Cars* by Janet Piehl.**

Piehl, Janet. *Formula One Race Cars* (Motor Mania). Lerner, 2007. ISBN 0822559293. 48 p. Grades 4–8.

"If it moves, people will race it" (p. 8), says the author of this book. Ever since the first cars were built, people have wanted to race them. And Formula One cars are probably the most amazing racing cars ever made. They almost look more like planes than cars! Over the years those cars have killed many of their drivers in horrible accidents. But today, the cars have so many safety features that no one has been killed in one since 1994.

Here are some of the fun facts you'll find in this book:

- These cars can move at more than 225 miles an hour. They are especially made for racing, and you can't buy a car that looks like them.

- "The name 'Formula One' refers to the formula, or set of rules, that determines how the race cars are designed and built. The formula helped to even out the competition among cars" (p. 9).

- European and American racing tracks are very different. Americans like short, round tracks, so that all the people can see the entire race. Europeans like long road courses. The spectators can thus see only part of the race. American car races are clockwise; European are counterclockwise. Most Formula One races are not in America.

- Modern safety features are pretty amazing. Look at the picture of driver Ralf Schumacher in his fireproof suit on page 25.

- A lot of famous race drivers raced karts when they were kids.

- Pit crews have to practice hard and often to become quick and efficient at doing everything they have to do as quickly as possible.

And there is a lot more!

Other well-reviewed books in this series include *Hot Rods* by Eric Braun (ISBN 0822535319).

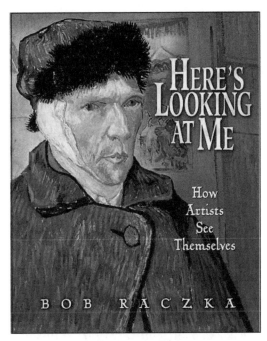

*Here's Looking at Me: How Artists See
Themselves* **by Bob Raczka.**

Raczka, Bob. *Here's Looking at Me: How Artists See Themselves.* Millbrook Press, 2006.
   ISBN 0761334041. 32 p. Grades 4–8.
   This book is just so much fun to look through.
   If you painted a picture of yourself, how would you do it? Looking at the mirror?
From memory? What would you wear? What would you paint—just your head, or part
of your body, or all of your body?
   All of the artists in history who painted pictures of themselves had to make those
choices. And, if you look at page 4, you will see the first known self-portrait in the his-
tory of art. Albrecht Durer, who was German, drew it himself, when he was only fourteen years old.
   On page 10, look at the extraordinary painting Diego Velazquez created in 1656.
It shows a Spanish princess with her playmates and maids, and she and the painter
himself are looking at her parents, the king and queen, as they have their portrait
painted. We can see them reflected in the mirror, and we can see Velazquez painting
them. This painting can play games with your mind!
   Or look at Goya, on page 14, who was able to paint at night before electricity: he
put candles on his hat!
   Norman Rockwell on page 23 shows us seven portraits of himself in a very funny
painting.
   This book will make you smile and make you think.

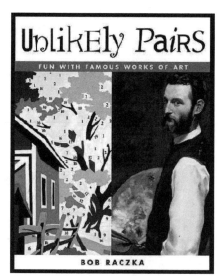

*Unlikely Pairs: Fun with Famous Works
of Art* **by Bob Raczka.**

Raczka, Bob. *Unlikely Pairs: Fun with Famous Works of Art.* Millbrook Press, 2006. ISBN
0761329366. 32 p. Grades 3–up.

As the author says, usually when we look at a work of art, we look at one work of
art at a time. Our thoughts focus on that one thing.

But in this book, Bob Raczka makes us look at two works of art at a time, and the
results are sometimes really a surprise! Try it and see what you think.

Note to booktalkers: This might be a great book for an art teacher or a writing
teacher to use with a class. Suggest that the students write a story about the two pictures that are on the same two-page spread. This should be a real creativity sparker!

*How Underwear Got Under There:
A Brief History* **by Kathy Shaskan.**

Shaskan, Kathy. *How Underwear Got Under There: A Brief History.* Illustrated by Regan
Dunnick. Dutton Children's Books, 2007. ISBN 0525471782. 48 p. Grades 3–5.

Underwear is often a pretty embarrassing word. First graders think it is the funniest word in the world. Most of us don't much want to talk about it, and most of us *really* don't want it to show.

But what would we do without it?

The first underwear of all was a loincloth—like Tarzan wears. Later, undershirts and shifts of all sorts appeared. Genghis Khan's Mongolian warriors used specially woven silk in their undergarments. If an arrow went in, they could twist the silk to help get the arrow out of the body!

That is just one kind of protective underwear. Other kinds are flameproof undergarments, religious undergarments, and pieces of clothing that protect a person from injury—like jockstraps and bulletproof vests. Of course, an important thing that all underclothing does is help keep you warm in cold weather.

This book is full of fascinating facts:

- Have you ever heard of long johns? They were named after John L. Sullivan, a great boxer in the late 1800s. He liked to fight in long underwear!

- Throughout most of history people have been almost unbelievably dirty. People used underwear as a sort of a dirt barrier. Many of their clothes were never washed or cleaned at all!

- Wealthy people often wore clothing that showed off the fact that they did not have to do any manual work. Their servants had much plainer clothing that let them move and do the job.

- Women's corsets and petticoats were almost unbelievable. They hurt, and they made it difficult to move or do anything.

- Astronauts wear underwear with water tubes running in it to keep them cool.

And that's just the tip of the iceberg. You will be telling your friends all about the surprising things you learn in this book.

Souter, Gerry. *Battle Tanks: Power in the Field* (Mighty Military Machines). Enslow, 2006. ISBN 0766026582. 48 p. Grades 4–9.

Tanks have been around since World War I, which lasted from 1914 to 1918. The British came up with an idea to make armored vehicles that ran on treads instead of wheels. The company that made them also made water tanks, and the tanks were shipped to France in crates. On the side of the crates, it said "tank." So that is what everyone started calling them.

If you are interested in tanks this is an excellent book for you. First you'll take a look at the history of tanks, starting almost one hundred years ago and going right up to Operation Iraqi Freedom. American tanks now are considered the best in the world, and they do some absolutely amazing things. Here are a few interesting facts:

- When tank crews start getting ready to fight, they "button up" the tank—closing all of the hatches and openings. Even with air-conditioning, which the newer tanks have, the temperature can still be in the 90s. The surfaces of equipment can be as hot as 120 degrees. It is hot in there!

- Most wars throughout history had front lines. When tanks were designed originally, they just went straight ahead. That kind of warfare is pretty much extinct. Now the tanks have to go any direction, and quickly, and all of the guns need to be able to turn around completely.

- Modern tanks have equipment that enables the crew to see in the dark. This can lead to some incredible hits.

You'll enjoy reading this and looking at the photographs.

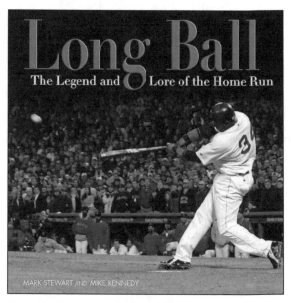

Long Ball: The Legend and Lore of the Home Run
by Mark Stewart and Mike Kennedy.

Stewart, Mark, and Mike Kennedy. *Long Ball: The Legend and Lore of the Home Run.* Millbrook Press, 2006. ISBN 0761327797. 64 p. Grades 4–8.

The Long Ball. Most of us think about it with another name: the home run. And is there anything that thrills a crowd much more than a home run? It's part of the reason people love baseball so much. They love to watch the batter connect with the ball and send it straight out of the ballpark.

This is the story of some of the greatest home runs in history and some of the greatest batters—the ones who could do it.

Some people still think the guy who could do it the best was a player named Babe Ruth. He had no training at all. He just hit the ball. He was one of the all-time greatest pitchers, and he could also hit home runs unbelievably well. He had fun. He loved to hit that ball hard, and he loved to swing as hard as he could. He often fell down because he swung the bat so hard! People absolutely loved to watch him. He made a big difference to baseball.

In the early years, there were not so many home runs. "Bats were heavier and had thicker handles than they do today, so it was difficult to produce the swing speed needed to hit a long home run. The balls in use … became mushy after being hit a few times. Finally, pitchers did not throw as hard as they do today" (p. 8). But when everyone realized that people loved homers, one thing the teams did was make sure they had lots of brand-new baseballs around.

This book is loaded with fun facts and great stories about the runs and the players. If you like baseball, you will enjoy this good read.

Szpirglas, Jeff. *Fear This Book: Your Guide to Fright, Horror, and Things That Go Bump in the Night*. Illustrated by Ramon Perez. Maple Tree Press, 2006. ISBN 1897066678. 64 p. Grades 5–8.

What are you afraid of?

Jeff Szpirglas, who wrote this book, says the scariest thing he saw when he was a kid was the movie *Jaws 2*. He immediately became scared of open water and, of course, sharks. He did finally get over it, but he tells us a lot of things that people are scared of.

Here are a few:

- Are you superstitious? How do you feel about the number 13? Do you ever knock on wood? (If you do, when do you do it? And do you know why?)

- Are you afraid of vampires? The dark? Ghosts? Monsters? Snakes or spiders? Bugs?

- Do you have any phobias? "A phobia is the fear of an object or situation that is out of proportion to the actual threat" (p. 50). If you are so afraid of tigers that you will not even go to a zoo, you have a phobia.

- Are you afraid of roller-coasters? Get some ideas as to what to do about it.

This is a neat book with fun pictures. Take a look at it.

Szpirglas, Jeff. *Gross Universe: Your Guide to All Disgusting Things Under the Sun*. Illustrated by Michael Cho. Maple Tree Press, 2004. ISBN 1894379640. 64 p. Grades 4–7.

This book is exactly what it says it is. You are going to learn about all sorts of gross things, from pus to slime, with many other topics as well.

Here are some of the gross things you'll want to know more about:

- Human beings have about 50 million bacteria living on every square centimeter (that is less than every square inch!) of their bodies.

- Cockroaches don't breathe with their heads, so a cockroach can live for up to one month without its head if it has had a recent meal because it breathes through its body. (It can't *eat* through its body, though!)

- On page 18, find out (yuck!) exactly why it isn't a good idea to pick your nose.

- On page 23 you will learn why ear wax is a really good thing.

- Have you ever seen pond scum? It is really biofilm, and there's a lot of it in a place we all know—inside our mouths! Read about it on page 28.

- There are lots of gross facts about animals. The Braconid wasp lays her eggs inside a caterpillar. She has a needle-like organ with which she pricks the caterpillar and lays her eggs—and when those eggs hatch, they eat that poor caterpillar from the inside out. It wouldn't be a fun way to die.

You will be wowed by the gross things you learn.

Szpirglas, Jeff. *They Did What? Your Guide to Weird & Wacky Things People Do*. Illustrated by Dave Whamond. Maple Tree Press, 2005. ISBN 1897066236. 64 p. Grades 4–8.

This book is just crammed with good stuff to browse through. You'll learn about some of the crazy fads in which people have participated, including doing things like swallowing live goldfish (one guy from Indiana claimed to have swallowed five thousand!), cramming themselves in phone booths or Volkswagen Beetles, sitting on flag-poles, sometimes for days, and buying pet rocks.

We also find out about gross stuff such as the ancient Romans using human urine to clean their clothes, weird and unsanitary hairstyles, and really strange shoes.

Do you know what an urban legend is? This is a story that people tell each other but isn't really true. Read the one about the Mexican Pet on page 15.

Learn about bird diapers, Turkey & Gravy soda, and people who have done daring things, such as going over Niagara Falls in a barrel and climbing up skyscrapers.

And all that is just the beginning. You will have a lot of fun telling your friends the weird things you'll learn.

Thomson, Sarah L. *What Athletes Are Made Of.* Illustrations by Hanoch Piven. Ginee Seo Books/Atheneum Books for Young Readers, 2006. ISBN 1416910026. Unpaged. Grades 2–5.

Hanoch Piven makes unique and original pictures using all sorts of unlikely objects. Take a look at the pictures in this book. He shows us some of his favorite athletes—men and women, alive and dead—makes portraits of each, and gives us some information about them. You'll have a lot of fun browsing, learning about the athletes, and figuring out what Piven used to create the portraits.

Read your audience the anecdote about Muhammad Ali—it is the first one in the book.

Mysterious Monsters by **John Townsend.**

Townsend, John. *Mysterious Monsters* (Out There?). Raintree, 2004. ISBN 1410905640. 56 p. Grades 4–8.

A lot of people must like monsters, because a lot of people sure like monster movies. Are monsters real? We know a lot of them are imaginary, but are some of them really out there?

Scientists aren't really sure, and in this book you will find out about some types of monsters that may be real—and some that definitely are made up.

Not many people think that werewolves and vampires are real, but what about dragons? In almost the entire world, there are stories about dragons. Does this mean that, perhaps, at one time huge lizard-like creatures—think dinosaurs—might have been around at the same time as prehistoric people? Dragons and dinosaurs do seem to be quite a bit alike. Komodo dragons, which were just discovered in 1912, are very real. They can be twice the size of a human being. They will kill any animal near it, including humans. All they have to do is bite something once. Their mouth is full of decaying meat, and the bite poisons the victim. After that bite, the komodo dragon can just wait around for its victim to die. Take a look at the picture of one on page 15.

Are there monsters that live in lakes, such as the most famous, the Loch Ness Monster, in Scotland? Is it real? If it is real, a lot of people think it is a leftover dinosaur that did not really become extinct. Some people think there is a monster they call Champ in Lake Champlain, and another they call Tessie in Lake Tahoe. Look at the information and see what *you* think.

There are photographs of real, known animals that look a lot like monsters, and that people may have once mistaken for monsters. Some of them are pretty scary looking!

You'll enjoy reading this book.

Mysterious Signs **by John Townsend.**

Townsend, John. *Mysterious Signs* (Out There?). Raintree, 2004. ISBN 1410905667. 56 p. Grades 4–8.

There are many strange things on our planet, and in this book the author takes a look at some of the most mysterious ones.

Everyone loves a mystery, and these objects and phenomena are surrounded with mystery. Sometimes people think they have solved the mysteries, but others don't agree with them.

You'll learn about things like:

• Crop markings—these are designs cut into fields. Who makes them? We know some of them are made by human pranksters, but, of others, we are not so sure. A great number of them happen in Wiltshire, in England. Why there?

• Carvings on the earth—this intrigues everyone. Why and how did ancient people, long ago, cut out huge designs on the earth? For what reason? How did they get up high enough to see the design? Or were they made by aliens?

• Mounds—some mysterious mounds are actually burial places, made long ago. But others we are not so sure of. In Ohio, you can see the Great Serpent Mound, probably made by Native Americans about 1,500 years ago. It is over a quarter of a mile long and shaped like a snake. Why?

• Ley lines—"Some people say they can sense a kind of energy at ancient human-made hills or stone monuments. Perhaps such places were built on invisible lines of mysterious energy that run across Earth. These lines are often called ley lines" (p. 40).

And these are just a few of what's inside this book. You'll have a lot of fun learning about and trying to figure out some of these mysteries.

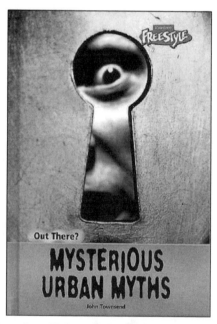

Mysterious Urban Myths by John Townsend.

Townsend, John. *Mysterious Urban Myths* (Out There?). Raintree, 2004. ISBN 1410905675. 56 p. Grades 4–8.

Have you heard the most amazing story? It sounds incredible, but it is really true. I do not know the person it happened to, but that person is a very good friend of my cousin. My cousin says this guy would never ever lie, so we can count on it being the truth.

That's how most urban legends start. Somebody knows somebody who knows somebody to whom an incredible thing happened. But no one *really* knows that person. Most of the time an urban legend is a really good story, but it is just that, a story, not the truth.

In this interesting book we are even told which legends are absolutely false, which are maybes and which—not very many—are true. While you are reading it, see how many of the urban legends in here you have heard.

Here are a few of the true ones.

- In Norway, in 1932, a four-year-old little girl was captured by a huge, flying sea eagle. He flew her to a cliff a mile away.

- "A lawyer in a Toronto skyscraper was showing some students how tough his office windows were. He pushed hard against the glass to show its strength, but he crashed through the window. He plunged twenty-four floors to his death on the street below" (page 43).

- In 2000 a woman brought home a fried chicken dinner for her family dinner. One of the pieces was really gross. It was a chicken's head, complete with eyes and a beak, and it was deep fried too!

Those are some of the real ones. Wait till you read the ones that are even more un-believable!

Acknowledgments

Chapter 1

Cover from *Up Close: Robert F. Kennedy* by Marc Aronson. Used by permission of Penguin Young Readers Group.

Cover from *With Courage and Cloth: Winning the Fight for a Woman's Right to Vote* by Ann Bausum. Reprinted with permission of the National Geographic Society.

Cover from *Where Washington Walked* by Raymond Bial. Published by Walker Books for Young Readers.

Cover from *Nauvoo: Mormon City on the Mississippi River* by Raymond Bial. Jacket photographs © 2006 by Raymond Bial. Reprinted by permission of Houghton Mifflin Company. All rights reserved.

Cover from *Journeys for Freedom: A New Look at America's Story* by Susan Buckley and Elspeth Leacock. Jacket art © 2006 by Rodica Prato. Reprinted by permission of Houghton Mifflin Company. All rights reserved.

Cover from *Kids Make History: A New Look at America's Story* by Susan Buckley and Elspeth Leacock. Jacket art © 2006 by Rodica Prato. Reprinted by permission of Houghton Mifflin Company. All rights reserved.

Cover from *Hero of the High Seas: John Paul Jones and the American Revolution* by Michael L. Cooper. Reprinted with permission of the National Geographic Society.

Cover from *Cowboys and Coffin Makers: One Hundred 19th-century Jobs You Might Have Feared or Fancied* by Laurie Coulter. Cover illustration by Martha Newbigging. Published by Annick Press, 2007. Reprinted with permission.

Cover from *New York: The Empire State* by Margery Facklam and Peggy Thomas. Used with permission by Charlesbridge Publishing, Inc.

Cover from *Vinnie And Abraham* by Dawn Fitzgerald. Used with permission by Charlesbridge Publishing, Inc.

Cover from *5,000 Miles to Freedom: Ellen and William Craft's Flight from Slavery* by Judith Bloom Fradin and Dennis Brindell Fradin. Reprinted with permission of the National Geographic Society.

Cover from *The Founders: The 39 Stories Behind the U.S. Constitution* by Dennis Brindell Fradin. Published by Walker Books for Young Readers.

Cover from *The Silent Witness: A True Story of the Civil War* by Robin Friedman. Jacket art copyright © Claire A. Nivola. Reprinted by permission of Houghton Mifflin Company. All rights reserved.

Cover from *Alaska* by Shelley Gill. Used with permission by Charlesbridge Publishing, Inc.

Cover from *Thomas Jefferson* by Cheryl Harness. Reprinted with permission of the National Geographic Society.

Cover from *The Tragic Tale of Narcissa Whitman and a Faithful History of the Oregon Trail* by Cheryl Harness. Reprinted with permission of the National Geographic Society.

Cover from *Delivering Justice: W. W. Law and the Fight for Civil Rights*. Text copyright © 2005 by Jim Haskins. Illustrations copyright © 2005 by Benny Andrews. Reproduced by permission of Candlewick Press, Cambridge, MA.

Cover from *Up Before Daybreak: Cotton and People in America* by Deborah Hopkinson. Scholastic, 2006. Reprinted with permission.

Cover from *Double Cheeseburgers, Quiche, and Vegetarian Burritos: American Cooking from the 1920s Through Today* by Loretta Frances Ichord. Used with permission of Lerner Publishing Group.

Cover from *Pasta, Fried Rice, and Matzoh Balls: Immigrant Cooking in America* by Loretta Frances Ichord. Used with permission of Lerner Publishing Group.

Cover from *Skillet Bread, Sourdough, and Vinegar Pie: Cooking in Pioneer Days* by Loretta Frances Ichord. Used with permission of Lerner Publishing Group.

Cover from *O, Say Can You See? America's Symbols, Landmarks, and Inspiring Words* by Sheila Keenan. Scholastic Nonfiction, 2004. Reprinted with permission.

Cover from *A Woman for President: The Story of Victoria Woodhull* by Kathleen Krull. Published by Walker Books for Young Readers.

Cover from *1607: A New Look at Jamestown* by Karen E. Lange. Reprinted with permission of the National Geographic Society.

Cover from *Bushnell's Submarine: The Best Kept Secret of the American Revolution* by Arthur S. Lefkowitz. Scholastic, 2006. Reprinted with permission.

Cover from *A Dream of Freedom: The Civil Rights Movement from 1954 to 1968* by Diane McWhorter. Scholastic Nonfiction, 2004. Reprinted with permission.

Cover from *Roanoke: The Mystery of the Lost Colony* by Lee Todd Miller. Scholastic Nonfiction, 2007. Reprinted with permission.

Cover from *Children of Alcatraz: Growing Up on the Rock* by Claire Rudolf Murphy. Published by Walker Books for Young Readers.

Cover from *Quiet Hero: The Ira Hayes Story*. Copyright © 2006 by S. D. Nelson. Permission arranged with Lee & Low Books Inc., New York, NY 10016.

Cover from *Nobody Gonna Turn Me 'Round: Stories and Songs of the Civil Rights Movement*. Text copyright © 2006 Doreen Rappaport. Illustrations copyright © 2006 by Shane W. Evans. Reproduced by permission of Candlewick Press, Cambridge, MA.

Cover from *Haym Salomon: American Patriot* by Susan Goldman Rubin. Abrams Books for Young Readers, 2007. Reprinted with permission.

Cover from *Hockey: Miracle on Ice* by Michael Sandler. Bearport Publishing, 2006. Reprinted with permission.

Cover from *John Smith Escapes Again!* by Rosalyn Schanzer. Reprinted with permission of the National Geographic Society.

Cover from *Escape to Freedom: The Underground Railroad Adventures of Callie and William* by Barbara Brooks Simon. Reprinted with permission of the National Geographic Society.

Cover from *Make Your Mark, Franklin Roosevelt* by Judith St. George. Used by permission of Penguin Young Readers Group.

Cover from *Texas, 1527-1836* by Michael Teitelbaum. Reprinted with permission of the National Geographic Society.

Cover from *Remember Little Bighorn: Indians, Soldiers, and Scouts Tell Their Stories* by Paul Robert Walker. Reprinted with permission of the National Geographic Society.

Chapter 2

Cover from *M.L.K.: Journey of a King* by Tonya Bolden. Abrams Books for Young Readers, 2007. Reprinted with permission.

Cover from *The Other Mozart: The Life of the Famous Chevalier de Saint-George* by Hugh Brewster. Abrams Books for Young Readers, 2006. Reprinted with permission.

Cover from *Bright Path: Young Jim Thorpe* by Don Brown. Roaring Brook Press, 2006. Reprinted with permission.

Cover from *Amelia to Zora: Twenty-six Women Who Changed the World* by Cynthia Chin-Lee. Used with permission by Charlesbridge Publishing, Inc.

Cover from *Jump! From the Life of Michael Jordan* by Floyd Cooper. Used by permission of Penguin Young Readers Group.

Cover from *Sawdust and Spangles: The Amazing Life of W. C. Coup* by Ralph Covert and G. Riley Mills. Abrams Books for Young Readers, 2007. Reprinted with permission.

Cover from *Extraordinary Ordinary People: Five American Masters of Traditional Arts.* Text copyright © 2006 by Alan Govenar. Reproduced by permission of Candlewick Press, Cambridge, MA.

Cover from *The Forbidden Schoolhouse: The True and Dramatic Story of Prudence Crandall and Her Students* by Suzanne Jurmain. Copyright © 2005 by Suzanne Jurmain. Jacket cover photo © Doug Mindell. Reprinted by permission of Houghton Mifflin Company. All rights reserved.

Cover from *Walt Whitman: Words for America* by Barbara Kerley. Scholastic Press, 2004.

Cover from *Isaac Newton* by Kathleen Krull. Used by permission of Penguin Young Readers Group.

Cover from *Sigmund Freud* by Kathleen Krull. Used by permission of Penguin Young Readers Group.

Cover from *Up Close: Rachel Carson* by Ellen Levine. Used by permission of Penguin Young Readers Group.

Cover from *Houdini: The Handcuff King* by Jason Lutes and Nick Bertozzi. Hyperion, 2007. Reprinted with permission.

Cover from *Julia Morgan Built a Castle* by Celeste Davidson Mannis. Used by permission of Penguin Young Readers Group.

Cover from *Different Like Coco*. Copyright © 2007 by Elizabeth Matthews. Reproduced by permission of Candlewick Press, Cambridge, MA.

Cover from *Liftoff: A Photobiography of John Glenn* by Don Mitchell. Reprinted with permission of the National Geographic Society.

Cover from *Be Water, My Friend: The Early Years of Bruce Lee*. Text copyright © 2006 by Ken Mochizuki. Illustration copyright © 2006 by Dom Lee. Permission arranged with Lee & Low Books Inc., New York, NY 10016.

Cover from *Walker Evans: Photographer of America* by Thomas Nau. Roaring Brook Press, 2007. Reprinted with permission.

Cover from *John Lennon: All I Want is the Truth* by Elizabeth Partridge. Used by permission of Penguin Young Readers Group.

Cover from *John's Secret Dreams: The Life of John Lennon* by Doreen Rappaport. Hyperion Books for Children, 2004. Reprinted with permission.

Cover from *The Longest Season: The Story of the Orioles' 1988 Losing Streak* by Cal Ripken, Jr. Used by permission of Penguin Young Readers Group.

Cover from *Dickens: His Work and His World*. Text copyright © 2005 Michael Rosen. Illustrations copyright © 2005 by Robert Ingpen. Reproduced by permission of Candlewick Press, Cambridge, MA, on behalf of Walker Books Ltd., London.

Cover from *Andy Warhol: Pop Art Painter* by Susan Goldman Rubin. Abrams Books for Young Readers, 2006. Reprinted with permission.

Cover from *Sequoyah: The Cherokee Man Who Gave His People Writing* by James Rumford. Jacket art copyright © 2004 by James Rumford. Reprinted by permission of Houghton Mifflin Company. All rights reserved.

Cover from *Bethany Hamilton: Follow Your Dreams!* by Michael Sandler. Bearport Publishing, 2007. Reprinted with permission.

Cover from *The Hero Schliemann: The Dreamer Who Dug for Troy*. Text copyright © 2006 by Laura Amy Schlitz. Illustrations copyright © 2006 by Robert Byrd. Reproduced by permission of Candlewick Press, Cambridge, MA.

Cover from *Barnum Brown, Dinosaur Hunter* by David Sheldon. Published by Walker Books for Young Readers.

Cover from *Jesse Owens: Fastest Man Alive* by Carole Boston Weatherford . Published by Walker Books for Young Readers.

Cover from *Dizzy* by Jonah Winter. Scholastic Inc., 2006. Reprinted with permission.

Cover from *The Perfect Wizard: Hans Christian Andersen* by Jane Yolen. Used by permission of Penguin Young Readers Group.

Chapter 3

Cover from *The Mutiny on the Bounty* by Patrick O'Brien. Published by Walker Books for Young Readers.

Cover from *We Gather Together: Celebrating the Harvest Season* by Wendy Pfeffer. Used by permission of Penguin Young Readers Group.

Cover from *Trapped In Ice! An Amazing Whaling Adventure* by Martin W. Sandler. Scholastic, 2006. Reprinted with permission.

Cover from *When the Wall Came Down: The Berlin Wall and the Fall of Soviet Communism* by Serge Schmemann. Copyright © 2006 by *The New York Times*. Reprinted by permission of Kingfisher Publications, an imprint of Houghton Mifflin Company. All rights reserved.

Cover from *The Medieval World* by Philip Steele. Copyright © Kingfisher Publications Plc 2000. Reprinted by permission of Kingfisher Publications, an imprint of Houghton Mifflin Company. All rights reserved.

Cover from *The Secret of Priest's Grotto: A Holocaust Survival Story* by Peter Lane Taylor with Christos Nicola. Used with permission of Lerner Publishing Group.

Chapter 4

Cover from *Nic Bishop Spiders* by Nic Bishop. Scholastic, 2007. Reprinted with permission.

Cover from *Extreme Animals: The Toughest Creatures on Earth*. Text copyright © 2006 by Nicola Davies. Illustrations copyright © 2006 by Neal Layton. Reproduced by permission of Candlewick Press, Cambridge, MA.

Cover from *The Fossil Feud: Marsh and Cope's Bone Wars* by Meish Goldish. Bearport Publishing, 2007. Reprinted with permission.

Cover from *Saber-Toothed Cats* by Susan E. Goodman. Used with permission of Lerner Publishing Group.

Cover from *Wilderness Search Dogs* by Dan Greenberg. Bearport Publishing Company, 2005. Reprinted with permission.

Cover from *Owen & Mzee: The Language Of Friendship* by Isabella Hatkoff, Craig Hatkoff, and Dr. Paula Kahumbu. Scholastic Press, 2007. Reprinted with permission.

Cover from *Owen & Mzee: The True Story of a Remarkable Friendship* by Isabella Hatkoff, Craig Hatkoff, and Dr. Paula Kahumbu. Scholastic Press, 2006. Reprinted with permission.

Cover from *The World's Greatest Elephant* by Ralph Helfer. Used by permission of Penguin Young Readers Group.

Cover from *Ham the Astrochimp* by Richard Hilliard. Reprinted with the permission of Boyds Mills Press, Inc.

Cover from *Dogs and Cats* by Steve Jenkins. Jacket art copyright © 2007 by Steve Jenkins. Reprinted by permission of Houghton Mifflin Company. All rights reserved.

Cover from *Animals in the House: A History of Pets and People* by Sheila Keenan. Scholastic, 2007. Reprinted with permission.

Cover from *Watching Sharks in the Oceans* by L. Patricia Kite. Heinemann Library, 2006. Reprinted with permission.

Cover from *First Dive to Shark Dive* by Peter Lourie. Reprinted with the permission of Boyds Mills Press, Inc.

Cover from *Army Ants* by Sandra Markle. Used with permission of Lerner Publishing Group.

Cover from *Little Lost Bat* by Sandra Markle. Used with permission by Charlesbridge Publishing, Inc.

Cover from *A Mother's Journey* by Sandra Markle. Used with permission by Charlesbridge Publishing, Inc.

Cover from *Musk Oxen* by Sandra Markle. Used with permission of Lerner Publishing Group.

Cover from *Octopuses* by Sandra Markle. Used with permission of Lerner Publishing Group.

Cover from *Slippery, Slimy Baby Frogs* by Sandra Markle. Published by Walker Books for Young Readers.

Cover from *Oh Rats! The Story of Rats and People* by Albert Marrin. Used by permission of Penguin Young Readers Group.

Cover from *Saving the Buffalo* by Albert Marrin. Scholastic Nonfiction, 2006. Reprinted with permission.

Cover from *Quest for the Tree Kangaroo: An Expedition to the Cloud Forest of New Guinea* by Sy Montgomery. Jacket photograph © 2006 by Nic Bishop. Reprinted by permission of Houghton Mifflin Company. All rights reserved.

Cover from *Mastodon Mystery* by Taylor Morrison. Jacket art copyright © 2001 by Taylor Morrison. Reprinted by permission of Houghton Mifflin Company. All rights reserved.

Cover from *Polar Bears in Danger* by Helen Orme. Bearport Publishing, 2007. Reprinted with permission.

Cover from *Face to Face with Grizzlies* by Joel Sartore. Reprinted with permission of the National Geographic Society.

Cover from *Ballet of the Elephants* by Leda Schubert. Roaring Brook Press, 2006. Reprinted with permission.

Cover from *Look What Mouths Can Do* by D. M. Souza. Used with permission of Lerner Publishing Group.

Cover from *Look What Whiskers Can Do* by D. M. Souza. Used with permission of Lerner Publishing Group.

Cover from *Packed With Poison! Deadly Animal Defenses* by D. M. Souza. Used with permission of Lerner Publishing Group.

Cover from *Bengal Tiger* by Louise Spilsbury and Richard Spilsbury. Heinemann Library, 2006. Reprinted with permission.

Cover from *Saving Manatees* by Stephen R. Swinburne. Reprinted with the permission of Boyds Mills Press, Inc.

Cover from *Shark vs. Killer Whale* by Isabel Thomas. Raintree, 2006. Reprinted with permission.

Cover from *Mystery Fish: Secrets of the Coelacanth* by Sally M. Walker. Used with permission of Lerner Publishing Group.

Chapter 5

Cover from *Tracking Trash: Flotsam, Jetsam, and the Science of Ocean Motion* by Loree Griffin Burns. Copyright © 2007 by Loree Griffin Burns. Reprinted by permission of Houghton Mifflin Company. All rights reserved.

Cover from *Junk Food* by Vicki Cobb. Used with permission of Lerner Publishing Group.

Cover from *The Quest to Digest* by Mary K. Corcoran. Used with permission by Charlesbridge Publishing, Inc.

Cover from *Venus Flytraps, Bladderworts, and Other Wild and Amazing Plants* by Monica Halpern. Reprinted with permission of the National Geographic Society.

Cover from *It's Not the Stork!: A Book About Girls, Boys, Babies, Bodies, Families, and Friends* by Robie H. Harris. Text copyright © 2006 by Bee Productions, Inc. Illustrations copyright © 2006 by Bird Productions, Inc. Reproduced by permission of Candlewick Press, Cambridge, MA.

Cover from *Looking at Glass Through the Ages* by Bruce Koscielniak. Jacket art copyright © 2006 Bruce Koscielniak. Reprinted by permission of Houghton Mifflin Company. All rights reserved.

Cover from *The Story of Salt* by Mark Kurlansky. Used by permission of Penguin Young Readers Group.

Cover from *Hurricanes, Tsunamis, and Other Natural Disasters* by Andrew Langley. Copyright © Kingfisher Publications Plc, 2006. Reprinted by permission of Kingfisher Publications, an imprint of Houghton Mifflin Company. All rights reserved.

Cover from *Diving to a Deep-Sea Volcano* by Kenneth Mallory. Jacket art copyright © 2006 The Stephen Low Company. Reprinted by permission of Houghton Mifflin Company. All rights reserved.

Cover from *Tsunami Warning* by Taylor Morrison. Jacket art copyright © 2007 by Taylor Morrison. Reprinted by permission of Houghton Mifflin Company. All rights reserved.

Cover from *Wildfire* by Taylor Morrison. Jacket art copyright © 2006 by Taylor Morrison. Reprinted by permission of Houghton Mifflin Company. All rights reserved.

Cover from © *Switched On, Flushed Down, Tossed Out: Investigating the Hidden Workings of your Home* by Trudee Romanek. Cover illustration by Stephen MacEachern. Published by Annick Press, 2005. Reprinted with permission.

Chapter 6

Cover from *Mural on Second Avenue and Other City Poems*. Poems by Lilian Moore. Illustrations copyright © 2004 Roma Karas. Reproduced by permission of Candlewick Press, Cambridge, MA.

Cover from *A Wreath for Emmett Till* by Marilyn Nelson, illustrated by Philippe Lardy. Jacket painting © 2005 by Philippe Lardy. Reprinted by permission of Houghton Mifflin Company. All rights reserved.

Cover from *Once upon a . . . Poem: Favorite Poems That Tell Stories*. The Chicken House, 2004. Reprinted with permission.

Cover from *3-D ABC: A Sculptural Alphabet* by Bob Raczka. Used with permission of Lerner Publishing Group.

Cover from *Song of the Water Boatman and Other Pond Poems* by Joyce Sidman, illustrated by Beckie Prange. Illustrations copyright © 2005 by Beckie Prange. Reprinted by permission of Houghton Mifflin Company. All rights reserved.

Cover from *This is Just to Say: Poems of Apology and Forgiveness* by Joyce Sidman, illustrated by Pamela Zagarenski. Jacket art copyright © Pamela Zagarenski. Reprinted by permission of Houghton Mifflin Company. All rights reserved.

Chapter 7

Cover from *Unexplained: An Encyclopedia of Curious Phenomena, Strange Superstitions, and Ancient Mysteries* by Judy Allen. Copyright © Kingfisher Publications Plc 2006. Reprinted by permission of Kingfisher Publications, an imprint of Houghton Mifflin Company. All rights reserved.

Cover from *Debatable Deaths* by Gary L. Blackwood. Marshall Cavendish Benchmark, 2006. Reprinted with permission.

Cover from *Enigmatic Events* by Gary L. Blackwood. Marshall Cavendish Benchmark, 2006. Reprinted with permission.

Cover from *Legends Or Lies* by Gary L. Blackwood. Benchmark Books, 2006. Reprinted with permission.

Cover from *Perplexing People* by Gary L. Blackwood. Marshall Cavendish Benchmark, 2006. Reprinted with permission.

Cover from *Encyclopedia Horrifica: The Terrifying TRUTH! About Vampires, Ghosts, Monsters, and More* by Joshua Gee. Scholastic, 2007. Reprinted with permission.

Cover from *Gee Whiz! It's All About Pee* by Susan E. Goodman. Used by permission of Penguin Young Readers Group.

Cover from *The World of Disasters* by Ned Halley. Copyright © Kingfisher Publications Plc 2005. Reprinted by permission of Kingfisher Publications, an imprint of Houghton Mifflin Company. All rights reserved.

Cover from *Mysteries of the Mummy Kids* by Kelly Milner Halls. Used with permission of Lerner Publishing Group.

Cover from *Tales of the Cryptids: Mysterious Creatures That May or May Not Exist* by Kelly Milner Halls, Rick Spears, and Roxyanne Young. Used with permission of Lerner Publishing Group.

Cover from *Werewolves* by Stephen Krensky. Used with permission of Lerner Publishing Group.

Cover from *Superfast Trucks* by Donna Latham. Bearport Publishing, 2006. Reprinted with permission.

Cover from *Rescues!* by Sandra Markle. Used with permission of Lerner Publishing Group.

Cover from *Roller Coaster!* by Paul Mason. Raintree, 2007. Reprinted with permission.

Cover from *Aliens and UFOs* by Marc Tyler Nobleman. Raintree, 2007. Reprinted with permission.

Cover from *The Mystery of the Bermuda Triangle* by Chris Oxlade. Heinemann Library, 2006. Reprinted with permission.

Cover from *Formula One Race Cars* by Janet Piehl. Used with permission of Lerner Publishing Group.

Cover from *Here's Looking at Me: How Artists See Themselves* by Bob Raczka. Used with permission of Lerner Publishing Group.

Cover from *Unlikely Pairs: Fun with Famous Works of Art* by Bob Raczka. Used with permission of Lerner Publishing Group.

Cover from *How Underwear Got Under There: A Brief History* by Kathy Shaskan. Used by permission of Penguin Young Readers Group.

Cover from *Long Ball: The Legend and Lore of the Home Run* by Mark Stewart and Mike Kennedy. Used with permission of Lerner Publishing Group.

Cover from *Mysterious Monsters* by John Townsend. Raintree, 2004. Reprinted with permission.

Cover from *Mysterious Signs* by John Townsend. Raintree, 2004. Reprinted with permission.

Cover from *Mysterious Urban Myths* by John Townsend. Raintree, 2004. Reprinted with permission.

Author Index

Title Index

About the Authors

Kathleen A. Baxter served as the Coordinator of Children's Services in the Anoka County Library for over twenty-five years. In addition to four previous *Gotcha* books, she has written "The Nonfiction Booktalker" column for School Library Journal since 1997. She has presented at hundreds of national and state library and reading conferences all over the country. Kathleen has also taught classes in children's literature, served on the 2001 Newbery Committee, consults for publishers, and now presents all-day seminars on children's books for the Bureau of Education and Research. Visit her online at http://www.kathleenbaxter.com.

Marcia Agness Kochel has been a school media specialist in grades K-8 in North Carolina, Indiana, and Minnesota. She is currently Media Director at Olson Middle School in Bloomington, Minnesota. Marcia reviews nonfiction books for School Library Journal, served on the 2006 Sibert Award Committee, was a judge for the 2006 Children's and YA Bloggers' Literary Awards (The Cybils) for middle grade and YA nonfiction, and blogs about middle school books at http://omsbookblog.blogspot.com/. She has an undergraduate degree from The College of William and Mary in Virginia and a Masters of Science in Library Science from The University of North Carolina at Chapel Hill.